From 49 to 95

Lessons Learned on The Road to Success

Lee "Gino" McQueen

Cover design by Asghar

Editing and formatting by Lina Parker.

If you are interested in bulk purchases, booking the author to speak, or to use any part of this book, please email ctras2736@gmail.com

Printed in the United States of America

Copyright @ 2025 Lee "Gino" McQueen

ISBN: 979-8-9927762-0-1

Table of Contents

FROM 49 TO 95 LESSONS LEARNED

I served 20 years in the Army, starting at the rank of Private and retiring as a Major. I learned many life lessons from the greatest uncle in the World which is Uncle Sam better known as Uncle Sugar for Servicemembers. I traveled the World, experienced different cultures, met numerous people with different backgrounds, and worked with some of the smartest and most athletic people in world. Many days were spent traveling up and down Interstate 95 going from base to base. I traveled on I-95 so often, I can drive it blind folded.

EARLY CHILDHOOD

I grew up in Ramseur, North Carolina which had one stop light until the mid-eighties and the majority of the Black Residents lived on Highway 49 within a mile of each other. There were only three career options for people on 49; Military, College, or a mill which you definitely didn't want to go to. My Aunt Cora worked 3rd shift seven days a week for 30 years without air condition and only took vacation when the mill closed for a week during Christmas and 4th of July. Seventy-five percent of the males who were descendants from my great-grandparents, Fletcher and Goldie Goldston, joined the military. My goal ever since I was eleven years old was to join the military based on the stories which I heard from my older relatives.

My grandmother, Pauline Hill, told me stories about her father Fletcher who died about six-months before my birth. She said her dad joined the Army at the age of 14 because he was tired of walking backwards when he left town. He did this because his pants had too many holes in the back of them, and he did not want people to see how poor he was. He was able to join the Army at 14 because he was big for his age. Once in the Army he was deployed to France during WWI. He told my grandmother when the Germans saw black soldiers, they ran away frightened because they thought the white soldiers who they killed, returned as black burnt ghosts which enabled my great-grandfather's unit to succeed in battle. My grandmother said grandpa did not talk about his war experience, but she knew he was proud of his military experience because he would go into the attic and put on his military uniform from time-to-time. The military provided my great-grandfather the determination to succeed in life even though he could not read or write. Goldie, his wife, asked him how he signed his check in the military if he could not read or write and he said the Army told him to just make an "X" and it will suffice as his signature. His

2

wife eventually taught him how to sign his name. Grandpa Fletcher was a brick mason. He was the first Black man in Ramseur to have a car and lights in the inside of his house. He used an AC/Delco generator to light his house and the money he made as a brick mason to buy a car. Grandpa Fletcher's determination and hard work enabled him to own a small store/club, five houses, and over 50 acres of land while not knowing how to read or write.

Grandma Goldie had a difficult life. She lost her father when she was 10 and had her first child at 14. She told me her family was so poor that her mother did not have money to buy her children Christmas gifts one year, but she told her children she would give them a gift which would last a lifetime and the gift was she taught them how to read and write. Grandma Goldie eventually earned her high school diploma at the age of 70.

Lessons Learned

1. *You are never too old to learn* – Grandma Goldie achieved in her 70's despite growing up poor and in segregation.

2. *You can do anything you set your mind to it* – Grandpa Fletch could not read or write, but through hard work and determination he set his family up for success for many generations through the acquisition of land, building houses, and saving up money. He was a go-getter because he owned a small farm, store, and was a moonshiner. Selling moonshine was a way for Black Men to survive in those days.

3. *Teach your kids something to better their lives* – Grandma Goldie's mom taught her kids how to read which bettered her children and their descendants' lives.

Grandpa Fletch and Grandma Goldie

4

Grandma Goldie Goldston – When the fireplace went out in her house, they had to go to the neighbor's house to get fire.

Grandma Pauline and her Uncle Richard, along with her sisters Pattie, and Cora. I was trying to get in a picture any time someone had a camera.

5

My favorite uncle was Alfred Siler who served in WWII. When I was 11, he told Grandma Pauline, his sister, to leave me alone because I was going to grow up and be somebody. He said those words because I told him, I wanted to join the Army like him and become a General. I did not become a General, but I became an Officer and Uncle Al was proud of me for the accomplishment.

Uncle Al enjoyed telling his nephews some of his old war stories and showing us his old WWII equipment. He told us he was the guy who distributed condoms in the Pacific, but he ended up getting a penicillin shot. I used Uncle Al's rubber rucksack and mess kit on my Boy Scouts' Camping trips. The rucksack was heavier than today's equipment, but it allowed me to have the only dry equipment out of the other scouts when we went camping.

Uncle Al was the first family member to achieve his high school diploma which was a landmark back in those days. The community wanted him to become a teacher because of his achievement, but he had bigger plans and moved to Philadelphia. He was always trying to teach us young guys something. He taught me deep sea fishing, how to shoot a shotgun, operate a riding lawn mower, and use a chainsaw. His instructions on using a chainsaw and riding lawn mower were comical. One day Uncle Al asked me to help him cut wood, but I told him I did not know how to use a chainsaw. He told me he would hold the board and I would operate the chainsaw. He said using a chainsaw is easy, just press the trigger and cut the board he was holding. I looked like a cartoon character when I operated the chainsaw. When I pressed the trigger, the chainsaw went in the air and landed on his pickup truck which I cut in three places. Although I cut the bed of his new truck, he corrected my mistakes and we cut a truck load of wood. I learned how to operate a chainsaw that day and never cut another pickup truck bed.

One day I asked him if I could use his riding lawn mower to cut Grandma Hill's yard which was two acres in size because I was tired of pushing it for $5.00, a bag of popcorn, Kool-Aid, and a peanut-

6

butter jelly sandwich. Uncle Al told me to use the clutch to stop the lawn mower because the brakes didn't work. I drove the lawn mower down the steep driveway of his house to my grandma's house. I pressed the clutch to stop before I crossed the rode, when I pressed the clutch the lawn mower sped up, I flew across the road without stopping, jumped a ditch, and made a sharp left turn to slow it down. My uncle Douglas, an Army Veteran, saw this spectacular event and laughed hysterically. He asked me if I knew how to operate a riding lawn and I told him, Uncle Al said to use the clutch to stop the lawn mower because the brakes didn't work. My uncle told me to press on the brake and when I did, they worked. I learned a valuable experience that day and it was to never take advice from an intoxicated person. I later found out, Uncle Al had PTSD from WWII and the drinking of alcohol was his way of coping.

Uncle Nathan Gales was another favorite uncle of mine because at the age of 10, he allowed me to work with him putting in septic tanks. I will not call it hiring because the only things I received were hamburgers, soda, and a German Shepherd puppy which turned out to be the best dog I ever had. The only work I did was dig ditches for pipe emplacement and bring equipment to the workers.

One day I told Uncle Nathan I was tired of digging ditches and I wanted to learn how to use the backhoe, he told me to get my ass back on the shovel and no 10-year-old was going to mess up his $30k piece of equipment. Fred Alston, backhoe operator, was tired of hearing me whining and told me to climb on board so he could teach me how to operate the backhoe. I learned how to operate the backhoe in 5 minutes thanks to his teaching, but 15 minutes later I was back to digging ditches. I always looked up to Fred after this for taking the time to teach me how to operate the backhoe.

Lessons Learned

1. ***Test out equipment before using it*** – I should have tested out the breaks instead of taking Uncle Al's word for it.
2. ***Show a willingness to learn*** – If you show a willingness to learn, people will teach you. I did not hesitate to help Uncle Al cut wood despite not knowing how to operate a chainsaw.
3. ***Making mistakes is a learning process*** - If you make a mistake learn from it and move on. I cut Uncle Al's tailgate, but he corrected my mistake and I never cut another tailgate.
4. ***Persistence pays off*** – I requested daily about learning how to use a backhoe despite numerous denials. My persistent requests paid off when Fred taught me how to use it.

Uncle Nathan with my mom, Jean, at her wedding reception.

Uncle Al

HIGH SCHOOL

I was a very sociable kid in high school. My high school had almost 1,000 students and I knew everyone except for 47 students. I was able to do this because I played sports and drove a school bus. Bus drivers had to leave early and were assigned to the Freshman Study Sessions which was the last period of the day. I knew all of the freshman my junior and senior year of high school. I should have graduated in the top 10% of my class instead of in the middle, but I had too many outside distractions such work, sports, and friends. I was one of the few black students who took college preparatory courses. There were only three black students taking geometry and we were each in different classes. I took Algebra II and Geometry only because Pat Snyder, a classmate, told me she would help me pass those classes and get into college. Although we were never in the same class, she helped me out and I named my daughter after her. I was accepted into several colleges, but I was bored and burned from school because I worked at a movie theater, drove a school bus, and wrestled while taking college preparatory courses. My cousin, Tony Goldston, who was in college to become a teacher told us young guys, the hardest thing about college was not having enough food to eat. He told us there were plenty of nights where he would eat a Wish Sandwich which was two pieces of bread where you wished you had a piece of meat in between the bread. Once I heard the story, I made a decision to join the Army because I did not have money to go to college and I sure did not want to eat a Wish Sandwich.

If you want something you must work for it. I had several jobs before graduating from high school. I emptied trash cans for senior citizens in the neighborhood for .50¢, washed cars, worked as a cook, cashier in a movie theater, drove a school bus, helped put in septic tanks, picked tobacco, chopped wood, cut lawns, and sold black

10

berries. If someone said they would pay me for helping them, I would show up no matter the job.

Everybody in my neighborhood worked. The alcoholics would come to the tobacco fields smelling like a still. They would work in the fields all day and drink afterwards. The owners of the tobacco fields which I worked in paid us $3.00 an hour while other owners paid their workers $5.00 an hour. Their reasoning for paying us less was because we were young and they drove us to the fields. We worked from sun up to sun down with a 15-minute lunch break and the owners gave us a soda, peanut butter/cheese crackers, or moon pies. I became sick after eating a moon pie and never ate one again. Sometimes they would cheat us out our weekly earnings and their reasoning for it was because they said it was too much money for us young people. One day they asked us to remove the tops from the tobacco plants. The job normally takes an hour, but this day I told my friends to go slow. We played and went slow which upset the owners. We told them they owed us for four hours for our work and if they didn't pay us, we were going to quit. They paid us and we quit the next week.

I worked as a cook and used to hook my friends up with extra hamburger on their order. I rode my bicycle to and from work. They did not officially fire me; they just didn't put me back on the schedule. I must have been a sorry cook or they were tired of coming up short on inventory.

Work at the movie theater allowed me to see movies for free. I saw the original Star Wars 25 times, Empire Strike Back 20 times, and the first Indiana Jones movie 20 times. People would ask me how much was the $1.00 popcorn and I would say $2.00. Some gave me strange looks and others paid $2.00. I would give the money back to those who over paid. I made deals with my friends who worked at McDonald's. A Big Mac meal for a free movie theater ticket. I never paid for my dinner. One day the manager went in the movie theater and saw 40 people in the movie and only 10 tickets sold. She scolded me for because I took advantage of her policy which stated we could

11

allow one-person free entrance per movie.

I cut lawns for extra money up until I graduated from high school. The definition of a self-propelled mower was a person gets behind a mower and pushes it himself. I used to push my two-acre sized lawn on Thursday, my grandmother's two-acre lawn, and two quarter sized lots in the trailer park. I made $5.00 per yard for each lawn except for mine. Crash who lived in the trailer park would give me two glasses of Kool-Aid after cutting his yard. I later found out he was serving me daiquiris. The older guys were our mentors. They roughed us up sometimes to teach us to be better than them.

My aunts, Mable, Bessie, and Patti would take me fishing on the condition I would get the worms. I would dig through the trash at Aunt Bessie's house and search through leaves at Aunt Pattie's house gathering worms. I'm lucky I didn't get tetanus or bitten by a snake from those two locations. Aunt Mable used an old Coca-Cola cooler to raise worms which made it easier for me. She was the first person who taught me how to fish. I out fished her the first time we went fishing using a cane pole so she took the cane pole away from me and taught me how to use a casting rod. I cried like a baby when she took my cane pool away. Our summers would be spent fishing in the morning and playing cards in the afternoon. Marcus Charles, Vietnam Veteran, would take us teenage guys fishing. He would always say "boys if you want to eat, you better learn how to fish". We never went hungry, but I am surprised we didn't end up with mercury poison from eating the fish from the river.

12

High School Lessons

1. *Words of encouragement go along way* – Pat Snyder's words of encouragement helped me to pass College Preparatory Courses. I would have never taken those hard courses if it was not for her encouragement and help.

2. *Put education first* – Making money was prioritized over education in my area. Students could get excused absences for working in tobacco fields. The school would let students leave two hours early to go work in the mills. Mills encouraged students to quit high school and they would pay for their GEDs. When those mills closed, people were left behind the rest of society. I worked two jobs, wrestled, and took college courses in high school. If school work was prioritized over making money, I could have earned an Academic Scholarship.

3. *Do not be afraid to do things outside of your comfort zone* – I took Typing, Accounting, and Consumer Math which taught students how to do taxes, open up a savings account, and balance a checkbook. I did people taxes afterwards for a small fee. I was the only male in my accounting and typing classes and the females in those classes laughed at me because I was the slowest typist and I did not understand accounting. I could type 45 words per minute after two weeks and I achieved the second highest grade in Accounting after the first semester. I learned to crochet in middle school.

4. *If you are not prepared for college do something else beforehand* – Do not waste your time or money on college if you are not ready. You can join the Military or work for a couple of years before attending college. I served two years in the Army before going to college.

5. *Pursue your dreams no matter what everyone else thinks* – One of the worst things you can say to yourself is "I wished I had done this". It is your life, and it is up to you to make the best of

13

it; pursue your dreams no matter what anyone says.

6. ***Seek advice from people who have traveled the same road which you are preparing to travel on*** – Several people told me not to go into the Military because the only thing I would learn was how to curse. Twenty years later those same people told me they wished they had joined the Military.

7. ***Learn about money*** – Know the difference between Wants and Needs when dealing with money. I made a lot of money, but I blew a lot of it picking up the tab for friends. I wished someone had given me a class on investments when I was making money instead of living the good life. I saved up about 20% of it, but it should have been 50%.

8. ***One must read to learn*** – I read my parents collection of Biblical Stories, Encyclopedia Brittanica, and Ebony Black History books.

BASIC TRAINING

I joined the Army for two years after high school as a Military Policeman. This upset some family members, but my grandmother, Uncle Al, and other family members who were former service members thought it was a great idea and said it would make me a man. My recruiter was Staff Sergeant Billy Martindale, who I greatly respect till this day. I told him I wanted to join the Infantry and he told me I was crazy and to join the Military Police Corps so I can ride around in an air-conditioned car instead of sleeping on the ground. I never rode in an air-conditioned vehicle my entire two years in the military. My primary transportation during my enlistment was a jeep and the faster you went the cooler it became, and half of the time the heat was out in the winter.

I went to Fort McClellan, Alabama for Basic Training which I later found out is where my Uncle Al attended Basic Training. I think I was more excited about taking my first airplane ride than attending Basic Training.

I arrived at Ft. McClellan on 3 August 1982 and saw the biggest white man which I have ever seen in my entire life, he was a Drill Sergeant who made Hulk Hogan look like a 98-pound weakling. The first words out of his math were "We better take this training serious because the United States is involved in a conflict every 10 years and the majority of you will see combat". I never forget those words which became true to me because I was deployed to Grenada 14 months later.

The first night in Basic Training people hardly slept because of the constant yelling from the Drill Sergeants. They called us idiots and druggies because people could not fill out papers correctly and guys had long hair. Later that night while in bed, I began to cry and asked myself what in the hell did I get myself into. I was sleeping on the bottom bunk when I heard the person on the top bunk say "Oh Shit"

15

followed by a loud thud. The person on the top bunk fell off his bed. Nobody laughed because we were scared shitless of what would happen if the Drill Sergeants heard us.

The next day the Drill Sergeants took us to the barbershop, and they had a field day laughing at us receiving our haircuts. The barbers asked guys how they would like their haircut and guys would respond with "A little off of the top". The barbers would give them a Mohawk cut or other crazy design first and then proceed to cut it all off and laugh at the new recruits. Guys with long hair would be upset, but there was nothing they could do. One guy told the barber he had a large mole in the back of his head and asked if he would be careful in cutting his hair which the barber responded "Sure. The barber cut the guy's hair so close that he cut the mole off, and the Drill Sergeants and other barbers laughed hysterically. The barber gave the guy a Band-Aid and said, "Welcome to the Army".

A couple of days later, they boarded us on buses and shipped us out to our companies. My company was Foxtrot 12 and my Drill Sergeants were SSG Honaker, SSG Farmer, and SSG Farr. SSG Honaker, who sounded like SFC Herniaka on Stripes, met us on the bus at the company. He told us we had 30 seconds to get off of the bus and 29 of them on gone. We moved so fast that one soldier wasted his entire washing powders on the floor of the bus which resulted in the Drill Sergeants smoking us by making us do push-ups and mountain climbers for over an hour. I was so scared that I probably knocked out 300 push-ups. The Drill Sergeants gave us a brief on what is expected of us in Foxtrot 12. The First Sergeant asked, "Who is the toughest person in the group" and this one black guy stood up and said he was. The 1SG told him to report to the back of the stage. We never saw the guy again and it set the tone for the entire training. I believed the event was staged, but it kept us in line.

The Drill Sergeants had us practicing marching the next day because we had a new commander, Captain Greene, coming in. I later ran into Captain Greene while I was in college at NC A&T State

16

University in Greensboro. When we started marching, I could not stay in step for a minute, and we were getting chewed out because of it. The other soldiers kidded me about my marching and told me that I could not be black because all black soldiers had rhythm and could march. Well, that night I did double fire guard duty for two hours practice marching while doing my duty. I do not understand why the Army calls it fire guard when the building has fire alarms. The next day SSG Farmer put me in the first squad so that he could get a good laugh at my marching. He was blown away that I could march so well after yesterday's comical performance that he gave us 5 minutes extra free time.

My relatives told me to never volunteer for anything while in the military. Of course, I didn't listen. One day I had a chance to fire a M60 machine gun, a gun Rambo used in First Blood. I was very excited about firing the M60. Once I completed firing the M60, the Drill Sergeants asked for volunteers to turn them in. They told us that we just had to wipe them down and that we could drink sodas while we were cleaning them. We had 26 M60 machine guns between the 7 of us to clean. Once the weapons were cleaned, you turned them into an Inspector for cleanliness. The Inspector would make you do a function check and disassemble the weapon for inspection. The inspector checked the weapon with a Q-Tip. The inspectors rejected my 5 M60 machine guns about 5 times each. To this day I can take a M60 apart blind folded and put it back together in less than a minute. I think the instructors rejected them as a joke, because each time they found only a small amount of carbon on the gun.

We had good Drill Sergeants in Basic Training who spoke to us like people, but who did not hesitate to administer punishment when needed. Once a female Drill Sergeant hit me in the eye with a tennis ball for sleeping in a class, she apologized. I was wrong because the Drill Sergeants told us to stand up when we feel tired, but if you stood up, they would make you do 50 pushups which I could not do. I also dropped my weapon while climbing into the bleachers and a Range

17

Instructor, Vietnam Veteran, picked-up my weapon and inspected it. He was impressed that my weapon was spotless and then he threw my weapon back at me very hard. I caught the weapon, and he told me to never drop a weapon again and that if I did not catch that weapon, he would have kicked my ass. I never dropped a weapon again my entire time in the Military because of that incident, but I sure as hell dozed off in a lot of Military classes. I ended up meeting Drill Sergeant Farmer in Panama. He was a 1SG in Panama. He did not remember me, but I sure as hell remember him. I also had a good M60 instructor for our End of Cycle Test who was a former Marine in Force Recon. He taught us how to breakdown and put together M60 machines gun the by-the-book. He was an evaluator at the M60 station and when I came to his station, I was the only soldier who took it apart and put it together just liked he showed us. He was astonished and told me that I should make the military a career because I was the only student in his Military career who ever got it right after one round of instruction. Little did he know that I spent an entire day at the M60 turn-in point tearing down and putting machine guns back together, plus I was scared shit of him, and I did not want to get recycled that's why I put it together correctly.

I got in trouble a couple more times in Basic Training, once for leaving my key under my pillow which was forbidden. SFC Farmer flipped my bed over and trashed my wall locker. Another time I had extra rifle training because I kept getting 2 out of 3 inside the circle during rifle zeroing practice. The Drill Sergeants let us practice shooting drills on our own in an air-conditioned room. SFC Farmer came in the room and spotted me napping and told me to just roll over and do pushups. I learned in the Army whenever you get a chance to sleep then sleep. The Army says soldiers only need 4 hours of sleep per night and scientists say an individual needs 8 hours, so I am trying to figure out who is telling the truth.

I enjoyed the people who I met in Basic Training. We came in as individuals and left as a team. I was surprised to meet white guys

18

who had only seen African Americans on television. The white guys all wanted hair like mine because they thought I didn't have to comb my hair in the morning. At night I would wear a stocking cap to keep my so-called waves in. The white guys thought this was cool and would wear stocking caps also.

There was a soldier from Kentucky, Kurns, who said he joined the Army so he could get a new pair of shoes. Kurns would tell us stories about how poor he was and that he purchased three cars for $100 each. I thought I was from the country, and he made my one light town sound like New York City. Kurns was chaptered out of the Army, but he did achieve his goal of getting a pair of boots.

Golan was a fat kid who could not do one push-up or sit-up. The Drill Sergeants put him on the Fat Boy Plan in which he could only drink water, no fried foods or bread, and he had to do push-ups every time he saw a Drill Sergeant. Sometimes Drill Sergeants would call up on the intercom and make him do push-ups for no reason. This crazy routine resulted in Golan losing over 100 pounds in four months. Their weight loss plan was better than the Jenny Craig's Diet.

Soldiers in Basic Training came from different backgrounds and had different reasons for joining the Army. Jersey, whose bed was next to mine, was from New Jersey and joined the Army instead of going to jail. He would always tell stories about hustling on the streets of New Jersey and stealing purses from women and the Army made him a Policeman. Half of the people I served with in the MP Corps had records. The Army's requirement in those days for becoming an MP was supposedly to pass the Military Entrance Test, ASVAB, and the physical. I believe Recruiters had someone to take the test for some of the soldiers I attended Basic Training with because they were dumb as a rock.

Basic Training was an enjoyable experience to see people of different backgrounds come together to form a team and become good friends. Regretfully I failed to maintain contact with them. While my

19

parents were vacationing in the Bahamas one of my former classmates who was a Customs Agent recognized the last name and told my family that he attended Basic Training with me.

The hardest things about Basic Training to me was that you only had two minutes to eat each meal and the Gas Chamber. I gained about 10 pounds of muscle. The physical part of it was easy because I was in shape before I left home.

The Gas Chamber was the worst part about Basic Training. The Drill Sergeants had on their Gas Masks the entire time and would make us do exercises with the mask on and then make us take off the masks and say our names, rank, and social security number before exiting the chamber. If you messed up, the Drill Sergeant would make you go back through. I said my name and began choking, coughing, and crying. When the door opened, I ran out and vomited over a railing. The Gas Chamber was the worst feeling which I ever had. I gained a lot of respect for tear gas after that experience. Tear gas affected everyone except for a soldier from Louisiana. The soldier from Louisiana took off his masked and walked calmly back in to help those of us who were puking all over the place.

I along with seven other soldiers in Basic Training applied to attend Airborne School which was a goal for me. We were held over in Basic Training for three months waiting on orders for Airborne School. We did all sorts of jobs such cleaning the company area, Kitchen Patrol (KP), and preparing for the Inspector General (IG) Inspection, better known as the White Glove Inspection. KP was one of the worst jobs which I had in the Army because I felt like a bus boy in a restaurant. We washed dishes and tables, peeled potatoes, and served food.

The IG Inspection was worse than KP. During the IG Inspection we cleaned floors and toilets with toothbrushes, picked weeds out between rocks with our hands, cut grass, mopped, waxed, and buffed floors. Afterwards the cadre inspected the area wearing white gloves and if they found any dust then you had to clean all over again. It was a horrible experience preparing for that inspection. Until this day, I can clean better than any woman and operate a buffer with one finger. The unit passed, but I swore to myself, I would never go through another IG Inspection.

Lessons Learned

1. ***Teamwork beats individualism*** – You can't accomplish difficult tasks without teamwork. We had 15 minutes to clean the barracks before inspections. We established teams for floor cleaning, bathroom, bed making, and trash. There was no way we could have accomplished those tasks individually in a short amount of time.

2. ***Work on improving your short comings*** – I could not march worth crap, but I worked to improve my marching skills during Fire Guard.

3. ***Pay attention in class*** – The class which the former Marine gave us on breaking down and putting back the M60 machine gun enabled me to pass the Basic Training End of Cycle Test (EOCT) and it helped me throughout my military career. He taught me so well that 40-years later I can still break down and put back an M60 machine gun.

4. ***Think outside of the box*** – The Drill Sergeants plan of having Golan drink only water, eat healthy, and do push-ups throughout the day resulted in Golan losing over 100 pounds in less than 4-months.

Field Training at Ft. McClellan, Alabama

Saunders and I on day before graduation

Martin, me, and Tyrone kneeling

24

AIRBORNE SCHOOL

We finally received our orders for Airborne school in January. I wanted to be a Paratrooper because I thought it was cool to wear a beret and I could easily pick-up women, and plus, I needed the extra money for a car. Ft. Bragg was only 62 miles from my house.

I arrived at Airborne School in January along with seven other soldiers from my Basic Training unit and we were all sent to separate companies. Airborne school was hard because we ran in boots all of the time and were treated like crap. The Jumpmasters lined us up for inspections every morning and then they would fail 75% of the students just for fun. When you failed inspections, they sent you to the Gig Pit which was a sawdust pit. Once you were in the Gig Pit, they would wet the sawdust down and have you doing push-ups, flutter kicks, and any other screwed-up exercises they could think of. I was never sent to the Gig Pit and the reason I believe is because our Jumpmaster had an unwritten code in which he would pass the first four people in the squad and fail the rest. He would say "Gig Pit" without looking at the other soldiers' uniforms.

There was a Black Marine Sergeant who all Army TACs hated only because he was a Marine. They failed him every day and recycled him to another company three times just for being a Marine. The TACs would laugh at him while telling him, he was being recycled. The Marine Sergeant told me, "I do not care what they do to me, I am never going to quit". He graduated with me. There were three other Marines goofing off in formation one day and he gave them the stare of death and told them, he would kill them if they don't stop playing around and Marines don't act that way. Those three Marines stopped goofing around and came to attention which impressed me.

25

I made it to the second week in training which was called Tower Week. I was hoisted on a 200 feet tower and when they released me, I crashed to the ground. I was chewed out for not paying attention. I was more concerned with the view than paying attention to the TACs. They sent me back-up and this time I landed with my legs apart which resulted in me being recycled to another class. I wanted to quit, but an instructor talked me out of it and then I remembered I needed the extra $83 to buy a car. I calculated my pay in my head, and I figured my take home pay with Jump Pay would be $135 every two weeks after deductions of $100 a month for my GI Bill, taxes of $110, and a car payment of $235 a month. If I did not complete Jump School then my take home pay would be $99 every two weeks. Money was the primary reason I went into the Army. I wanted to attend college and not have to eat a Wish Sandwich so the Army was my ticket to riches.

I was moved to another company and then I made it to Jump Week. I cannot recall my first jump from an airplane because my eyes were closed the entire time. As a matter of fact, I think everyone's' eyes were closed. The second jumped I landed in a creek which had ankle deep water and chewed out for missing the Drop Zone. Half of the candidates landed in the creek.

The following day one of the students brought talcum powder to the TACs' office and told them they could not smoke us. Those TACs' ran the shit out of us. We ran 5 miles in less than 30 minutes in boots which 80% of the people fell out of the run and then they proceeded to smoke us in the Gig Pit. The TACs had never done ran us like that before. We later found out why and the student who brought the talcum powder had to do exercises between breaks while everyone else relaxed and told war stories. They smoked the shit out of him.

26

Lessons Learned

1. *If you have a goal in mind do not let others deter you* – The Marine Sergeant did not quit no matter how much the other Sergeants screwed with him.

2. *If you Brag, you better be able to back it up* – The Sergeant who boasted to the TACs about them not smoking us was one of the first ones to fall out of the run.

3. *When in a leadership position act like a leader* – The majority of the TACs used their position to act as Hazers instead of leaders. I have great respect for the Marine Sergeant because most soldiers would have quit because of the unnecessary harassment. Some leaders forget people volunteer to serve in the Military to be trained not to be hazed.

Airborne School. The best parachute jumps I made was from a C-130 Tailgate.

28

118TH MP COMPANY

My first duty assignment was the 118th Airborne Military Police Company at Ft. Bragg, NC in March 1983. I was so happy because I was going to be assigned to an Airborne company which enabled me to afford a car. The 118th and the 82nd Airborne Military Police Companies were the only Airborne MP companies in the Army at the time. I spent the first week at the reception station and could not sleep at all because I heard people running an obstacle course and calling cadence at 2:00am. It was the CCF Company better known as the Correctional Facility Company where the Army sent soldiers to, who failed to maintain discipline. CCF was worse than Basic Training. You marched in cadence everywhere you went, could not talk while eating, did physical training all hours of the day, endured daily inspections, and cut grass with scissors. Soldiers hated to go to CCF. The Army stopped the program because too many minorities were being sent to CCF. I had a white Squad Leader who spent 30 days in CCF and he said it was the best thing for him. I feel getting rid of CCF was a mistake because CCF saved the Army money and time by keeping a soldier in service instead of putting them out. Seeing other soldiers going through CCF made me more focused and disciplined. Twenty-five years later I saw Marines on Ft. Story breaking big rocks into little rocks in 95° weather. I bet they didn't make the same mistake again.

I reported to the 118th Airborne MP Company after spending a week at the reception station. The 118th was a company filled with a lot of characters. There was a beer machine outside of the unit and soldiers above the rank of Sergeant could have two beers for lunch. The new Commander, Russell Cancilla, removed the machines because too many soldiers were returning from lunch drunk.

29

The post bus would drop all the incoming students at their respective units after soldiers completed In-Processing. The driver told me the 118th had a bad habit of hazing new soldiers when they came to the unit, and he was right. As soon as I exited the bus the SSG Mills, Re-enlistment Sergeant, and Sergeant Grant made me do push-ups with my duffle bag on my back. SSG Mills, told me to call SGT Grant a "Motherfucker and a Son of a Bitch" if I wanted to get out of doing push-ups. I told him a Private can't say those words to a Sergeant and SSG Mills told me I was disobeying a Direct Order. After doing more than 100 push-ups, I finally called SGT Grant a SOB. Well, SGT Grant put me back to doing more push-ups. He told me if I wanted to stop doing push-ups, I had to call SSG Mills an "Asshole". I refused so I did another 100 push-ups. This went on for almost an hour. If I could not do push-ups, they made me do flutter kicks. I left a pool of sweat in their office. Later my Platoon Sergeant, SFC Surom, picked me up and asked me where I was from. I told him I was from Ramseur, NC and he asked me if knew the name of his mother-in-law who owned a radio station in Asheboro, NC which was the town next to mine. I knew the name of the station and the street it was on, but I did not know his mother-in-law's name which resulted in me doing more push-ups. I was truly smoked after being in the unit in less than 2 hours. SFC Bennett, who was in the same Platoon and from Randleman, NC, was laughing during the entire ordeal. Randleman is a town in the same county where I grew up at.

I was assigned to a room with 6 other soldiers. I thought this was Heaven because my room was one of two rooms which contained a bathroom and a shower. The room was 12 x 12 not counting the bathroom. It would not work in today's Army because only two soldiers are allowed in a room of that size now.

The unit made me an M60 gunner primarily because no one wanted to carry it and it weighed 26 pounds. They didn't know my dream was to become a M60 machine gunner and I knew the weapon better than a M16 because of my experience with it in Basic Training.

30

The other reason they made me a M60 Machine Gunner is because I achieved the highest score on the M60 Qualification in the platoon. Since I received the highest score qualification score on the M60, I was rewarded a chance to shoot a 50 Caliber machine gun. SFC Surom trained me on the use of the 50-caliber. After three rounds of practice, I was consistently hitting targets a mile away. I enjoy shooting machine guns because I can't hit the backside of a barn with a pistol. Almost every time I go to a pistol range it takes me two times to qualify.

118th Soldiers

The 118th was a good unit with a lot of crazy soldiers. I don't know how the Army let some of them become Military Policemen because they had a lot of issues. The unit would even fight other MP Companies. They would talk crap to the other MP Companies and throw snowballs at them because they were not on Parachute status. My roommates were Chuck, Frank, Conway, Sutton, and Jay. Chuck and Frank were from New York. Chuck ended up making a career out of the Army and achieving the rank of Command Sergeant Major (CSM).

Frank was a rich kid from New York who was told to join the Army or go to jail because he was caught joy riding. Frank introduced me to Classical Music which helped me fall asleep after a 12-hour work shift. Frank was a weightlifter who was always showing off his muscles. One day I was tired of hearing Frank talk about how much he could lift, so I locked the door then put 135 pounds on the bench which stuck to my chest like a magnet to steel. I tilted the bar to the left and then to the right resulting in the weights crashing to the floor. A couple of soldiers came knocking on the door when they heard the sound. I told them I dropped some weights and everything was okay. Thank goodness I didn't have any weight collars on the bar. Once I left the Army, I became a weightlifting king and if saw Frank today I would out bench press him by a hundred pounds.

Jay was the youngest soldier in the unit and a virgin when he arrived at the unit. He went crazy after his first sexual experience and began to pick-up hookers on Bragg Boulevard against our advice. He told us he picked a hooker up and the hooker was going to give him a blow job and when he reached to touch the person's behind, he felt nothing but hair. Jay said he stopped the car and threw the man out, we all laughed hysterically after hearing the story.

Conway was the senior guy in the room and drove a green Chrysler with rims on it. He was very laid back and professional. He was the first person to introduce me to Popeye's Chicken.

SGT Sutton was a country boy from Kinston, North Carolina who lived in our room temporarily. He was a very calm and outstanding leader who I looked up to. His uniform was always immaculate, and he enjoyed showing off the scar on his leg from a pig bite. He had just arrived from Germany and showed the platoon his $1,200 stereo system which had a Reverb system, equalizer, cassette deck, turntable, receiver, and two huge speakers. I still don't know the purpose of Reverb. I was in shock when I saw SGT Sutton's stereo because where I came from people only had a turntable or an eight-track player. SGT Sutton's bragging about his stereo system resulted in me purchasing almost $20k of Bose equipment. Bose should put me in a commercial for the money I spent on their equipment. Most soldiers who went to Germany returned with an expensive stereo or a German Shrunk (Cabinet). I later ran into SGT Sutton 11 years later at Ft. Leonardwood, Missouri. Sutton retired as a Command Sergeant Major.

My first Squad Leader was SFC Houston, Veteran who claimed he was filmed running in Airborne School during the movie Green Berets Starring John Wayne. He was out of the Army for a while and returned to the Army for retirement benefits. He could not run due to bad knees.

The Squad Leader who took over after SSG Houston's retirement was nicknamed hardcore, but when we went to Grenada, he whined liked a two-year-old because he was afraid, he would be killed. He felt I should know more about soldiering, but I was Private wet behind the ears. In fact, Privates were not highly thought of in the unit. The only things I could do were shoot, march, run, and shine boots. I remember the time I was placed on Flag Duty. I told the squad leader I have never done Flag Detail before. The instructions I received were to salute the flag and just stand there. The flag touched the ground which made him upset and then he went ballistic on me for not

33

knowing how to fold the Flag. The night after the Flag incident, I asked someone to train me on it because I knew I was going to be placed on Flag Detail again, and I was right. This time I did such an outstanding job they placed me on the Color Guard Team for a Change of Command and a Funeral Detail. It takes about 18 months for a soldier to really learn the ins and outs of the Army.

My Team Leader Bobby, roommate Chuck, and the Brigade Commander's Driver rode Harleys and at one time they talked about joining the Hells' Angels. I asked them why and they said for protection, and I replied you are Military Policemen a person who is responsible for upholding the law so why would you need protection? They never answered the question, and I just shook my head and told them they were crazy. Several soldiers thought it was a rite of passage to get busted down in rank, but I associated rank with money, and I knew if I was busted down then I wouldn't be able to afford my car payment.

SGT Kowalski, a female, was one of the best soldiers in the unit. Out of 200 soldiers there were only about 3 females, but they were tough, and SGT Kowalski was one of the toughest ones. She did everything by the book and she really cared about the soldiers in the unit. I have a lot of respect for SGT Kowalski till this day.

SGT Brown who was 6 foot 4 and married to a German National was funny. He told me his wife would not give him sex before 6:00am so he changed the clock in the bedroom two hours ahead. That only lasted a day because he forgot to change the other clocks in the house. SGT Brown and I were M60 gunners on our deployment to Grenada.

SGT Crosby, a very sharp, laid-back, and professional soldier who took time out of his schedule to help others. I later ran into Crosby at a football game at NC A&T State University where I was attending college. I met Crosby at the 118th reunion and he retired as a CSM and became a Minister.

34

PFC Hollaway, a friend of mine from South Carolina was the first person I met with a 42-inch vertical jump. He was about 5'7 and could only dunk a basketball two-handed because his hands were too small to palm the ball.

PFC Lee from Philadelphia was another good friend of mine who would do anything for you, but sometimes he wouldn't listen to good advice given to him. Lee wanted a car very badly and we warned him about the shady practices of used car dealers around Ft. Bragg. I went with him one day and asked the used car salesman could we look at the engine and he replied, "What for", we left in a hurry. The next day Lee went by himself to a car dealership which we warned him about. He purchased a Toyota Celica and within a week he was putting a $1,500.00 transmission in it which was almost as much as the car cost. Lee retired from the Army and the Government.

Specialist Wooten from Georgia a stocky chain-smoking individual with a neck which looked like the Spike, cartoon dog that Droopy used to fight. He drove a Yellow Ford Thunderbird which we called the Yellow Banana. Dwight was the biggest shit talker in the unit. Although he was a Specialist, he would tell the Sergeants to kiss his ass. He knew his job, but he had a mouth on him and he still does. I remember when they sent him to Force Recon school, he was back on the bus before the bus left the site. Force Recon Cadre sent him back to the unit 5 minutes later because he told the Force Recon Cadre that they were not going to holler at him like a Private.

Sergeants Reese and Jenk knew their jobs well but loved chasing women. They would be on duty trying to pick-up women. Rese retired from the Army.

The Army sent Jenk to college for 6 months and he came back wild as hell. Jenk and Reggie, who was trying to become a Professional Football Player, drove Cadillacs. When Jenk returned from college, he asked to borrow my Toyota Celica so he could pick-up something from the Post Exchange. He returned about three hours later cruising

35

with a hand hanging out of the sunroof. I believe he took my car over to a girl's house.

Bland, a boxer on the Post-Boxing Team also drove a Cadillac. I would later serve in Panama with Bland's younger brother who was a character too. I have never seen so many young guys driving Cadillacs before in my life. Where I was from only big fat old men drove Cadillacs.

We had two soldiers who were best buddies, one had black hair and the other one blond. They were so close that they even shared toothbrushes. One night they got drunk and went to the Dragon Club which was located close to our barracks. They met two girls and flipped a coin to see who would take the pretty girl home. The soldier with black hair flipped the coin and lost, but told his buddy the blonde hair soldier he lost. The soldier with the black hair took the pretty girl home and caught a venereal disease. We burst out laughing when he told us this story.

SGT Worth was another good soldier in the unit. He was the person who made me realize I had screwed up teachers and family members. One day I was boxing Dwight in the motor pool, and I was tagging his head boxing Southpaw, but when I boxed right-handed Dwight would land some punches. SGT Worth told me to switch back to boxing him Southpaw which I did and won the fight. I shot a rifle, bow, and pool stick left-handed, but wrote right-handed. My teachers would always get on me for the unorthodox ways I held a pencil and fork. I discovered after the boxing match I was actually left- handed and everyone made me use my right hand because they thought left-handed people were weird.

There was a lot of hazing occurring in the unit. Soldiers would hang newbies out of the second-floor window in sleeping bags. The zipper broke on a Private's sleeping bag and he landed in the bushes head first. When he stood up the first thing he said was "Where is my cigarette".

One day a MP picked up a soldier from jail at the Fayetteville Police Station and put him in the back seat. They were having a conversation and the soldier jumped out of the at a red light. This incident resulted in us handcuffing everyone we were transporting back to posts. Fayetteville Police back then would arrest you for anything. I picked up a soldier who blew a .01. He wasn't drunk, did not smell like alcohol or disrespectful to the officer who was a former soldier himself. I felt sorry for the soldier because he was leaving the Army the next day. Fayetteville police loved messing with soldiers whom they arrested on Hayes Street.

PFC Edwards, who arrived in the unit around the same time as me, received the worst hazing case. One night some sergeants took Edwards to a trailer park and got him drunk. They took off all his clothes, tied him to a telephone pole, sprayed whip cream on him, and made him say "I am a Cherry". All new soldiers were called Cherries until they completed their first jump with the unit.

Dog handlers in our unit were crazy on a different level. There was SGT Parks who the unit made grow his hair when he first arrived. The leaders said he looked too hardcore and crazy, therefore; he was ordered to grow his hair. One day he was in a bar and a girl had a pet mouse on her shoulder and Parks grabbed it and ate it. He had diarrhea for three days. The other dog handler who I can't remember was not that crazy, but the unit sent him to a psychologist because he was eating dog biscuits. His reason for eating dog biscuits was if it's good enough for his dog then it's good enough for him. The psychologist said he was okay and he was no crazier than rest of the soldiers in the 118th.

We had a Motor Pool Sergeant who was on steroids and reduced in rank a couple of times. He enjoyed asking us what we were doing in 1973. I responded I was in the 2nd grade, and he laughed and said "He was the Radio Operator for his Commander in the 82nd during their preparation for a Combat Jump into Africa". The mission never happened, but it was his claim to fame.

37

The Motor Pool Sergeant and a former Basic Training friend of mine got drunk and broke into the base swimming pool one night. They were caught because one of them left their flip flops behind with their name on them. They both were busted down in rank. I associated rank with money, and I was going to do everything in my power to ensure I wasn't going to be busted down, but the other soldiers thought it was a rite of passage to lose rank.

I constantly spoke to the Hispanic soldiers in the unit: SFC Rosa, SSG T, SGT Torres, and SGT Rivera. The only Hispanic person I ever met prior to them was an exchange student from Mexico during high school. SFC Rosa, a Vietnam 101st Combat Veteran would always say the Purple Heart is one medal he did not want because it meant you were shot in Combat. SSG T was a former Ranger Battalion who drove a Black SAAB which kids in my neighborhood said looked like a casket. I later found out SSG T was great at exaggerating stories. SGT Rivera would go on to become a Command Sergeant Major. SGT Rivera chewed me out for not securing rounds which another soldier placed beside me in Grenada. I spoke to CSM Rivera 25 years later because I was trying to get assigned to the 118th as my last duty station. We talked for almost an hour about the good times in the unit. The Puerto Ricans treated me like a person and not like a Private and where always giving me advice on how to become a better soldier. They would be shocked today if they knew I spoke Spanish.

SFC Surom our Platoon Sergeant who later became our 1SG was an outstanding leader who I looked up to. He looked like the cartoon character Howdy Doody. I thought the man knew everything. He was MacGyver before MacGyver was a tv show. One day we had to clean a stove and we could never get the soot out of the bottom. He told us to put dirt in it, shake it up, and then wash it out. It worked. He loved the A-Team and made everyone watch it when it came on. He would quiz us the next day about what happened on the A-Team and if you answered incorrectly, you either did push-ups or you were assigned to a crappy duty. He was so American he only drunk Red,

38

White, and Blue Beer which was worse than Schaefer Light. I spoke with SFC Surom during a 118th Reunion about these stories and of course didn't remember them.

1SG Buck the 1SG when I arrived in the unit had a rough look and voice and the only time, I saw him smile was for a picture in Grenada. A soldier broke a urinal after a night of drinking which pissed 1SG Buck off so much, he stood in front of the formation and told us the soldier would be buying a new urinal for use as a flower pot. The soldier received an Article 15 which included a forfeiture of two months of his base pay which equaled a about $1,200 and he was restricted to the company for 30-days. Soldiers did not want to be restricted to the company because the 1SG came with details such as cutting grass, cleaning grass out between the rockets, cleaning floors which included buffing and waxing, picking-up trash, washing vehicles, answering phones at night while others were sleeping and any other shitty detail he could think of. There was never another broken urinal in the company. I remembered when 1SG traded his white Mazda RX-7 for a gray one just because another soldier brought a white Mazda RX-7 like his.

Soldiers in the unit were always doing crazy things. A soldier asked me did I have my blood wings and I replied "no". The Blackhat Instructors in Airborne School would ask graduates of Airborne School if they wanted Blood Wings. Instructors would pin the Airborne Wings on the soldier's chest without the safety clasp. The soldier laughed and said" that is not what I meant". He said "you earn your Blood Wings by eating your girlfriend out on her period". I said, "Hell No, you sick SOB" and he laughed. I said to myself I would never share a drink with his dirty ass even if it is the last drink on Earth.

39

Patrol Duty

Our unit was responsible for policing the main post and protecting the headquarters during field training. My first experience with policing was a disaster. The training which we received in Basic Training was not like what a soldier experience in the real world. We first had an inspection before assuming shift and the Officer on duty asked everyone questions such as "Who is the Secretary of Defense"? Everyone in the line-up failed to answer the questions. The only thing my leaders told me was to make sure I had my license and a clean uniform. I was given a vehicle, map, radio, and told to patrol an area. Five minutes after I started duty, I oversaw a minor vehicle accident. A young soldier hit a car in the rear and confessed that he was wrong. I did not know what paperwork was required and thank goodness there was a Sergeant in the area to help me out. I was on the case for three hours.

The next day I had duty, but I was prepared this time. I knew the entire Chain of Command from the President on down which shocked everyone.

Two weeks later I was assigned along with Bobby to patrol the ROTC camp. One day we encountered a sergeant who had been drinking and Bobby told him to leave his car and call a friend to pick him up. Well, the soldier started walking and when he saw us leave, he jumped back in his car, and we caught him a mile away and took him to the station. He started arguing with Bobby and another Military Policeman and they gave him wall to wall counseling. Back then soldiers would fight MPs just for the hell of it. I witnessed a lot of beatings. I never hit anyone, but we had a couple of crazies who enjoyed issuing beatings. One day a soldier who was arrested told a group of MPs that he would beat their asses and began to fight everyone. The Desk Sergeant jumped in, and it was an 8 on 1 fight which did not go well for the soldier. Amazingly the soldier did not get

40

hurt and his only punishment was a reduction in rank. Once a soldier was telling MPs that he was going to hurt them and was calling everyone names. Jones became tired of his antics and smacked him on the back of his neck. That soldier shut up and started crying. Another time a soldier who was arrested said he was going to beat every MPs ass in the room if we took the handcuffs off him. When I went to take his handcuffs off, he begged me not to. He knew if those handcuffs came off, he was going to get a beat down. Those times were crazy.

Another crazy event occurred when the unit made SSG Bran a Desk Sergeant. SSG Bran should never have been an MP. He always talked about his desire to go to war. A man who wants to experience war is off in the head. SSG Bran should have been Court Martial previously for shooting a Special Forces Soldier. SSG Bran responded to a fight and the Special Forces Soldier broke down in a Karate Stance and SSG Bran shot him in with a 45. The Army said he was justified in shooting him because he thought his life was in danger. Really, SSG Bran shot the soldier because he was scared shitless of the ass whipping coming his way.

The unit installed Cameras in the MP Station and the senior Non-Commissioned Officer warned us about doing crazy things in front of the cameras and the consequences we would face. He told us if we need to straighten someone up to do it outside of the station. There was this Korean lady who would come to the MP Station every weekend and beg us to arrest her husband for cheating or not giving her money. She would cry and scream at us every weekend. She never came on weekdays. One Saturday on a pay day weekend she showed up crying. We were extremely busy responding to fights and domestic disturbances all over the posts. She would not stop crying and was hollering at SSG Bran who was the Desk Sergeant. SSG Bran jumped across the desk and slapped her. It was caught on camera, and he was relieved on the spot. I don't know the outcome of the situation because I left the unit.

I was on patrol one night and encountered a hit and run incident involving a boxer. I requested an ambulance and back-up. A traffic patrol officer came, followed by Reese and Jenk. Reese and Jenk thought they were Billy Dee Williams and Denzel Washington and left the scene to talk with two females who were driving by. The females were nothing to bragged about and ended up leaving those two stranded on the side of the road. The traffic officer and I stayed with the boxer until the ambulance arrived. I don't know what happened afterwards with the boxer, but he was so high he didn't feel a thing.

My mentor was SSG "Bigfoot" Davis. SSG Davis was a tall guy who drove a red Lincoln LTD. I was his driver because he did not have a license for some reason, but he drove to and from work every day. Our first day was like the movie Training Day with Denzel Washington. Our first call was in a housing area on post where a woman was having a baby in the living room. The neighbor was helping, and the husband was outside smoking. We walked in and I just stared because I had never seen anything like that before. SSG Davis laughed hysterically afterwards and told everyone in the unit that I froze, which was true. I was the joke of the unit for a week. After we left the scene, we were driving through the same neighborhood and SSG Davis had me stop the car so that he could catch a guy who was stealing uniforms from clotheslines of other soldiers. The thief ran in front of the car and if I wasn't so green behind the ears, I would have run over him. The guy ran a 4 second 40 because he left Davis in his tracks. The thief did throw down the clothes and we returned them to their rightful owners. Later that evening we responded to a fight between two brothers. The younger brother stabbed the older brother with a knife because the older brother would not change the TV channel which contained an inappropriate movie for the younger children. The father was upstairs sleeping. There was always something going on at Ft. Bragg. A Military Base is a reflection of society. The same things which occur in society happens on base, but not as much.

42

Davis would catch soldiers having sex in the cars with their girlfriends. Once he caught a couple having sex in the car, Davis told her the guy was cheap and no good because he didn't take her to a hotel on a payday weekend. Well, the girl ended up giving Davis her number and the rest is history. He would always tell me these amazing stories, probably 99% were lies.

We used to patrol Smith Lake at night and find couples having sex. Davis said that he used to catch another Squad Leader and his wife having sex in their van every weekend. We patrolled the area every weekend looking for the Squad Leader's van which we never spotted.

The Brigade Commander came to our checkpoint and I made him show his ID and registrations because our instructions were to check every car. The Brigade Commander followed my instructions and told me "Good job". Davis chewed me out and told me I was crazy for stopping the Brigade Commander, but senior officers would always chew us out for not checking their IDs and registration because they wanted to know if we knew our jobs. The next day Davis was driving to our checkpoint in his big red Lincoln, I flagged him down to stop and he punched the accelerator and drove through the checkpoint, and everyone laughed afterwards. I learned a lot from him including what to do if someone becomes belligerent. He was a tall intimidating figure with a deep baritone voice and when a suspect disrespected him, he just told them if they did not comply with his orders then they would face a reduction in rank, reduced pay, and they could face a Court Martial. When you say you are going to take a soldier's money and rank, they usually cooperate.

Drugs were rampant in the Military in the 80s. The Army started making units test all their soldiers for illegal drugs. The 118th had some soldiers who used drugs illegally and the leadership team administered a urinalysis test hoping to catch them. The Sergeant in charge of the urinalysis told the leadership team that everyone involved with administering the test had to be school trained. The first time the unit

43

administered the test; seven soldiers came up positive. The test was thrown out because one of the administrators was not school trained. The craziest thing about the test was the main druggies beat the test because one of them was good friends with the Command Group's secretary and she told him about an upcoming drug test which he gladly shared with the unit. The leadership team continued testing soldiers for drugs which resulted in the unit having more professional and drug free soldiers.

SSG Damron was a great and caring leader who would go the extra mile to help soldiers be successful. He would send soldiers to schools to advance their careers. I later ran into a soldier who had SSG Damron for a Drill Instructor and SSG Dameron would show the trainees who were misbehaving his knife which he killed a Cuban Soldier with while serving in Grenada. I just laughed because it was a tall tale.

Parachute Jumps

My first Airborne jump with the 118th was almost a disaster. When you were a new Private the unit made all new soldiers wear a helmet with cherries painted on it to let everyone know that it was our first jump with the unit. The 118th had so many new soldiers that they ran out of helmets for me. We were jumping out of helicopters, and I started counting in my head and when I reached 3 seconds my parachute didn't deploy, I was getting ready to pull my reserve parachute at 4 seconds then the parachute opened. When I landed on the ground a fellow soldier told me that your parachute doesn't open until 6 seconds after you exit a helicopter. They never told us this during pre-jump training.

My next jump was a C-130 Tailgate with senior personnel in the Command Group. It was CPT Cancilla's first jump with the unit. Jeff Carpunky and I were the lowest ranking people on the plane. Jeff had to jump in order to receive his Jump Pay and the jump was my reward for making up my bed.

No one in the unit made their beds before work. My mom made me make my bed every day before school and the requirement was reinforced in Basic Training. Soldiers would tease me for making up my bed before work. One day Captain Cancilla conducted a room inspection and my bed was the only one made. 1SG Surom made everyone sleep outside in tents for a week. The tents had to be in alignment with each other. The other soldiers asked me if I would join them and I replied, "Heck No". I enjoyed having a room and television to myself. Captain Cancilla told me at a Reunion, the Battalion Commander called him to his office and told him he understood why he was doing it, but he wished he would not do it in front of the unit where everyone could see. Captain Cancilla responded, 'That was the only available place". There were no more unmade beds afterwards.

45

The worst jump I ever experienced was on Ft. Bragg when we were flying around the post for over three hours waiting to get clearance to jump. Everybody on the plane was getting sick. I was on the verge of vomiting when we received clearance to jump. When the Jumpmaster, a Lieutenant, said go the red light came on 5 seconds later. It came on when I was at the door, and I wasn't stopping because I was sick. When I landed on the ground, I noticed the 1SG and 10 other people who were behind me gathering their Parachutes for turn-in. The Commander and 1SG who had over 100 jumps each said they were not about to stay on the plane because it was the worst plane ride they ever experienced. We later saw the Lieutenant and she looked visibly upset because she allowed people to jump during the red light and thought she was going to get punished for it, but no punishment ever occurred from the incident.

The 118th normally made soldiers who missed formations, drunk on duty, or broke a Military or unit rule to cut the grass. One day I was assigned grass cutting duties, although I never broke a rule. I was mad because we had soldiers who were on punishment for various reasons and who should have been assigned to cut the grass. Although I was mad, I cut the grass as I was told. SFC Surom came out in front of the formation and asked who cut the grass. I was scared to confess because I thought I did something wrong. I finally said it was me and he said good job and the soldiers in my squad gave me the thumbs up sign. I was surprised everyone was congratulating me for cutting the grass. I later found out when leaders would assign grass cutting duties to the other soldiers, the soldiers would leave uncut sections and not cut around buildings or objects. I grew up cutting yards, so I knew the correct way to do it. I was never assigned grass cutting duty again.

Ft. Carson

We went to Ft. Carson, Colorado a month after I arrived at the unit. I was a late substitution because a Private suffered a broken jaw at the hands of some Samoan soldiers at the Dragon Club. The Private got drunk and mouthed off to some Samoan soldiers who beat the crap out of him. Soldiers used to fight every weekend at the Dragon Club and the Yutema Club which was in 82nd Airborne Division. We called the Yutema Club the stab and jab club because of the numerous fights and stabbings which occurred there.

We were the opposing force at Ft. Carson. One day we went to aggress the other unit and my Squad left me out in the middle of nowhere with no compass, radio, and map. I had captured one of the soldiers from the other unit. I waited for 3 hours for the squad to return. I still remember hearing coyotes hollering to this day. I finally told the soldier to take me to his unit. The unit leaders thought it was a trick and did not believe me. The unit later called SFC Surom to picked me up. He asked me where Chuck was and I told him I did not know, and Chuck told me to stay put and he would return later which he never did. I could see the stress on SFC Surom because a Marine had died in California earlier that year when his unit left him in the desert and SFC Surom knew if he lost a soldier the entire Chain of Command would be fired. Chuck finally returned around 8:00am and SFC Surom wanted to kill him, but he just shook his head and walked away. We dodged a big bullet. The only other time I saw worry on SFC Surom face is when we lost a soldier to a DUI incident on post. The soldier wrecked his vehicle and died about a week later.

Dwight and Frank

Field Exercises

We went on another field exercise at Ft. Bragg a month later which was a disaster. It rained on us heavily and our equipment became wet. Everyone's clothes were wet and SFC Surom wondered how our clothes became wet in our rucksacks. He later found out no one in the platoon knew about putting a waterproof bag in their rucksacks and then placing their clothes in the waterproof bag. It was one lesson which I never forgot, and I do this with my clothes when I travel. We came in early from the field exercise and that's when Conway introduced me to Popeye's Chicken. I have been hooked on Popeye's Chicken ever since 1983.

I had cousins who lived in Fayetteville. On my first weekend off from the field exercise, I took a cab to their house and the cab driver asked me if he could stop and pick up something at a store. I said "Sure", and he stopped at one of Fayetteville's National Landmarks, The Bottoms-Up which was a strip club. The cab driver went in, got a shot of liquor, looked at the girls, then he took me to my cousin's house. I was shocked, but I had a similar experience when my Uncle Al took me the work with him and stopped in a bar for a drink.

I finally purchased my car after been at Ft. Bragg for 4 months. It was a used 1982 Toyota Celica, black in color, sunroof, and a radio with an equalizer. It cost $9500 and I put $2,500 down on it. After my car payment of $235 and $100 a month for my College Fund, I had a whopping $135 every two weeks to spend. I thought I was rich because I had a car and it was more money than I made in the tobacco fields. Little did I know insurance, maintenance, and gas come along with a car.

Lessons Learned

1. *Learn from your mistakes* – The platoon learned to put their clothing in waterproof bags before deploying. To this day, I put my clothes in waterproof bags when traveling.

2. *Read the weather forecast* – If we read the weather forecast before deploying, we would have been prepared for bad weather.

3. *Never admit guilt in a vehicle accident* – The other person may not have license or insurance, therefore; they should have never been on the road.

4. *Know the responsibilities of owning a car* – Insurance, maintenance, and gas are associated with car ownership. Ensure your car payments or no more than 20% of your monthly income.

GRENADA I

In October of 1983 I deployed to Grenada with the 118th to guard Prisoners of War (POWs) and rescue college students. I was scared shitless. I was an M60 gunner and weighed 147lbs. I carried the tripod, spare barrel, and 1100 rounds of ammo in addition to my food and clothes. My equipment weighed more than me. When we landed the Air Force Pilot told us to get the hell off of his airplane and Captain Cancilla lead us to the POW camp which was about a mile away, but it seemed like 5 miles away with all of the equipment I was carrying. He was in such a hurry that he left his M60 gunners 100 meters behind the formation. SGT Brown was mad as hell and I was struggling with the weight, but he told me don't worry when we come under fire, we will be good because we had all the fire power. A leader should never leave their main fire support behind which is something I later learned in the Infantry. The Navy was firing artillery rounds over our heads as we were going to the POW camp. I would later see the accuracy and the destruction of Naval Gunfire on enemy forces. I saw a couple of downed helicopters and Rangers preparing for their next mission. Two of those Rangers who were in Grenada; Skip and McMahon were in my Officer Candidate School Class.

My unit finally made it to the POW camp and some of us went to evacuate the college students where we encountered sniper fire during the process. We put all the college students on airplanes then we relieved 82nd MPs who were guarding the POWS. I saw my friend PFC Powell who was in my Basic Training Unit and one of the seven soldiers from Basic Training which attended Airborne School.

We were assigned barracks previously used by Cuban soldiers. We had 12 soldiers assigned to a 12x12 room with 6 bunk beds and no bathroom. SGT Kowalski was the only female in the room. We were assigned 12 hour shifts so rotated the use of the beds. PFC Greene

51

would complain about SGT Kowalski hanging her panties to dry over his bed. Two weeks later 3 soldiers moved out. I volunteered for night shift security because it was cooler, and I had no problems staying up at night. The only bad things about night shift were the mosquitos, the heat, and the daytime cleaning of the latrines which consisted of burning shit like in the movie Platoon. I did not mind sharing a bed, but latrine duty was the worst. PFC Fair, whose father was a 1SG in the Infantry was so upset his son joined the Army as a MP that he told him, told him, he would rather his daughter be a whore than his son to be a MP. Everyone in the room burst out laughing afterwards.

The first night in Grenada I pulled security for an Infantry Company and SGT Bobby tried to sneak up on us and I spotted him. He was shocked I was awake. I was scared, is the reason why I was awake. The next morning the Infantry soldiers woke up and went to the beach for a swim. Their Platoon Leader, a big white soldier, told us "It's not the size of the dog that counts, but the fight that's in him and then he said, "I have a big dick with a lot of fight" and he stripped off all his clothes and jumped in the ocean. We laughed, and I could not believe it we were at War, and he was going swimming. I couldn't blame him because the beaches around Grenada were crystal clear, and the water was warm. We later acquired clothes from the Cubans to go swimming. The next night another soldier and I had security on a remote beach. We were only supposed to be on duty for 12 hours, but the unit left us out there for 24 hours. It was the first time I ever stayed up for 24 hours straight and of course my reward was cleaning out toilets.

A roommate received a package containing a 5th of Jack Daniels and some chocolate chip cookies. We had a social event that next night. It was my first-time drinking liquor and after one shot, I was feeling good. My roommates were laughing at me the next day because I ate most of the cookies. They later told me the cookies were laced with Marijuana. I said previously some of the people in my unit should never have been MPs.

52

The unit asked for volunteers to build a bunker. I was the first one to volunteer because I wanted to get out of cleaning toilets. SGT Kowalski, I, and a couple of other soldiers constructed a concrete bunker overseeing the POW Camp and Airfield. It was a work of art. The bunker was cool in the day; roomy enough to put chairs in it; and it provided better protection than the barracks.

The POWs were evacuated about 30 days after the mission. Our mission once the POWs left was to search for enemy soldiers. We responded to reports of people who were helping out the Cubans. We received Sniper fire a couple of times and recovered a few grenades and AK-47s.

I spent my Birthday and Thanksgiving in Grenada. We ate Thanksgiving Dinner in an old barracks which had been shot up and had blood stains on the wall, but it the best Thanksgiving Dinner which I ever ate because we had been eating C-Rations for the past 30 days. The only things I remember about C-Rations were the peanut butter, crackers, John Wayne Chocolate Bars, and the P-38 which was the can opener. I still have my P-38. Our reward after Thanksgiving Dinner was MREs which was like steak to us.

We finally left Grenada about two weeks before Christmas. The day before departure, the leaders brought us beer and we had a party. One thing about combat, it brings people together. After Grenada the unit became closer. When we returned from Grenada, we had a party with food and a keg in the Dining Room. Mostly everyone departed the area except for a couple of female Sergeants and myself. It was my time drinking from a keg and I thought I could drink about a quarter of it. After 4 drinks I was finished. When I left the females told me don't worry, they were going to finish it off. I don't know if they finished it off, but I know they out drank me.

We had an outstanding soldier, SGT Wesson, who left the Army right before we deployed to become a Highway Patrolman. SGT Wesson called the unit after our return to congratulate us and stated he felt sad because he did not deploy with us. His gesture showed me how much he cared for his fellow soldiers. We told him "Thank You" because his training helped us prepare for combat.

Lessons Learned

1. ***Be prepared*** – I was in shape physically which allowed me to carry equipment weighing more than me.
2. ***Train your subordinates*** – The Sergeants and lower Corporals/Specialist were strong leaders who lead by example. The POW camp ran smoothly because everyone knew their job and were properly trained.
3. ***Do not leave your fire power behind*** – If we had come under attack enroute to the POW Camp, our unit would have suffered heavy casualties because the M60 machine guns were nowhere near the leaders.

118th MP Company at Airfield in Grenada

GRENADA II

In January we were told we of an upcoming IG Inspection and the unit needed volunteers to deploy with another MP Company to perform police duties until the Grenadians can get a police force together. I was the first one to raise my hand because I did not want to go through another IG Inspection. I was traumatized from the IG Inspection I went through in Basic Training. I can't believe I choose getting shot at over cleaning. The other reasons why I wanted to return to Grenada were because I wanted to spend my winter in a warm environment and to find out if my girlfriend and I relationship could survive being away from each other. Our relationship ended less than two weeks after my arrival in Grenada. The only things I ended up with in that relationship were a huge phone bill, broken heart, and a break- up letter. My college friends later called it a "Dear Gino letter" instead of a Dear John Letter when their girlfriends broke up with them by a letter. I hated the break-up at first, but I am so glad it ended because my Military career would have ended and I would be stuck working in a mill.

We stayed in an old house which was near a complex which Navy SEALs captured. The house also provided a view where some SEALs drowned enroute to the complex. I was assigned Patrol Duty in the city. In less than 5 minutes on the ground I was involved in an accident. I was a passenger in a jeep driven by SGT Sutton, and we hit a civilian vehicle head-on traveling less than 5 mph. We were not wearing seatbelts and I tried to brace myself by putting my hands on the dashboard, but I landed on the hood. Thank goodness we had the windshield down. I was convinced from that day forward, seatbelts save lives. We were also responsible for assisting Grenadians with traffic control because the Grenadians had no stop lights. Two MPs had duty directing traffic for 12 hours in the sun. I hated traffic duty

55

so much that I volunteered to search for weapons and sightings of Cubans left on the island.

One day the patrol which I was in charge of as a Private First Class encountered a Grenadian who was sympathetic to the Cubans being surrounded by other Grenadians. The other Grenadians were getting ready to kill the Grenadian affiliated Cubans, so we convinced the group not to kill the man and then we escorted him to his house. The Private and I never told anyone because we considered this as doing our job. Most people do not know the responsibilities placed on soldiers and this incident could have become an International Incident.

The other soldiers would always mess with me as a Private. One day I was sent to the Motor Pool which was in a hotel 30 minutes away to bust tires. The Motor Pool Sergeant asked me if I ever busted tires before and I told him "Heck No, I never worked in an auto shop before" and I asked him has he ever worked in a tobacco field"? My response resulted in me doing 50 pushups. The busting or breaking down of tires consisted of deflating tires and using a crowbar to separate the tires from the rim. He showed me one time and I ended up breaking down 26 jeep tires while the Motor Pool section sat in the shade drinking sodas. I never complained because I was used to manual labor, and it surely beat directing traffic. I didn't receive a congratulation, just two orange sodas.

Games

I would go play basketball against the Grenadians or watch the Cricket matches during my spare time. I still do not understand Cricket to this day. I was assigned to another MP Company in Grenada and the 1SG of the unit scheduled a basketball game between the Americans and Grenadians. The Grenadians recruited an American Soldier who was a good basketball player to play point guard for their team. They beat us by 2 points and the 1SG was furious not because we lost, but an American helped the Grenadians win. I lead the teams in rebounding, steals and block shots for a 5'10 guy. The 1SG congratulated me and told me, he didn't think highly of me because I was quiet and didn't hang around soldiers from his unit. I just smiled at his comment, because he did not know I played baseball, basketball, football, and wrestled before joining the Army and I played against the Grenadians in a 3 on 3 game a month prior in which we lost 50 - 48. I scored 42 points the game because my teammates did not know how to play basketball. I'm not good, but I know how to play. The 1SG got his revenge on me in Spades. We needed 10 hands to win, and I was confident we were going to get it, but my partner was not. I won hands 9 hands in a row and the 1SG won the last hand with an Ace of Spade and smiled at me, I was crushed.

57

Promotion

A Platoon leader from the company we were attached with, promoted me to the rank of Specialist after being under his command. I was extremely happy because this meant my pay went up to $235 every two weeks. The other soldiers could not believe I made Specialist in fifteen months. Most of them made Specialist at the two-year mark of their enlistment. The Lieutenant promoted me because my uniform was immaculate, I showed up for work 15 minutes prior to shift, and I was the only one who cleaned the house we stayed in without being told. The other soldiers thought the lieutenant was racist because he rarely talked to other soldiers and he did things by the book. I told them he was not racist and my reasoning for this was because he considered Eddie Murray the best baseball player in the Major Leagues at the time. I explained to the other soldiers who Eddie Murray was, but it did not change their opinions about the Lieutenant. The Lieutenant and I talked about baseball every day. Most of the soldiers were basketball and football fans. I followed all sports and as a child and read the newspaper daily. I could recall the statistics of the top 50 players in each major sport because I was good at remembering numbers.

The other soldiers took me to lunch at St. Georges Hotel for my promotion and threw me in the pool with my uniform on. I struggled to get to edge, and they just stood there laughing. The funny thing is they never asked me if I knew how to swim. Their reasoning for not asking me if I knew how to swim was that all Country boys know how to swim. Thank goodness my grandmother made me take swimming lessons with my cousins a year before joining the Army. My grandmother put a lot of trust in me. She would let me drive family members to Church on Sunday although I had no license. Her reasons were, I was big enough to see over the steering wheel of her Buick 88, Church was only a mile away, and I needed the experience. She would be arrested in these times for her actions.

St. Georges Hotel

The Grenadians later took over most of the policing duties and we were moved to the St. Georges Hotel. This was great because the hotel had a swimming pool, beach, bar, and there were only 2 people in a room instead of 12. The hotel had a Dining Facility which provided us with two hot meals a deal. We lived like kings at the hotel.

I would shoot basketball by myself every day. One day a 12-year-old Grenadian asked if he could shoot some basketball with me, and I told him "Sure". He would ask me questions everyday about America. I later learned that he did not have a father or many friends and that he would hang around the base for our MREs. I would give him my MRE's because I hated them, and I could get food from the Dining Facility. When I told him I was leaving, his mother gave me a gift full of Island Spices which was a pleasant surprise. His mother told me they did not have any food and because of my generosity they were able to eat. It felt good, but I wished I had done more for the boy and his family.

Guard Duty at St. George was relaxing. A Grenadian who was very intelligent worked with us on Guard Duty. He spoke Spanish, French, and English. The government before the invasion wanted him to study medicine in Russia, but he refused. He probably should have taken the assignment because Europe produces outstanding doctors.

A Special Forces Colonel would come through the gate drunk every night in uniform and pass curfew hours. He would just smile at us because he was too drunk to say anything. We were told he was on a Secret Mission which was probably to go out and scout the local clubs and meet women. He never gave us a hard time.

We laughed at a Major and his girlfriend having sex in the ocean. The Major thought if he took his girlfriend to waist deep water, we would not know what he was doing. We would call the entire platoon to the beach to watch the Major and his girlfriend. He was lucky, smartphones were not invented because his activities would have been posted on the internet.

One day a civilian invited a group of soldiers in the platoon to visit his island. The Coast Guard transported us there and I became seasick on the trip to the island. There were European ladies on the island walking around topless. We would walk up to them trying to carry on a conversation, knowing they did not speak English, so we could look at their breasts. I did not know the mission of the Coast Guard at the time because I always saw them tubing and fishing in Grenada. I later learned the true mission of the Coast Guard and I tried talking my son into joining them.

A soldier from another unit bet us $300 he could do 500 push-ups. We put our money together for the bet. I left the area after he reached 373. I was later told he did 736 push-ups.

Grenada was the first time I heard Reggae, and I became a fan of it. When I first introduced Reggae to my college friends they hated it, but after listening to me play it every day for a year they became fans of it also. Grenada was stressful, but I enjoyed it because it made me a better soldier.

Lesson Learned

1. ***Do things without being told*** – Soldiers in my platoon could not believe I made Specialist (E4) in 15 months. The Platoon Leader who was with us in Grenada observed me cleaning the house by myself without being told and meritoriously promoted me to E4 which was the quickest in the unit for someone without a college degree.

2. ***Seatbelts work*** – A person is not strong enough to prevent themselves from being ejected in an automobile accident. Thank goodness we had the windshield down and were going slow, if not I would have been seriously hurt.

3. ***Be nice to everyone you meet because you may not know their situation*** – I gave the little boy food daily not knowing this was the only food his family had for the day.

End of Enlistment

We returned from Grenada around April 1984 which left me with 4 months on my Army Enlistment. The unit put me on Charge of Quarters (CQ) for those remaining months. I just answered the phones and picked up trash.

The Supply Sergeant sent me along with his assistant who I later met in Panama to pick-up equipment at a warehouse. I was the driver and he told me to back up the jeep which had a trailer attached to it. It took me over two hours to do it and the assistant and the warehouse supervisor were laughing at me the entire time. I was the joke of the day. The next day the Supply Sergeant sent me back to the warehouse to pick up some items and to get a good laugh out of me trying to back up a trailer. Well, they I surprised them because I backed-up the trailer in less than 10 seconds. I was never sent to the warehouse again after that, and I became an expert at backing up jeeps with trailers. SGT Sumptner, Assistant Supply Clerk, later became a Green Beret which I could not believe because he was not physically fit in the 118th. I ran into him in Panama and he denied being in the 118th, but I told him I never forget an ugly face and I definitely remembered his ugly ass and **we** laughed. He told me he joined Special Forces because it was the only way he could stay in the Army after the problems had at the beginning of his Army Career.

I learned a good lesson on CQ. I was picking up trash one day and the jeep broke down 10 minutes before I was scheduled to get off. I was 300 yards from the unit when it happened. I waited for two hours until the Motor Pool Sergeant arrived at work. When he went out to check the vehicle it was out of gas. The gas hand said full, but jeeps were notorious for having broken gas hands and I knew to do a visual check before driving the jeep, but I skipped visually checking the gas tank because I was in a hurry to get to sleep.

My last jump was a Hollywood Jump which happened on a Saturday. We called jumps Hollywood Jumps because you jumped without equipment. I was in jeopardy of losing my Jump Pay because I haven't jumped in three months due to being stationed in Grenada. It was so quiet on the plane you could hear a pin drop. I began shouting, trying to get everyone motivated. I was clapping and shouting "Let's do this and saying WOOO! A captain turned around and gave me a thumbs up. I had never acted like that before. It was my last jump and I was going to go out with a bang.

1SG Surom and others tried to talk me into reenlisting, but my mind was set on going to college. I was glad I was going to college, but sad because I was leaving my buddies.

The 118th was a wild and crazy unit, but it was a great learning experience. I had great mentors especially CPT Cancilla, 1SG Surom, SFC Bennett, SFC McIntosh, SSG Davis, SSG Damron, SSG Brown, SGT Reese, SGT Jenkins, SGT Kowalski, SGT Bobby, SGT Roster, SGT Sutton, SGT Torres, SGT Worth, SPC Wooten, SPC Frank, SPC Conrad, and a host of other soldiers in the unit. The Sergeants and Corporals/Specialist knew their jobs. Most of the soldiers in the unit performed their duties in a professional manner. In any job there will be some screw-ups. I will not trade my experience in the 118 for anything. I learned how to become a soldier, policeman, mechanic, construction worker, and a host of other skills which prepared me for life in and out of the Military.

Lessons Learned

1. ***Do your best because you never know who is watching you –*** When I left the 118th, the company presented me with a Plaque for outstanding work. I was surprised and very appreciative of the award.

2. ***Shortcuts lead to disaster –*** I was in such hurry to go to sleep that I looked at the gas hand instead of looking inside the gas tank after being told numerous times to look inside the gas tank.

3. ***Take care of your subordinates –*** A lot of senior soldiers watched out for me and took time to ensure I understood the duties and responsibilities of being a soldier.

118TH REUNION

I attended the 118th MP Company Unit Reunion in April 2021. I could not believe so many former soldiers stayed in contact with each other and attended the reunion. I was very excited several soldiers stayed in and made a career out of the Army. I met Major Cancilla, CSM Damron, CSM Sutton, CSM Crosby, 1SG Buck, 1SG Torres, 1SG Surom, MSG Bennett, Greene, Doug Worth, Grant, and a host of others who were in the unit from the 70s to the 90s. It was the most organized and best reunion which I have ever attended. I told MSG Bennett I was a Cherry back in those days, and he responded "We were all Cherries because no one knew what the hell they were doing" which made me feel like I wasn't so lost after all. 1SG Surom was a very caring leader who would do anything to make a soldier successful. An example of this, is when he helped SGT Sumptner revive his career which led to Sumpter becoming a Green Beret. It goes to show you a person can redeem themselves if given the opportunity.

118th Second Platoon – I was in Grenada for the second time when this photo was taken.

Unknown LT, me, CPT Cancilla, and 1SG Buck

Crosby, Trimble, LT Bradford, unknown SGT, and Wooten in Grenada

POW Camp in Grenada

Guarding the beach with Jeff Carpunky

Woods and unknown soldier

68

PFC Lee retired from the Army and the Federal Government.

PFC West and me

Cuban Barracks (Kolwaski, Parks, Knoll, Carpunky, Henderson, Jim, and unknown soldier). Park's dog would bark at Americans and not Cubans. SGT without a shirt was sent chocolate chip cookies from his family laced with marijuana. I unknowingly ate the majority of the cookies.

Bunker which I helped build it and volunteered for guard duty there because it was cool and it kept me off crap burning detail.

70

Night before departure – Carpunky, Knoll, me, Greene, Jim with unknown soldier, Henderson, Kolwaski, and unknown soldier.

Al Cohen my roommate. His dad was a professional gambler who called us when he won, but never when he lost.

71

Posing with cheap sunglasses and a Grenadian beer. We lived in the building behind me in Point Salines and staged our operations from there which included Search Missions and Traffic Control.

72

Group from Trinidad who I met at a restaurant on the beach. We moved from Point Salines' where we slept 10 to a room and ate MREs twice per day to the hotel by the beach where we slept 2 to a room and ate hot meals twice per day.

PHOTO, DATED JAN. 22, SHOWS McQUEEN, EXTREME RIGHT, IN GRENADA

Newspaper Article which was distributed across America. Henderson is second from the left. Soldier on the far left and I prevented a Grenadian from being killed by a group of people. I was a Private 1st Class and he was a Private.

73

COLLEGE

I went to NC A&T State University in August 1984 to major in Computer Science. It was a great decision going to NC A&T, but a dumb decision to major in Computer Science because A&T was not known for its Computer Science program during that period. There were about 20 computers on campus, and a third of them were broken. Computer Science Major consisted of mostly math courses and I was weak in math.

The funny thing was I picked up my roommate's Calculus book and answered the first three questions correctly and decided I could major in Computer Science and Math. I enjoyed Calculus, Statistics, and Physics. When I reached Engineer Math and Geometry classes I received a wake-up call which said, "Change your Major Now" because I failed those classes. I graduated with a Bachelor of Science in Economics and the reasons why I selected Economics was because they accepted a lot of my math classes, and it allowed me to graduate in 4 years.

The only thing I remember about Economics is the Supply and Demand Curve. I constantly bragged to other Army Officers, I graduated with a degree in Economics and a Minor in Math because most of them barely passed their Economics Classes. This worked well until I was assigned to an Engineer Unit. An Engineer Officer told me to sit my ass down with that crap about my educational background because all Engineers are Math Majors.

My friends who I attended high school with were amazed because I spent two years in the Army and graduated within a semester of them. I was good with numbers and sciences and I should have majored in Biology or Accounting. I did not think college was hard because I learned how to study in high school, and I knew if I did not graduate then I would be back doing Police Call. The Army called it

Police Call which I never understood why because it never involved any policing duty, just picking up cigarette butts and other trash every morning before work.

College Jobs

I wasn't afraid of work and during college I worked at Goodyear Tire Company, Black and Decker, two different truck loading jobs, washing cars, and scraping plaster off house ceilings which clogged up my lungs for two weeks.

I worked at Goodyear in the summer and over Christmas Break making $300 a week and during Christmas, I made $700 for 3 days of work because employees received 2 ½ times their pay for working on the holidays. I recall my grandmother becoming upset with me when I left the Christmas Dinner early to go to work. I told her no one here is paying me $300 so I am going to make money.

The employees at Goodyear were always talking dirty and betting on NASCAR. The husbands would tell other men sitting at the table they gave their wives a good beat down last night and the wives would tell me they were just hollering so they could get the fool off of them.

I worked for a Temp Agency loading and unloading trucks. The Temp Agency scheduled me and another person to unload a Levi Truck for $125.00 each. The other employee did not show up, which made the truck driver nervous because he had to pick-up another later on. I told him I could unload the truck without any help which he didn't believe. I had gloves and a dolly cart and unloaded the truck in two hours which normally takes two people 6 hours. This shocked the driver and because I did the job in record time the Temp Agency gave me the check of the absent employee.

I worked with another Temp Agency, but this time it was an easy job. I worked third shift for a company which only had six employees for third shift. We had to load steel beams on 8 trucks before 8:00am using cranes. Most of the guys were Veterans and they had the loading procedure down to a science. They would load 5 trucks in two hours, take a three-hour break, then load the other 3 trucks at 6:30am. The boss thought they were working all night. I don't why they needed me. I would go home and take a nap during the break and then go to class at 9:00 am. They offered me a full-time position, but my priority was graduating from college. It was the easiest job I ever had and thank goodness I did not accept the position because they ended up laying off most of their employees.

Black and Decker was the most boring job which I ever held. I worked on an Assembly Line packaging Dust Buster Vacuum Cleaners for shipment. I could package 350 Dust Busters Vacuum Cleaners in an 8-hour shift. The supervisor threatened to fire us one night because we only packaged half of what we did the day prior. Everyone smoked, except for me and two other students. I never understood why people smoked until I worked there. I believe people smoked there to die early so they didn't have to package anymore vacuum cleaners. The company did shut down which prevented people from dying of boredom.

I washed cars in college for spending money. My Uncle James, Air Force Veteran, would pay me $5.00 to wash his Ford Aerostar Van which used $3.50 of quarters. I enjoyed washing his van because I always found $2.00 in change which enabled me to get a meal from Libby Hill or Bojangles. I lived in those two restaurants while in college. I almost fell out when he gave me $20 and told me to keep the change. He later fired me for putting his floor mats upside down in his van. I put his floor mats upside down because he kept tracking mud in the van which costs me more money to vacuum clean. I could get a meal for $3.00 and his dirty floor mats took $1.00 from my meal money. Little did I know that one day he would be a passenger in his van and take off his shoes. The floor mats had sharp points on them which poked the bottom of his feet. Although I was fired, he gave me a great investment tip which was to invest in an Individual Retirement Account (IRA). I was hesitant at first because I was making 10% off of Certificate of Deposits (CDs) and Savings Bonds. I made a lot of money from his investment tip when I cleaned the wax out of my ears.

I do not know how my friends and I made it through college without Facebook or Cellphones. Everyone talked with each other face-to-face and shared information on tests, difficulty level of the teachers, parties, and jobs. Someone would spread the word on which movie theater would let us in free and what restaurant had meals on sale. Greensboro Coliseum would hire college students for concerts which enabled us to get in for free and meet the stars. Companies would hire us for parties. My friends were hired to be bartenders for an airline party. The only mix drinks they knew were how to mix beer, liquor, and Mad Dog 20/20 in one sitting. An airline company hired them and told them the party goers would tell them how to mix their drinks. They made $1,200 that night and the company gave them 3 half gallon bottles of liquor which we tried to consume over a weekend. If today's technology was available during my time, I would have been a professional college student.

Interact with other students and people in the community. The people who you meet in college may be someone who can help you out later in life. Facebook and cellphones were nonexistent when I was in college, so you had to talk to people. Some of my college friends are judges, professors, teachers, engineers, Community Leaders, and Military Officers who supported me in funding scholarships or getting jobs for my students.

Lessons Learned

1. ***Do your research on the college you wish to attend*** - Ensure they have the Majors you are pursing.

2. ***Major in something which pays the bills*** – Some majors are only worth the piece of paper which they are printed on, so major in something which society needs.

3. ***College exposes you to people from around the world*** – Learn from everybody and everything you do in college. I thought of plays as boring until a college professor made the class go to a play for a grade. The play was outstanding which changed my thinking of plays. Now I enjoy going to see plays.

4. ***If you don't learn something new every day, then you have wasted your day*** – A college professor told our class this which influenced me to read the newspaper daily.

5. ***Take a course in swimming or golf*** – A lot of business is conducted on the golf course and swimming saves lives. I should have taken a second swimming class which would have better prepared me for other jobs.

6. ***Exercise in college*** – College is a great time to get into shape. Gyms are free and there are plenty of running areas.

7. ***Stay in contact with classmates*** – Staying in contact with classmates may lead you to better opportunities.

8. ***Do not get caught up in the college party life*** – The goal is to graduate from college. There are many scholarships offers available to help students make it through college. Join the National Guard or Reserves because they offer scholarships, work experience, and are a good source of networking. I have met CEOs, Bank Managers, and high-ranking Government Officials who are members of the National Guard or Reserves.

9. ***Hustle*** – There are job opportunities for college students. I bailed hay, worked in factories, unloaded trucks, and washed cars to pay my tuition.

10. *Give back to your community* – My church gave $5 each year to every college students. Five dollars wasn't much money, but it did provide funds for beer and a Bojangles Meal. I donated a $2,000 to the church after I became a lieutenant.

College Classmates
Front Row: Michaela Brewington, Monica Patterson, and Angie Neal
Middle: Gwen Smith, Tam Dowdy, Harry Washington, Eugene, and me with the mustache
Back Row: Marcus Staley, and Robert Melton
Four became Engineers, Three retired from the Military, and the others worked for the Federal Government or in Education.

80

NAVY PRE-OFFICER CANDIDATE SCHOOL

I attended a Navy Pre-Officer Candidate School in Newport Rhode Island after college with the intentions of being a SEAL or Flight Navigator, neither worked out. I met a Naval Officer Recruiter at a job fair at NC A&T. The Non-Commissioned Officer (NCO) who was helping the Recruiting Officer was drunk on duty and smelled like he was on a 3-day binge. I asked what the requirements were to becoming a SEAL and the NCO stated I needed to swim 250 yards, which I could do. Little did I know that he left out treading water for 5 minutes, 5-mile ocean swim, and a host of other requirements.

I arrived at Newport Rhode Island, along with about 10 other candidates and we were required to take a swim test. I took a Beginning Swimming class in college which was the hardest "A" I ever earned. I should have taken Advanced Swimming, but I was cocky because I was the best swimmer out of all my friends. I passed the 50-meter swim test and high dive test, but failed the 5-minute treading water test. There was a 350lb plus female civilian instructor who chewed out all the Black students for not being able to pass the test which pissed me off. There were a couple of Navy SEALs who gave us remedial training. Chief Snow was one of the instructors who helped me, and the other African Americans pass the test. The way Chief encouraged me to pass the treading water test was he asked me if I could run for 5 minutes and I replied yes, and he told me to treat treading water like a 5-minute run and I would pass the test. I passed on the next try. The other SEAL whose name I can't recall taught me the side stroke which became my strongest swim stroke. My swim teacher at NC A&T was a Coast Guard Veteran whose motto was Save a Life instead of Take One. He encouraged me to take Advance Swimming and go into the Coast Guard, but I knew little about the Coast Guard at the time and

I did not want to take swimming in the wintertime because the pool was cold. I later became a Lifeguard and Swim Instructor Trainer at the age of 55.

The Navy Pre-OCS School was a great learning experience, but I wanted an adventurous job or any jobs associated with weapons instead of a Surface Warfare Officer. I didn't learn about the duties of a Surface Warfare Officer until I arrived at Newport Rhode Island. The Recruiter told me, I get to choose my job after completion of Pre-OCS school which was not true. I never understood why Recruiters lie. When I became a Recruiting Commander, I made sure I told recruits the good and bad parts of the jobs which they were requesting and let them make the decision on their career choice. Recruits have access to a lot more information about their future jobs now than what I experienced.

Once I found out more information about the duties of a Surface Warfare Officer, I wanted to switch jobs. One instructor told me to become an Admiral in the Navy a person would have to be a submariner or an Aviator. Another instructor told me he hated being a Surface Warfare Officer and the job took 5 years off his life. When I heard these comments, I asked the Commander to be released from the program to return to the Army. He was upset, but I explained to him what my goals were and I was willing to recycle if he would switch me to a more adventurous job, he offered me Supply Officer which I declined. I later ended up working as a Supply Officer in the Army. The Commander granted me my request. I called SSG Bill Martindale after my release from Naval Pre- OCS. I wanted to go in the Infantry and then to OCS. SSG Martindale was a smooth talker and convinced me to return as a Military Policeman. I later found out I could have went directly to (OCS), but recruiters want people to join immediately and prefer not to do an OCS Packets because it takesabout three months to complete an OCS. When I became a Recruiting Commander, my company sent three people to OCS.

82

Lessons Learned

1. *Research the job you are seeking* - Speak with someone who is currently in the job or previously held the job. The internet and cellphones are now available, so there are no excuses for a person not knowing what their potential job is about.

2. *Your attitude about your job makes a big impression on potential hires* – I probably would have stayed in the Navy, if instructors did not say Surface Warfare was a dead-end job.

3. *Don't be afraid to switch careers* – The Navy is a great organization, but I was unable to work in a field of my liking, therefore; I switched back into the Army which was a great decision.

4. *Assign your best people to represent your company* – The Navy had a drunk and unknowledgeable sailor as a representative.

Enlisting in the Navy OCS Program. I drove Angie's, college classmate, Ford Escort with a broken front seat, 75-miles to the Recruiting Station.

24TH MP COMPANY

I was assigned to 24th MP Company at Ft. Stewart, Georgia. I'm glad I went to Ft. Stewart because I met people who prepared me for the rigors of OCS. When new soldiers reported to the 24th, they had a private meeting with 1SG McGarrah, who later became a Command Sergeant Major. I reported to his office, and he told me about himself, the unit, and the expectations of every soldier in the unit. He spoke to me for an hour with his eyes closed the entire time. I was asking myself is this a trick because I should be the one sleeping not him. He asked me what my career goals and I replied I wanted to go OCS and be an Infantry Officer. He replied, "Why you want to be an Officer instead of an NCO and you will probably be Rifted which meant put out of the Army" and I said I wanted to make the big dollars and not pick up cigarette butts anymore. He finally opened his eyes and laughed. I returned to my platoon after I left his office, and I asked the other soldiers was the 1SG trying to get me to go to sleep by talking with his eyes closed and they started laughing and said he always talks with his eyes closed. We said the next time he gets in front of the formation and talks with his eyes closed, we were going to leave, but it never happened.

The platoon was wild, but not like Ft. Bragg. Weeks before I arrived two soldiers were caught robbing a bank and a shootout ensued. About 1000 rounds were fired and only two rounds hit the robbers. One robber was killed and the other wounded. The rounds which hit the robbers belonged to the Civilian Police. The commander couldn't believe not one round belonging to an MP hit the robbers, therefore; he ordered a review of all MP Qualification Records and noticed that every MP had achieved a score of Expert on Pistol Qualification. The Commander sent everyone back to the range. It was a known fact that soldiers forged their Qualifications Records because a higher score equaled more promotion points. Officers were

85

the worst at forging records.

I was assigned to the 2nd Platoon and my roommate was a nice guy who knew his job, but kept his area dirty and was weak on Physical Fitness. I was tired of cleaning the entire room by myself and one day Command Sergeant Major Cornell, a former Green Beret, performed a room inspection. The Sergeant Major was pissed because we had the dirtiest room in the Platoon, and he threatened to pull my OCS packet. My side was cleaned, but the Squad Leader said since I was trying to become an Officer, I should have informed someone about my roommate's area. All leaders knew my roommate was not a neat person, but I did not report him because I knew nothing would happen to him because he hung out with the Sergeants.

My best friend in the unit was Tony McGee who later became the head of General McCaffery Security Team in Desert Storm. Tony, a South Carolina native, was always singing a "Tear in My Beer" and telling stories about the time he was in Korea and rejected a Dallas Cowboy Cheerleader who wanted to seduce him. Tony and I lifted weights and played tennis every day after work. Tony would always tell me I was not Black because I spoke proper English and wore Polo Shirts.

One day while we were on a joint patrol, we noticed a fire approaching a Tactical Operation Center (TOC) and no one inside the tent noticed the fire. We jumped out of the car and put out the flames. Tony put me in for an Achievement Award. I later ran into Tony in Panama when I was a Captain and we joked about how a Sergeant put a Captain in for an award. Tony later became a Command Sergeant Major in the Military Police Corps. He probably could have been Command Sergeant Major of the Army, but he retired from the Army because he spent so much time away from his family.

Monroe was another friend from North Carolina. We were out in the field guarding a Checkpoint and bullshitting when the Commander's vehicle approached. I popped up from behind a tree which scared the Commander. He said good job and told the entire

86

company that is the way you are supposed to conceal your Checkpoint Position. The incident reminded me of Bill Murray in the Movie Stripes when the unit performed Drill Movements out of Uniform.

Monroe had some bad experiences during the first year of his Army career. Monroe was a small and short guy which made him the target of bullies. He did not talk crap like most small guys, but it did not stop people from taking advantage of him. He was robbed at the bus station enroute from Basic Training to his home while he was sleeping in the waiting area. Someone reached in his coat pocket and stole his money. The station was full of people, and no one spoke. When he arrived at Ft. Stewart, he was at a club dancing when someone who he did not know struck him on the head with a bottle for no reason. Monroe danced like Michael Jackson, so I guessed that's what made the guy jealous.

One night we were taking equipment to Atlanta, Georgia for repair and stopped overnight for rest because the facility was closed when we arrived. Monroe asked a white man "where are all the Black People at" and the man responded "the last one was hanging in that tree right there". Monroe did not sleep a wink that night.

We had a going away party for a couple of soldiers at the Non-Commissioned Officer Club (NCO) club where they would have dancers once a month for entertainment. When we went there were two wives dancing in two-piece bikinis (Nudity was not allowed). The women were of German descendants and one of them looked like Marylyn Monroe. I could never figure out why she was dancing because I would have gladly given her my paycheck for 15 minutes of fun. Monroe had everyone laughing because of the dirty dancing he was doing with the dancers.

Hughes and Rick were also good friends of mine. Hughes was a big country boy from Alabama who took his police job seriously because he wanted to be a sheriff in Alabama. He was strong as an ox, but could not run worth crap. When Hughes' mother died, he asked Monroe to drive him to Alabama for the funeral. Monroe told us they drove over 100 mph and were passing cars on the median and anywhere else they could squeeze his little red Chevy through. When I was in the car, it couldn't go 70 mph downhill.

Rick was a former Marine from Detroit who was an excellent shot. I used to tease Rick that he learned how to shoot from being in the Hood and he would reply the Marine Corps taught him how to shoot. When Rick was in the Marine Corps, he was assigned Gate Guard Duties. He would salute the Navy Officers with his left hand and the Marine Officers with his right hand. His Captain noticed him doing this and laughed about the incident. Once Rick was caught speeding in South Carolina and the Sheriff took him to jail and told him he could pay a $300 fine on the spot or wait until Monday for the judge to come in. Rick paid the fine right there which taught me not to speed in South Carolina. It sounded like some Mayberry stuff.

When I was on vacation before departing to OCS, Rick carried me to Monroe's house in Raeford, North Carolina the day before Monroe's wedding. We were sitting on the couch and I looked out of the window and saw two men walking along a dirt road with one them wearing a robe with rollers in his hair. I asked Monroe who is the man wearing the robe and he replied it was his father. I kidded him the entire day about his town and the fact his dad's hair was better than his mom's.

There was another soldier who was house sitting for his Squad Leader, an E-6. The soldier started looking through his Platoon Sergeant's photo album and noticed his Platoon Sergeant was wearing a dress and lingerie. The soldier shared those pictures with other soldiers in the unit. The Squad Leader never knew why people were laughing at him when they saw him.

If you were a MP, you caught hell on Ft. Stewart. The Infantry would run past our unit and say you can't spell "Wimp" without a "MP", and we would respond that "You can't take a shit without a Grunt". We had a female MP who against all advice from fellow MPS, put a MP sticker on her car. One day her car broke down on Interstate 95 and someone broke the back window of her car. She never put another MP sticker on her car.

There were two MPs who stopped the Pizza Delivery lady for speeding, and she offered them 2 pizzas if they would let her off. They took the pizzas, and she reported the MPs to the Commander which resulted in them getting their rank reduced. Those pizzas cost them about $200 each.

There was a Squad Leader who had been in the Army for 20 years and only achieved the rank of Staff Sergeant, which showed how little he cared about getting promoted. I associated rank with money, and I never understood why soldiers never put in the extra work to get more rank. This Staff Sergeant would boast everyday about returning to Germany to visit the Red-Light District (Prostitution Houses). He said he never made it past the 1st floor. He had a great motto which I think about all the time and it was "Do what your career can stand". I guess his career meant he enjoyed not being promoted and not making money.

Our Reenlistment Sergeant, Sergeant Howard, was another character in the unit. I was his driver when we went on training exercises because he had no Driver's License. He was a Staff Sergeant until he was reduced in rank by the Garrison Commander, an African American whom everyone called Darth Vader. SGT Howard blamed his DUI on his sister who was riding on the back of his motorcycle. He said it was his sister's fault because when he leaned into the curve, she leaned the opposite way which caused the motorcycle to run off the road and hit a tree.

89

He told me a story about when he was his Captain's driver in Hawaii on how he drove his drunk Captain drive home from the Officer's Club. The First Sergeant in SGT Howard's Hawaii unit would challenge any soldier to a fight every Monday Morning and if they beat him, he would give them a week off. One day SGT Howard challenged him, and the First Sergeant told him "If he didn't get his ass back in formation, he would be Court Martialed". SGT Howard was from the streets of DC and the First Sergeant knew he could fight because Howard would be involved in a fight every weekend.

SFC McIntyre from Miami was our Platoon Sergeant. He was not the most physically fit soldier, but he was the greatest hustler I ever met. He knew everybody on base and could get any equipment a soldier needed and if he could not get the equipment then he knew someone who could get it for us. Everybody on the post owed him a favor. When we returned from any training exercise, we could not go home until our vehicles were cleaned. SFC McIntyre would call a friend from the Armor unit, and they would let us use their wash racks which were for tanks to clean our vehicles. In Turkey the Customs and Immigration Officials would not let us load our vehicles until they were cleaned, and we were supposed to be one of the last units to depart. SFC McIntyre called in one of his many favors and we were able to get our vehicles cleaned and we departed two days before schedule. I met SFC McIntyre in Panama when I was a Captain.

The platoon leader was an outstanding leader who was looking to attend Law School after his four-year commitment was up. He helped me prepare my OCS packet and sent me to an Armor Unit before I attended OCS, so I would learn about the duties and responsibilities of an Armor Officer.

Our duty in the field was securing the Tactical Operation Center (TOC) and we deployed with live ammo. One day an Infantry Platoon was sent out on a mission to see if they could enter the TOC. We were asleep when the Infantry Soldiers entered and started firing at us with blank rounds. The Lieutenant had us to stand down and he told the

90

Infantry Lieutenant we had live rounds, and somebody could have seriously been injured if we had responded to the blank fire. This came as a surprise to the Infantry Lieutenant because he thought MPs only carried blank rounds. The next night the Infantry came back out and we responded to their attack with blank rounds this time.

Turkey

The 24th MP Company provided security missions in Turkey and Egypt. My platoon deployed to Turkey for three weeks while the other platoon deployed to Egypt. That was the second time that I ever deployed overseas. The area which we occupied in Turkey was about an hour from Istanbul.

My platoon was in charge of controlling access to the base and perimeter security. One day a member of the platoon attempted to stop the Security team for a Turkish General from running through our checkpoint. The Turkish Security Team drew their weapons on the U.S. Soldier which scared the crap out of him, eventually we convinced the Turkey Security Team to drop their weapons. Once the situation was diffused the Turkish Soldiers pulled out cards of naked women and we all laughed. Naked women and alcohol are two things which can diffuse any situation.

A Captain from a Transportation Company said she would give Tony McGee and myself an award if we could help land three F-16 Fighter planes. Tony placed VS-17 panels on the ground where we wanted the pilots to land and I directed the pilots with hand and arm signals to their respective landing spots. Once I became an officer, pilots told me they land wherever they want to and those pilots were probably laughing their asses off at Tony and I. The captain never gave us an award for our work which pissed me off.

There was a SSG Sergeant from another unit who wanted to buy a Turkish prostitute, but he didn't have enough money, so the guys in my squad put our money together and gave it to him. The SSG went to the prison for a good time. Prostitution was illegal in Turkey and if a woman was caught prostituting, she was sent to prison. If she didn't have any money to pay her bail, she had to raise her bail money through prostitution. The SSG purchased a woman, and the woman asked him

92

to perform oral sex on her and he replied to her, "He was supposed to be enjoying it not her". It's the story he told us, but he probably did perform oral sex on her.

There was a Black Command Sergeant Major from another unit who I would speak with every day. He would boast about how women loved him. He was at another location when his unit came under fire. The CSM dived under a jeep while the Officers stood around wondering what was happening. CSM had been in Vietnam, and he knew what live rounds sounded like. No one was injured in the incident.

Three days before our deployment ended, the unit took us to the Bazaar in Istanbul which contained shops filled with gold and bronze items. The first person we met was a Turkish kid who was selling a variety of souvenirs. I pretended I wasn't American by speaking French to him and to my surprise he spoke French. I learned French in high school and college, but my French was nowhere near the level of this kid. The kid was extremely smart and was able to curse in seven different languages and he practiced them all on me. We were told not to bring any money before the deployment, but thank goodness I did not listen. I brought $30 on trip to Turkey, and I spent every penny. I would enjoy a return trip to Turkey.

Turkey – We spent three weeks in country and went to a restaurant where I ate lamb for the first time and toured the Bazaar in Istanbul after the dinner.

Patrol Duty

I didn't like Police duties because of the long hours, weekend work, and breaking up Domestic Disturbances. Military bases experience the same violence as Civilian Police, but on a lower level. I was partnered with Jimmy a Retired Green Beret. Jimmy was overweight with a Jheri-Curl. Jimmy would always tell stories about women chasing after him. Women were chasing after him because he had a pocketful of money.

Jimmy and I responded to a Domestic Disturbance involving two sisters in their twenties. They were drunk and the younger sister stabbed the older sister with a pair of scissors. The wound was superficial. The older sister pulled down her shirt and showed us the stab mark and breasts. Jimmy went crazy and asked the girl for her number which she gladly gave up. They both looked like crackheads. The ambulance took the older sister to the hospital and I never heard from her again, but said he did.

Another night we responded to a Domestic Disturbance involving a married couple. They were watching television when they decided to re-enact the television commercial referencing Robert Conrad and Eveready Battery. The wife put a battery on her shoulder and asked her husband to knock it off and of course he missed and struck his wife in the face. They were both drunk and we made the husband leave the house. We would respond to the couples' house every pay day weekend. Normally Domestic Disturbances occurred the week after payday and the week before payday because soldiers were broke.

Jimmy and I responded to a Domestic Disturbance involving a wife who stole her husband's last twenty dollars. She claimed she did not do it, but later confessed to being a recovering crack addict. We believed the husband's story that his wife stole the money, but

95

according to Ft. Stewart policy the husband had to spend the night in his unit's barrack to defuse the situation.

I patrolled by myself on numerous occasions. I spotted a new Nissan which cost over $20,000 with broken windshield wipers, spray painted, oil and Clorox dumped on it, and broken side mirrors. I knew it was a case of a spurned lover. I contacted the owner and asked him to come outside and look at his car. The owner showed up two hours later and I saw him leaving the room of his new girlfriend which was 200 meters away from the incident. When the owner saw his car, he wasn't upset. I asked him if he knew the person who did it and he smiled and responded "Yes". I asked him if he wanted to press charges and he said "No". I don't know how he kept his composure, but I would have gone ballistic seeing my new car destroyed. The female caused about $3,000 worth of damage to his car.

The Military Police had to perform Guard Duty at the Generals' houses because an upset soldier planted a sign with a Green Penis in the yard of a General. There was a saying by soldiers which stated that the Army was a Big Green Weenie and it was always screwing soldiers. People suspected who the soldier was, but no charges ever occurred since the soldier left the Army.

I was chewed out by Major General Taylor for the silliest reason. I was patrolling in my assigned area when I stopped to watch an Engineer Company perform water operations. General Taylor's vehicle pulled up behind me and he exited his vehicle and in a "loud voice asked what was I doing"? I explained to him this was part of my patrol area. He suspected I was sleeping which I was not, so he began screaming at me that I was unprofessional because I wasn't wearing my hat inside of my patrol car. I reported the incident back to my unit and the Commander made put out a silly order stating "all Military Policeman must wear their hats inside of patrol cars. The rule lasted about two weeks. General Taylor sent me a congratulation letter for being selected for OCS which I promptly threw away.

I was always putting my foot in my mouth. I hated patrol duty, so I convinced my leadership team to let me perform Radio Telephone Operator (RTO) Duties. I was boasting that it was easy duty; little did I know what lay ahead. All hell broke loose when I assumed RTO Duties. People were calling in for Domestic Disturbances, Traffic Stops, House lockouts, Escorts for Money deposits, Building Alarms, Military Policeman requesting permission for lunch breaks and other calls requesting Military Police assistance. I had to know the locations of all Military Policemen, give directions of locations to officers, answer telephone calls, and assist people when they entered the Police Station. When I sat down behind the radio, I did not get up. I thought I would get a 30-minute lunch break like Military Policemen on Patrol Duty, but I was totally wrong and received an eat as you go lunch which is the Desk Sergeant brought me a sandwich to eat behind the radio. RTO duty was hard and intense. I thought it would be a one and done deal, but my Squad Leader put me behind the desk every day for two weeks. I have a Country Accent and Hughes would call up the station and tell me to put some bass in my voice.

A funny and strange situation occurred during one of my RTO Duties. A 1SG brought a young man from Alabama to the station in order for us to press charges on him for impersonating a soldier. I called an Investigator over to assist with the situation. The young man showed up to the unit and said he was in the Army and did not have any money or uniforms. The Commander of the unit asked the 1SG to take care of the young man. The Army's motto is to take care of soldiers. The 1SG gave the young man some uniforms and began to fill-out paperwork to get him paid. The young man gave the 1SG an incorrect answer when asked where he attended Basic Training at. 1SG asked him to do a hand salute and other Drill Movements which all new soldiers know, and the young man failed the tests which made the 1SG very suspicious of him. The 1SG brought the him down to the Police Station where we began questioning him. He said his momma told him to join the Army because she was tired of supporting him, so he drove to Ft. Stewart which was nine hours away from his house and

97

the only post he could enter without a Military ID. The young man stopped at the first unit he saw with a group of soldiers standing outside. We were stunned to hear his story and then we explained to him the sequence of events a person has to do in order to join the Army. We later found out he failed the Military Entrance Test (ASVAB) which was the reason he could not join the Army. 1SG escorted him off post and returned to the station where we all began laughing historically about the situation because no one ever heard of anyone doing such a crazy thing to join the Army. We said to ourselves, he would have made a great soldier because of his determination to become a soldier.

The worst Domestic Violence Incident occurred after I finished a duty shift. A lady stabbed her spouse in the chest with a knife; the husband woke up and beat the spouse to death with a baseball bat; then wrecked the car in front of the Military Police Station. It was a strange sequence of events, but I was glad my shift ended because if not I would have been working another eight hours. I never found out if the husband survived incident.

I received orders to attend OCS (Officer Training School) and go to Germany at the same time. The civilian personnel officer asked me if I prefer to go to Germany or attend OCS and I told her "Heck No, I don't want to go to Germany, I want to attend OCS and become an Officer so I can make those big dollars", she began laughing hysterically. It was a $1,500 a month pay raise for becoming an Officer.

Armor Battalion

My Platoon Leader sent me down to 2nd Battalion 7th Infantry Division (Armor Battalion) because I wanted to become an Infantry or Armor Officer which was a great experience.

I worked with an Armor Platoon Leader who was a recent graduate of OCS. He gave me a book of almost 30 pages which all OCS students were required to know. It included quotes by General McArthur, Schofield Definition, Leadership Tactics, OCS Motto, and other Military Knowledge subjects. I learned the book word for word in 3 weeks which saved me from a lot of extra Drill and Ceremony at OCS.

I attended field exercises and worked in the Bradley Simulator Room with the unit. I went through the same simulation training as other soldiers. I learned how a Tank Commander called for fire and the weapon systems on the Bradley. The Lieutenant scared the crap out of me when he spun the turret around while we were crossing a bridge and I was beside him. I thought we were running off the bridge and I grabbed hold of him to get his attention. He burst out laughing from my reaction. I did field exercises with the platoon. I enjoyed watching people and animals through the Infrared Scope. The only thing I did not do which I should have done was walk 12-miles with the other soldiers. They asked me if I wanted to ride in the Bradley Tank or walk 12-miles with them. I looked at them like they were crazy and I chose riding over walking which was a cowardly choice. I should have walked with them to prove I was tough as them. Those soldiers were thrilled a MP wanted to be one of them and willingly shared all of their knowledge with me. The guys told me tanks are like women, you got to get some.

Soldiers of the Battalion were always telling stories. SSG Lee, was extremely funny. He joined the Army at the age of 31 and I asked him why he waited so late. Lee said he was working at UPS making $50K a year in the 80s and his supervisor made him upset so he quit not realizing he had no money saved up. Lee said after being broke for a while he joined the Army which was $25K pay cut. He told us that he was on a date, and he asked his date what do you want to do and she replied whatever he wanted to, so he drove his date to a hotel. We asked Lee what happened to his date and he replied, "he married her", and we laughed hysterically.

The guys would come up with ways to impress girls. Two Privates who were broke picked up their dates and convinced them to eat MREs for dinner. We asked them how did they do convince them and they replied by telling them, it was Astronauts food. The girls thought they were dating astronauts and had sex with them afterwards.

I asked an LTC in the 2nd BN, 7th Infantry Division for advice on what I needed to become a successful Officer in the Army and he told me to "Keep your Integrity". It was the best advice which I ever received because I met plenty of Officers who would lie for their own needs.

I learned a lot with from the unit. I owe a great deal of my success as Officer to LTC Canada, Battalion Commander of 2nd BN, 7th Infantry, and the soldiers under his Command. LTC Canada assigned me to a Platoon Leader who graduated from OCS and the Platoon Leader gave me his OCS booklet which I learned three weeks before my arrival to OCS.

When I left LTC Canada gave me a plaque and made me an Honorary Cotton Baler which was the Battalion's nickname. I enjoyed the experience of training with the Armor unit. Officer Branch granted me two dream jobs in the Army which were Infantry and Armor.

I-95 Travels

I enjoyed Ft. Stewart and met a lot of nice people there. I drove a BMW 325 and put over 68,000 miles on it in 14 months. I told all my friends and family members if you lived within 500 miles of Ft. Stewart, I would visit you. I went to every state from Florida to New York. New York was the first time I saw live Jazz. There were people coming off the street just playing for the audience, and they were very good. I was like a vampire in New York in that I partied all night and slept all day.

One Friday night, I took I-77 to North Carolina instead of staying on I-95 which was a mistake. I stopped at a small convenience store to get gas. As I was pumping gas, I looked up and saw a burning cross a distance away. I immediately jumped in my car and sped off. I never took I-77 again.

Ft. Stewart is very close to Florida and my goal in college was to attend Spring Break in Florida, but every year my car would have some type of mechanical problem which canceled my trips. I visited my cousin and her spouse in Tampa where I met Lee Paige a former Professional Football Player who later became a DEA Agent. He was a cornerback who could bench press 400 pounds. Lee taught me how to eat crab legs.

I was involved in a car accident two weeks before I was to attend OCS. My cousin and I were sitting at a stop light in her new Mercedes when a guy ran into the back of us at over 55 mph. We hit the car in front of us so hard that it flattened its tire. I was lucky I did not get seriously hurt because I always wore my seat belt under my arm pit, which is the incorrect way. Seat belts do work, and they will prevent serious injury when worn correctly. I was slightly injured, but I wasn't going to tell my unit because it would have delayed my OCS date. Thank goodness I recovered before attending OCS.

Lessons Learned

1. *Be careful what you ask for* – I thought being a Radio Operator was an easy job until I was placed in the job.

2. *If you see something wrong, confront the person or inform a supervisor* - I knew my roommate was not a neat person and I should have informed the leadership team of his shortcomings instead of keeping quiet.

3. *Reward people for their hard work* – Awards show a person their company cares about them and recognizes the hard work they put in to help the company to become successful.

4. *Don't be Content with your job* – I never understood why soldiers don't try to achieve higher rank. The Military provides numerous Civilian and Military schools for Servicemembers to obtain a better job and higher rank.

5. *Chase money not women* – The E-6 who told us "Do what your career can stand" was not interested in higher rank, but only in returning to Germany. I wonder how much money he spent on Call Girls. If he was focused on his career as much as women, he probably would have achieved the rank of CSM which is over $2,000 more a month in pay.

6. *You can't receive help if you don't ask for it* – I informed my Platoon Leader of my goals and he helped me to achieve it by getting me letters of recommendations and sending me to an Armor Unit to learn about the duties and responsibilities of an Officer. I owe a great deal of my success in becoming an Officer to him.

OCS

I arrived at Fort Benning, GA for OCS in March 1990. There were over 130 students in attendance and 95% of them were Prior-Service Soldiers ranging from E-4 to E-7. There were Green Beret and Ranger Soldiers in the school. TAC Officers would say the only reason we wanted to become Officers was for the pay and the Green Beret Soldiers would laugh and say they took a pay cut to become an Officer. The Green Beret Soldiers were making more than the TAC Officers because they were receiving Special Duty pay such as Airborne and yearly bonuses.

The TAC Officers were good soldiers and they cared about us. They ran everything because the Commander was never around. CPT Upshur was the senior TAC and a former football player at Appalachian State in Boone, NC. He was always talking trash about how he could outrun any cadet in OCS. One day we picking grass from between the rocks which was another menial task. While picking the grass between the rocks, CPT Upshur challenged me to a race in boots. When someone said go, I took off like I was shot from a cannon and as I turned around, I saw CPT Upshur's eyes pop out of his head. He knew he was in a race for his reputation. He beat me by 2 inches according to him, but I talked trash and told him he only won because I was in boots and I just finished eating. I would have smoked him in running shoes which is why he challenged me in boots.

CPT Burnett, my Platoon TAC, was an outstanding leader and a former college basketball player. He was with us at every training event. He would chew you out only if you deserved it. You could only eat with a spoon in OCS and cadets had 45 seconds to eat their food. When cadets finished eating, they reported to a TAC Officer for uniform inspection and a quiz on OCS required knowledge such as "Schofield Definition of Leadership". If you missed one word you

103

would receive 23 Demerits (The number of words in Schofield Definition of Leadership) or whatever they quizzed you on. CPT Burnett tried numerous times to get me on the Required Knowledge, but he could never do it because I knew the book like the back of my hand thanks to the Armor Lieutenant at Ft. Stewart. One day I reported to him, and I was extremely confident he could not trip me up on any Required Knowledge question. He asked me Schofield Definition of Leadership and I repeated exactly how it was written in the book and he said, "23 Demerits" and I responded, "What for?" and he said there was a doughnut flake on my uniform. My jaw fell to the floor. The only day we ate donuts; I ended up with a piece the size of a pin on my uniform. The Demerits meant I had to walk in the quad for 30 minutes in full uniform with weapon, stopping at each corner and conduct a Rifle Drill Movement (Left Shoulder Arms, Right Soldier Arms, Present Arms, and Parade Rest). I sucked at first until Cadet Armbruster, who used to be on the Marine Corps Drill Team, gave me some training which made me good at doing Rifle Drills while marching.

First Lieutenant (1LT) Wilson was a TAC and West Point Graduate. Students hated reporting to him because he knew the OCS Required Knowledge like the back of his hand from his time at West Point. He was the only TAC who did not need to look at the OCS handbook when quizzing students on Required Knowledge. One day I reported to him which did not bother me because I knew that OCS Handbook like the back of my hand. He asked me a quote from General McArthur, I responded with confidence and a smile on my face. 1LT Wilson said wrong and gave me 45 minutes of Drill Time for two days. I asked him what for and he said you missed one word, and I responded "I did not and showed him my OCS Handbook", and he showed me his OCS Handbook which was an updated version which read "that" instead of "and" which was written in my OCS Handbook. My mouth dropped to the ground. Those tours made me so good Drilling with a Rifle, that 30 years later I can still do it.

The TAC Officers would march us to the barbershop for haircuts then the Officers would return to their offices. We would get our haircuts and then pay the person next door to shine our boots. One of the students told the TAC Officers about students getting their boots shined. The TAC Officers rushed over to the barbershop and put a stop to it. The individual who told on the class mentioned my name and another cadet. I guess the person was jealous and cheap because they did not want to pay $4.00 for a boot shine. CPT Upshur and CPT Burnett called me and the other soldier in the Office and asked us to tell on the others which we both refused. The TAC Officers told us using the boot guy was creating an unfair advantage over the other cadets and I responded, I did not see the problem in using the boot guy because Officers are supposed to look their best; we were paying for the services; and Officer Candidates from other classes were using the service. Those excuses did not go over well, and the TAC Officers began to smoke the crap out of us. I probably did about 500 pushups and 1000 flutter kicks. When I left their office there was a pool of sweat on the floor where I was at, but I didn't talk.

Inspections

There were daily inspections at OCS conducted by respective TAC Officers and then four company inspections which involved TAC Officers from different platoons. The first inspection occurred two weeks after the arrival of cadets.

There was an unwritten rule for the First Inspection which everyone failed, no matter how they looked. My company stated we were going to be the first company to pass the first inspection. We cleaned for three days and conducted our own inspection before the TAC Officers' Inspection. In OCS you had to fold your clothes and roll your socks a certain way. The Lieutenant at Ft. Stewart told me to roll my socks and shirts in a way which creates Sad Face for all inspections except for the last Inspection. In the last Inspection, fold your shirts and socks so they resemble a Smiley Face because a Smiley Face means you are about to become an Officer. I did exactly what the Lieutenant said and when the TAC Officer came in; he began to chew me out and asked "Why did I have my items giving him a Sad Face when I should be happy to be in OCS". He failed me for my display of items. The truth is if I rolled my socks into a Smily Face, the TAC would have told me a Smily Face means you are a graduate and I would have failed for impersonating an Officer. The purposes of failing the company on the first inspection are to get everyone working as a team, show what the standards were for OCS, and to keep us focused. If a company passed the first inspection, they would have become cocky and slacked off for the next inspections.

The next day after the inspection, Lagat who was Hawaiian, a physical fitness stud, and serving as the Company CSM obtained the Master Key from one of the TAC officers to put our forbidden items such as electric shavers and make-up for the females into the storage room. Lagot opened the room which kept the suitcases full of civilian clothes and Care Packages. Care Packages were forbidden at OCS.

106

Members of Second Platoon who had Care Packages decided to open them and share it with other Platoon Members. Lagat's family sent him octopus which he shared with everyone. It was my first-time eating octopus and it was delicious. I don't why his mom sent him octopus knowing he would be not able to eat it for another three months. Jackie, my cousin who was a soldier in Korea, sent me chocolate chip cookies and a host of other sweets. We sat around, ate, and told stories about our lives before OCS. We had a great time and paid for it on a 5-mile run the next day, but it was worth it. Everyone became closer after the party.

Lindo was soldier who was formerly in the Ranger Battalion and Special Forces. He was extremely intelligent, but he did not like the mind games which the instructors played on us in OCS. Cadets had to stencil their T-shirts with their name in the center of the shirt and folded in a certain way. Lindo hand wrote his name in large letters on his T-shirts and put his clothes in his drawers like he wanted to. His TAC Officer would dump his clothes out every day and assign him walking Tours with his rifle. Lindo had so many Tours it would have taken him two years to complete them. He would not conform to any standard which he thought was useless. Once he was marching his platoon to the Dining Facility, he abruptly told them to turn left. There was no Column Left March, or any resemblance of a Military Drill Command given and the entire Company burst out laughing at Lindo which did not faze him at all. The TAC Officers wanted to put Lindo out of OCS, but McMahon and Strickland who served with Lindo in the Ranger Battalion talked them out of it. When we went on a field training exercise, the TACs gave Lindo an assignment which they did not think he could not accomplish, and he executed it to perfection which shocked them. I asked Lindo why he didn't follow the TAC instructions and he told me, he wasn't going to let soldiers who haven't been through the training he went through tell him what to do; he had suffered a lot worse harassment in Special Forces and Ranger Units than they could administer to him; and he enjoyed seeing them get upset. I asked Lindo how he became a Special Forces Soldier and he

107

told me while in the Ranger Battalion they put five soldiers in a circle and asked them to fight it out to determine who would attend Special Forces School and he beat everyone. Lindo was about 5'10 and 175 pounds and tough as nails.

Mind Games

The TAC Officers would assign us menial tasks. The majority of the students were Prior Service Soldiers with seven or more years of experience in the Army. A TAC Officer had this game called Human Laundry Mat. He found a student's closet unsecure; order the entire company outside in formation with all their clothes hangers at 12:00 am; and then instructed us to pass the clothes hangers from right to left like a conveyor belt in a dry cleaner.

Once we were waiting for the buses to take us back to the company area, a TAC Officer made the company walk-in knee-high water just for fun. There was no reason or any learning behind this exercise. We later got our revenge on him. We were doing a 12-mile foot march and half-way through the march the TAC supposedly fell and started screaming like a two-year old kid. A couple of students saw him jump in the ditch and pretend like he hurt himself because he could not complete the march due to him being out of shape. The entire company would imitate his screams and laugh whenever he walked by us.

The instructors would take us on runs at 10:00pm just for the kicks. We took showers at night and had to get up at 0400 in the morning to run again. The only thing this did was make us sleepy in class. There were 5 shower heads and 7 sinks for 80 males, and we had about 10 minutes to shower, shave, and use the bathroom between completing our Physical Training and First Formation. There would be six guys around 1 sink shaving and brushing their teeth and 5 guys around 1 shower head and our motto was "Don't drop your soap". I learned to shower and shave in less than 90 seconds. I refuse to do it now.

109

OCS Classmates

Soldiers who attended OCS came from various branches: Special Forces, Ranger Battalion, Infantry, Supply, and other branches. All soldiers in OCS were very intelligent and most of them had their college degree. We had a soldier in our company, Conrad, who graduated from West Point, but did not receive his Officer Commission due to an incident before his West Point graduation. West Point made him enter the Army as a Specialist for his mistake. The TACs told him he would be the smartest Corporal in the Army if he didn't graduate from OCS. Conrad graduated. TACs were always talking shit to us.

LT Treciokas told me about her flight on the Concord. Her father paid $5,000 a piece for their tickets, and they ate lobster and sipped champagne on the flight. I was amazed at her story because flying on the Concord was a dream of mine, and I never ate lobster or drank champagne in my life at that time. I was from the country, and we associated lobster with crayfish and no one in my family ate crayfish.

Les was another Special Forces Soldier who helped me through OCS. Les was the Distinguished Graduate of his Special Forces Class and he talked more to me than any other student for some unknown reason. The other students would always ask me what type of person Les was and I would tell them he is extremely intelligent and private. Les was a driven person who was focused on completing any goals placed before him and he did not believe in telling anyone about his life. I was more of a social person, and had conversations with everyone in the class. Les and Kris served over 40 years in the Army.

One day the TAC rushed the company over to the Chapel for a meeting with the Brigade Commander after lunch. I was in the front of the company which enabled me to use the bathroom quickly. The other students were lined up waiting to use the bathroom and the TACs immediately told everyone behind me to get out of the line and sit-down before the Brigade Commander arrived. We waited for 30 minutes, and the Brigade Commander had not arrived, other cadets asked to use the bathroom and the TACs said "No". I looked at Les and he was sweating profusely from holding his urine. The TACs finally allowed us to use the restroom and the entire class ran to the bathroom. In OCS you use the bathroom any chance you get whether you have permission or not. It wasn't uncommon to see three or four guys using one urinal at the same time.

Skip was a soldier from the Ranger Battalion who loved to tell stories about his time in Grenada. He told the same stories over and over that everyone in the company knew them word for word.

Another classmate who was in the Ranger Battalion would tell us the story of when he first arrived in the Ranger Battalion. Everyone in his squad was required to pay $50 every payday to a girl who maintained an apartment off base where Rangers could hang out after work. The girl was called a Bat Girl and her responsibilities were to always have beer and food for the squad, keep the place clean, and provide extracurricular favors for a few extra dollars. The Bat Girl enjoyed this privilege because she had a free apartment and protection.

OCS students had additional duties which were rotated among the students such as answering phones at night, cutting grass, cleaning the command hallways, picking-up trash, Fire Guard, and Parking lot guard. Married students would pay single soldiers to pull their parking lot guard so they could meet their spouses in the parking lot. I made over $100 doing this. I had a little hustle in me.

OCS was hard and fun. The TAC Officers enjoyed playing mental games with the students and we were always plotting on ways to get over on them.

The weekend before our final phase the TAC Officers gave us an 8-hour pass on Saturday and a 6-hour pass on Sunday. We were not

111

allowed to drive, but a lot of the students said their spouses or families were coming to pick them up, which was true for only about twenty percent of the students. On Saturday everyone went to fast-food restaurants and rented hotel rooms so we could relax and drink beer.

The TACs told us to stay around the area and not go to certain areas because of drugs. On Sunday we piled in Les car wearing our uniforms and went to Tuskegee University in Alabama looking for girls. We met some girls and the next time they saw us, they pretended they didn't know us. The girl from Detroit who I met, gave me the cold shoulder for not calling her over the summer. She gave me the wrong number and said I should have tracked down her number from people on campus. I looked at it as their loss because we all retired as Military Officers.

We went to the off-limits area after our return from Tuskegee because a passenger who was from the area told us it was safe. As soon as we pulled up in the area to watch a basketball game, we saw our TAC Officer there. He left his basketball game to chew us out for being there and said to us "What in the hell are you guys doing in this area" and we responded in unison "Sir, what are you doing here"? He told us to get the hell out of the area or he would Court Martial us, but he couldn't punish us because he was doing the same thing.

The last week of OCS, the TACs let us have some free time. Everyone went wild. Some of the students went to the NCO Club and some made a beer run. When we came back some of the students were running down the hall hollering, and Captain Upshur was chasing after them to no avail. I was passed out on the bed and students said Captain Upshur just walked by shaking his head.

Graduation Day in OCS was an exciting day. I had been preparing for it for two years and it felt like a ton of bricks off my chest. The Army tradition is an Officer must give a Silver Dollar to the first soldier who salutes them. Every student purchased 10 Silver Dollar pieces. As soon as graduation ended, the CSM stood outside

112

the door and rendered a salute to all new Officers. The CSM made over $100 doing this. Hopefully he held on to those Silver Dollars.

I graduated with a 94 average which was number 50 in a class of 96. I should have graduated in the top 15, but I failed Night Land Navigation the first time we tested on it. We had to get 3 out of 4 points right in a given amount of time. The points were located mostly off the road. I was worried about getting lost in the woods than finding my points. I arrived 30 minutes before the allotted time with 3 points and CPT Burnett told me to go and try for the 4th point, but I was confident I had 3 correct points. The TACs graded us, and I came up with only 2 correct points. I was upset with myself, and CPT Burnett told me being cocky knocked me out of the top 10% of the class. Chris, Special Forces Soldier, gave me a class on Land Navigation which helped me pass Night Land Navigation the second time. Chris was a Navigating expert. He jogged the Navigation course. Chris is the only person I know who eats entire peanuts including the shells.

OCS is harder than Basic Training because of the constant exercising, lack of sleep, and mind games being played by the instructors. We ran every day and males had to do 10 pull-ups before each meal while females had to do three. Majority of the females could do ten plus and there were a couple of males who could not do one pull-up, but by graduation everyone including females could do at least ten pull-ups. We learned Map Reading, Radio Operations, Military Tactics, Supply, First-Aid, and other skills soldiers needed. I had a lot of great classmates and fond memories of OCS.

113

Lessons Learned

1. ***Stay focus on the task at hand*** – I was focus on becoming an Officer. I learned the entire OCS Handbook word for word before arrival.

2. ***Cockiness can overshadow ability*** – We had to find 3 out of 4 locations to pass Night Land Navigation. I was too overconfident in my navigation skills that I only looked for three points instead four points. My cockiness resulted in me finishing in the middle of my class instead of near the top.

3. ***Do not be afraid to speak to leaders*** – The TACs would not let us use the bathroom because they were afraid to tell the Brigade Commander about us needing to use the bathroom. If a leader knows the situation, they will make the decision.

4. ***Time Management*** – You have to manage your time if you want to succeed in any occupation. There was little free time in OCS. We had 45 seconds to eat and 10 minutes to shower, shit, and shave between exercise and breakfast.

OCS   3-90

Excellence   begins here!

2nd PLATOON

I am standing in the rear

115

Field Training

LOCKED AND LOADED

HELLO . . . HELLO!

THIS WAY??

Les (upper right) and McMahon and Skip (middle left picture) were some of the class leaders. Skip is in the lower left picture. I am in the middle on bottom right picture.

"WHY US!" SHAVE!!?

Digging fighting positions. Chris, another class leader, is bent over looking at the camera. I am posing in the picture on the left and shaving in the field. Shaving was a daily requirement regardless of where training took place.

Horse playing around a couple of days before graduation. OCS has three phases which corresponds to the color of the ascot. White Ascot signifies Senior Phase.

Jackie, my cousin, who was stationed in Korea sent me a package full of cookies and other goodies trying to get me to hook her up with one of my classmates. I told her if I hooked her up with one of my friends then I will lose a friend.

118

INFANTRY OFFICER BASIC COURSE (IOBC)

The OCS students who were branched as Infantry Officers, reported to the Infantry Officer Basic Course the next day. We were tired because we had no rest time between OCS and IOBC. I needed a break in between classes to allow my bone spurs to heal up. I was afraid of going to see a doctor because Infantry Officers are taught to be tough and I was afraid of being assigned to another Branch. The Army gave me my dream request of becoming a Light Infantry and Armor Officer and I wasn't about to give up on my dream jobs.

I associated IOBC as a big fraternity which consisted of soldiers from OCS, College, and Military Academies, and Military Schools. It was an all-male unit with everyone having money to blow and at least one or two days off for the weekend. Guys would go to the club on the weekend and even drink during the week, despite having Physical Training the next day. There were plenty of characters in IOBC.

Our TAC Officer would get upset with Lindo, who was an OCS classmate of mine, for wearing his Green Beret because the uniform for training was soft caps. Everyday Lindo would come to formation wearing his Green Beret and everyday our TAC Officer would curse him out. He finally convinced Lindo to follow his instructions by threatening to take away his Lieutenant Rank.

We had a former teacher who had been in the Individual Readiness Reserves for 7 years and the Army called him to Active Duty for Desert Storm because they paid for his college scholarship. He was out of shape and he reminded us of Klinger on Mash. He hated the Army, and was trying everything to get kicked out, but to no avail. We had to complete peer reports on each other, and he would ask for the other lieutenants to rank him last in the platoon. When we conducted a 12-mile foot march for the Expert Infantry Badge, I saw him smoking on the march. He came in last. He did graduate, but I don't know what happened to his Army career.

Russell was a Norwich Graduate and the biggest person in the class. He was 6'4, 250 pounds and ran two miles under 11 minutes. Most of the students did not take the Expert Infantry Badge (EIB) Test seriously because the test would be conducted twice a year at our assigned units. Less than 5 out of 100 IOBC students earned the EIB during IOBC and Russell was one of them. We would go by Russell's room to ask him if he wanted to go out and Russell would be sitting on the floor naked camouflaging his face in preparation for the EIB test. We would tell him to put some damn clothes on before inviting us in his room.

I passed all of the requirements for earning my EIB except for the Marksmanship Test. I hit 35 out of 40 targets the first time I shot for the Marksmanship Test. Soldiers needed to hit a minimum of 36 targets to become an Expert Marksmanship. I shot three more times and scored less each time which was due to a lack of focus. I earned my EIB in Panama.

Doc was a Reserve Physician in our platoon. We didn't if he was telling us the truth about being a physician or the Army was stupid for sending a physician to the Infantry Officer Basic Course instead of Medical School. He would always leave the club with a different woman each weekend because when he told a woman he was a doctor, they would fall head over heels for him. The only doctoring which I saw him do was to put a bandage on someone's leg. I believe Granny from the Beverly Hillbillies was a better doctor than him.

The guys in IOBC were brutal. A classmate from Ohio, wife followed him to Ft. Moore (Formerly Ft. Benning). We went to a Strip Club and she was our waitress. The guys told him it would only be a matter of time before she gets up on stage and of course, she was on stage a week later.

Another soldier's wife was a stripper in Atlanta. He would tell us she made $75K a year as a stripper and encouraged us to go see her. I told him I'm not going to support his lifestyle.

The classes in IOBC were the same as OCS except we conducted Live-Fire exercises in IOBC. IOBC instructors would let former OCS students out of classes which did not involve Live-Fire exercises because we had the exact same classes and instructors in OCS.

I went to North Carolina after OCS to pick-up my BMW 325. I was driving around Ft. Moore when I met two girls. I described the girls to Skip, OCS Classmate, and he started to smile and said "They only talk to O-1 and Above" which means they only talk to Officers. Officers had blue stickers on their cars and Sergeants had red stickers. One of the girls looked like a short Patti Labelle. I asked Skip how he knew they only talked to Officers and he described the following scenario to me. Skip drove a red corvette and he went on a date with the girl who resembled Patti Labelle. The next day Skip showed up at her house with a red decal on his car which was the sticker for sergeants and the girl dumped him on the spot. I dated her friend until I departed to Panama. She dumped me when she found out I was going to Panama which didn't bother me because I knew her history. Those two girls reminded me of the movie An Officer and a Gentlemen. They knew the Officer Club better than I did.

121

Court

I was returning from a movie theater around 11:00pm when I noticed a policeman at an intersection looking for drivers who were not coming to a complete stop at the stop sign. It was the same thing I did as a MP. When I proceeded through the intersection, he noticed my license tag was expired and pulled me over. I showed him my registration which stated North Carolina Drivers had a 15-day grace period after the expiration of their license tag. The policeman did not believe the statement on the back of my registration and gave me a ticket anyway. I opted for court date instead of paying $200 to the city of Columbus. Columbus, Georgia policemen enjoyed messing with soldiers and we probably paid for their new headquarters and police cars through all the fines we received.

The court was packed when I showed up. The first case involved an old lady selling crack from under her wig. The judge gave her a 30-year sentence. The next case was a guy driving without car insurance. He told the judge he could not afford car insurance and the judge gave him 30-days in jail. The next case involved two high school girls who were fighting in school. The judge sentenced them to 4 days in jail. I was nervous and asked the police officer in the back if I was in the right court and he replied "yes".

The judge continued on with his rampage and gave a guy a 3-year sentence for stealing cigarettes from the house of his former girlfriend despite her pleading with the judge she wanted to drop the charges. I was scared when it came my time to appear before the Hanging Judge. I presented my evidence showing North Carolina gave their drivers a 15-day grace period to renew their license and a copy of my new registration card. The judge dismissed my case. Have your ducks in a row when you drive in Columbus.

A TAC Officer was involved in a head-on collision with the Commanding General's daughter. The General's daughter was drunk and driving the wrong way on a one-way street. The General's daughter received no punishment and the street sign was changed to a two-way sign the next day which is a total abuse of power.

RANGER SCHOOL

I attended Ranger School after finishing IOBC. Nine of us slept on the floor of Chris' apartment the night before Ranger School. One of my IOBC classmates took my running shoes and I reported to Ranger School without running shoes. A Ranger Instructor gave me a pair of secondhand shoes. I am very particular about my running shoes, and I would only run in Nike Air Max because they alleviated my bone spurs.

Ranger Instructors would fail people just for fun in those days. They failed the two highest physical fitness scores of my OCS class and one was a Special Forces soldier.

In Ranger Schools your Peers vote to see if you should move to the next phase. I was almost peered out in the Benning Phase because I was the only Officer in a Squad full of soldiers from the Ranger Battalion.

I heard from some of my friends say Russell had been dismissed from Ranger School because some members of his squad made some untrue statements about him. Russell is a trustworthy and honest guy who I would put my life in his hands. He was in a squad full of soldiers from the Ranger Battalion who were probably intimidated by Russell's size. Russell later became a Green Beret who I saw in Korea.

I passed the Swim and Physical fitness tests in Ranger School and aggravated my bone spurs from running in those secondhand shoes. Every morning, I would ask the medics for Motrin and an injection in my heels to ease the pain. I don't know what they injected in my heels, but it was more painful than the bones spurs. I suffered bone spurs in OCS, but the Nike Shoes helped ease the pain. I found out who took my shoes a month later and I wanted to punch the

124

individual for knowingly taking my shoes. He should have told the Ranger Instructors of the mistake instead of looking out for his own well-being. His shoes were a size smaller than mine.

I went to Mountain Phase, but did not pass. I failed a Patrol mission because the instructor saw a Squad Leader sleeping on the Operation Order and I failed to make the correction in a timely manner. I failed rope tying and received a failure for going to the medics for my feet. Twenty years later, I learned how to tie rope from my JROTC students.

Ranger Instructors would allow students who failed a subject to make it up by volunteering as a Radio Operator or carrying extra equipment. I did all sorts of extra work to make-up for those failed subjects and still failed Mountain Phase.

The Army later recognized a lot of Black Soldiers were failing the Mountain Phase of Ranger School and assigned a Black Commander. I met several former Ranger Instructors in the Florida who stated if a Black Soldier showed up at Florida Phase, they would do everything possible to ensure they pass because the instructors knew Black soldiers caught hell in the Mountain Phase. I deserved the failure on rope tying because I folded under pressure. I know I did not deserve the other negative reports, but some instructors took pride in failing officers. In those days, instructors walked on water and I never saw any Company Commanders at training. The biggest mistake I made was attending Ranger School injured.

Lessons Learned

1. *Never attend a Military school injured* – You must be mentally and physically prepared for any Military Training. I should have asked the IOBC Commander for permission to report to my unit to heal up before attending Ranger School.

2. *If you face a setback, continue* – Russell was dismissed from Ranger School, but he continued to strive for excellence and became a Green Beret.

3. *If you make a mistake, confess to it, and do the right thing* – The individual who took my shoes did not understand the importance of those shoes and should have returned them.

4. *Focus on the task ahead* – I should have earned my EIB in IOBC, but I was more focused on having a good time instead of shooting.

PANAMA

I arrived in Panama in January 1991. I never received a Welcome Packet from the unit, so when I arrived a Liaison Sergeant picked a group of us at the Airport and dropped us off at the Costa Del Sol Hotel. I received a phone call as soon as I arrived in my room. It was a lady who was looking for a guy she met the night before. She spoke no English and someone with her who spoke English asked if she could come over and I said sure. I could not believe I met a woman in less than an hour upon my arrival in Panama. I opened the door and standing in front of me was a beautiful lady who looked like Jennifer Beals the girl in Flashdance. She was in shock because the previous gentleman was a White Soldier. It was like two 1-year-olds talking to each other, she spoke no English and I spoke no Spanish. Nothing happened, but I said to myself if picking up women is this easy then I died and went to Heaven. The women in Panama made the Kardasian women look ugly. I was mad at myself for taking French in College and High School. The teachers at my school said French is the Language of Love, their minds would have changed if they went to Panama before studying French. A Sergeant from the Reception Station told all us single guys we would be married by the end of our tour in Panama. Four years later, I was in that category.

Panamanians drive crazy. The hotel driver would take us to and from the base for in processing. He would drive on the sidewalks and pass cars on double yellow lines. While he was driving crazy, he would look at me and laugh. I would smile back, but I was scared shitless inside.

The 508th Airborne Company sent their S-3 Officer to interview me to see if I was a fit for their unit. We talked and he asked me which unit I would like to be assigned to and I responded I would like to be assigned to the Armor unit in Panama. I read up on the history of

127

Panama and other Soldiers in my OCS and IOBC class told me about the Armor unit in Panama before my arrival. There was an Amor unit in Panama, but it deactivated a year prior to my arrival which I did not know. The Army says every soldier is assigned a sponsor before their arrival in a Unit, but back then this procedure was not followed often and since I did not receive a Welcome Packet or have a Sponsor there was no way I knew the Armor unit had been deactivated. I did not impress the S-3 so he called the 5/87 Infantry Battalion and told them they have a new Lieutenant. Messing up the interview was the best thing to happen to me because I was assigned to C/Co which had a great Company Commander.

C/Co 5/87

The 5/87 Infantry Battalion was located at Ft. Davis which was the Atlantic Side of Panama. Soldiers did not want to go to the Atlantic Side because Colon was a small city and there was not much to do there. The clubs in Colon were off limits to soldier when I arrived. The Pacific Side of Panama had more entertainment and restaurants. The Pacific Side resembled a small version of New York City while Colon resembled the town of Mayberry. The 5/87 was moved from the Pacific Side to the Atlantic Side a few months before my arrival. The Battalion had a reputation for fighting. The soldiers were cocky because most of them had participated in Operation Just Cause and a lot of senior Sergeants refuse to take a leadership position in the Battalion because they considered the soldiers undisciplined. When the unit returned from training they would go to the club and beat other soldiers up for sitting in their areas. They unofficially designated certain areas in the club for themselves and any soldier not knowing their section would suffer a beat down. The club would be packed with women and the soldiers from the 5/87 would order the girls to come over to their section and tell them to "Stand-up and turn around" and if the girls did not look good, the guys would tell them to leave. Soldiers on the Pacific Side said they were glad the 5/87 moved to the Atlantic Side. When the battalion arrived to Ft. Davis, soldiers put on their black T-shirts and red bandanas; went to the club and beat up the Special Forces soldiers there and hollered the club was theirs. The Battalion Commander banned the soldiers from attending the club for two weeks and forbade them from wearing their black t-shirts and red bandanas.

Captain Maxwell, my Commander, came and picked me up from the Pacific Side in his rust bucket Jeep which gave us time to talk about his expectations and my goals.

I was assigned to the 2nd Platoon of C/Co 5/87. The first night on Ft. Davis, I went with the outgoing 2nd Platoon Leader to a Boxing Match on Post. Every Infantry Soldier thinks they can box. Our Medic, who was boxing, wore a t-shirt which said, "You Fall, We Haul". Doc got his ass whipped. There were some outstanding boxers in the Battalion. We had Gold Glove Champions and a former Olympic Boxer named SSG Amanteen. SSG Amanteen was a Panamanian. I met a soldier from the Ranger Battalion who served with SSG Amanteen and he said SSG Amanteen would have been a Heavyweight Champion if he had left the Army sooner because he gave Ray Mercer, former Heavyweight Champion, the fight of his life. I would mess with SSG Amanteen by telling him somebody wanted to kick his ass and SSG Amanteen would respond "If he come over here, I will knock his ass out".

Soldiers

CPT Maxwell's priorities were to ensure his soldiers were well trained for combat and physically fit. He didn't care much about starched uniforms and spit-shine boots because he said there is no purpose in looking good if you can't fight. I came from a Military Police Unit and soldiers were required to have starched uniforms and spit-shine boots. He loved Charlie Company and the Soldiers loved him and his leadership style. If a soldier from Charlie Company was in a fight at the Club; CPT Maxwell would call an alert and order the entire company to show up at the club and take revenge on the perpetrators. CPT Maxwell's Friday Safety Briefing would be as follows: "Do not go to the club and start a fight, but if you go to the club take your Fire and Support with you" which meant always travel with a buddy who could fight. Every weekend Charlie Company would start a fight in the club and the Club Manager would call the 1SG to come and get his soldiers. The 1SG would shout in the club; "Charlie Company Formation Outside" and then march the soldiers back to the barracks. SPC Henderson who was in my platoon and loved to fight stated it was the reason why he re-enlisted in the Army and I told him he better not go back to the states with such crazy thinking or he would be put out of the Army. C/Co was a very tight company and soldiers took up for one another if things went haywire.

We called 1SG "Billy Dee Williams" because the first thing he would do before he stepped in front of the formation was comb his hair. 1SG Uniform and boots were immaculate. He would be in his office manicuring his fingernails. He was so clean; he didn't sweat on a 12-mile Foot March.

Keith was the Executive Officer who looked like Paul Newman. We were roommates for a short time. A former soldier of Keith's platoon loved to ride motorcycles and catch snakes. He caught 7 feet

131

long Bushmaster Snake, most poisonous snake in Panama, put it in a backpack, and rode it over to our house on his motorcycle with his friend who was carrying the snake in the backpack on his back. We did not believe him when he said he had a Bushmaster, so we asked him to show it to us. The soldier opened the backpack and placed the snake on our living room floor. He then pulled his mouth back and I placed a broom stick between his mouth which revealed the snake's almost two-inch fangs. We told him not to ride with the snake in his friend's backpack because the snake could bite through it. He probably did it anyway. The snake was given to the Smithsonian Institute in Panama.

The soldier caught a 10 feet long boa constrictor crossing the road near our house. The MPs stopped traffic to allow him to catch it. The snake knocked him down when he tried catching it, but he recovered his footing and brought the snake to our house. It was the prettiest boa constrictor I ever saw because it was gray with blue patches on it. He placed it in our storage shed and I told him after three days, he had to come and remove the snake. The only way he could capture the snake was to feed it a Kudamundi, an animal like a raccoon.

Lieutenant Steve was a good friend of mine from Oregon and the 1st Platoon Leader. A lot of people did not understand Cooper because he was not very vocal, but he was tactically strong. Steve loved guns, sky diving, mountain biking, and snakes.

Steve had an AR-15, shotgun, and two pistols in his room. He had more weapons in Oregon. We could set-up our own ranges in Panama almost anywhere we wanted to. We only had to set-up our left and right limits using Range Flags then shout, "Is there anyone down range". The Lieutenants would go shooting on the weekends. We would practice shooting out of the bed of a moving truck or any crazy positions we could think of. I would bring my 380 which jammed after every shot and had a range of 10 feet. I purchased the gun, fishing rod, and bike for $125. I called it my throw away gun because if I shot someone then I would throw it in the ocean.

Steve would sky dive from apartment buildings and bridges.

132

Security guards would leave the door unlocked for Cooper to make his morning jumps. One day he decided to jump from Bridge of America before 0600hrs on a Saturday because there would be no one on the bridge at the time. When Steve decided to jump somehow every Panamanian showed up to watch. He landed safely. A Special Forces soldier who was trying to impress a schoolteacher on her first Jump resulted in the teacher suffering a broken leg. She should have linked up with Steve for her first jump. Steve had over 500 jumps before he left Panama.

Steve ended up in a bad situation when the Battalion Commander assigned him to be the Mortar Platoon Leader. The Sergeant in Charge was in Short Timer's Mode because he was retiring soon. C/Co was constructing an assault area when mortar rounds began landing within 30 feet from their location. Soldiers were leaping over three strands of concertina wire to get out of the area. The investigator found the mortar soldiers aim was 45° off their intended target. It was Steve's first day on the job and the Mortar Sergeant failed to inspect the soldiers' aim. The Army had the bright idea of assigning AIT Straight Leg Infantry Soldiers (11Bs) as Mortar men with only one day of training and then assigning them to units as 11Bs. The soldiers who were firing the Mortar Tube were Privates who haven't touched a mortar in two years. The responsibility was on the Mortar Sergeant who should have never assigned two Privates on a Mortar Tube and he should have inspected his soldiers. The blame was unfairly placed on Steve because the Army says a leader is responsible for all the good and bad things which happen in their command. Steve was eventually moved to another company and he ended up leaving the Army. What a loss of a great soldier.

Steve loved snakes and ended up purchasing a small boa constrictor. Steve would invite me over to his apartment to watch the snake feed. Steve was tired of purchasing mice, so he came up with the idea of raising his own mice. His experiment failed miserably and he ended up with more mice than his snake could eat and a smelly apartment.

133

Dave was a Lieutenant who graduated from the Citadel and had a forever tan. His nickname was Super Dave. Dave's father infiltrated a Motorcycle Gang in an undercover operation and said he had more respect for the Motorcycle Gang than the Police Force because they lived by a code while the police members were always turning on each other. Dave left the Army because of bad leadership. He could have been a General if we had more caring senior leaders on Ft. Davis.

Frank Mata was the Assistant S-2 who married a rich Panamanian of Chinese descent. There were five Americans at his wedding including me. There were a lot of rich Chinese present. People were dropping off envelopes filled with money and every table contained a bottle of Johnny Walker Red. Very few people drank the liquor and Frank gave me permission to take every unopened bottle. I ended with a case of Johnny Walker Red which I shared with the Panamanians who did favors for me. I received free cable and transmission work for two bottles of Johnny Walker Red. The transmission work was a $400 job. I always kept liquor and beer especially Seco Herrerano and Old Milwaukee in my house. Panamanians loved Old Milwaukee, they considered Budweiser headache beer and I agreed with them. We could only buy a certain amount of alcohol per week. A six-pack beer was $1.60 and a six-pack of coke was $2.00. Americans would complain about the cost of beer compared to soda and I would tell them to shut up and go back to the states if they don't like it because they were messing with my Influencing Product. I called my alcohol products Influencing Products because I used it to influence people in giving me things cheaply.

Lt. Beane, Fire Support Officer and a Prior Service Soldier who served in the Personnel Department of a Ranger Battalion. Beane knew the Army's manual on Leave and Passes (670-8-10) like the back of his hand. He told me soldiers can take a 3-Day Pass during the week without including a weekend unlike a 4-Day Pass. I told the 1SG about this and he told me not to tell anyone because soldiers would be asking for a Tuesday, Wednesday, and Thursday off constantly. I told them

134

anyway, but he denied many of them.

Beane drove with his family from the States to Panama while other soldiers traveled by plane. The Army did not allow soldiers to drive from the States to Panama because it was too dangerous. Beane's wife was from Guatemala. He told us the problem of driving to Panama was some nations closed their borders at certain times especially for lunch. The Army paid Beane well for his travel to Panama.

SFC Bonilla was my Platoon Sergeant from Puerto Rico. He called everyone "Chingo" which he said means friend in Puerto Rico, but Panamanians said it means monkey. I don't know who is correct, but I learned in Panama to stay away from words which began with "Ch" because they are normally bad words. SFC Bonilla was probably calling everyone "Friendly Monkey".

SFC Bonilla and I worked like a team. He told me he would take care of everything in Garrison such as Sergeant Evaluations, Barracks clean-up, Guard Duty Schedule, and handle the Support Team during Field Exercises while I handled things associated with Physical Fitness, Field training, and the Assault team for Field Exercises. SFC Bonilla and I discussed everything involving the Platoon and he helped me to become a successful Platoon Leader. He also showed me how to prepare and eat land crabs.

Every May there would be millions of crabs crossing the street for breeding purposes. Panamanians and soldiers who were from Latin American Countries would be on the road catching them. SFC Bonilla told me once you catch the crabs, you need to place them in a cage and feed them corn meal for a week which cleans out their systems before you cook them. SFC Bonilla and his wife served the best tasting crabs which I ever eaten. SFC Bonilla retired as a First Sergeant and became a JROTC Instructor in Ft. Lauderdale, Florida.

The Squad leaders were SSG Duran, SSG McGrath, and SSG Locklear. SSG Duran was from the Dominican Republic and fluent in

135

English, French, and Spanish which he combined when writing evaluations.

SSG McGrath was the Battalion Sniper along with PFC Burson. SSG McGrath was sent to Special Forces Qualification School, but did not pass because of a lack of support. My request from the Battalion Commander to allow SSG McGrath three months to prepare for Special Forces School was denied. The Battalion only allowed SSG McGrath three weeks of training time while soldiers who wanted to attend Ranger School were given three months. In those times many senior leaders looked at Special Forces Soldiers as Renegades. I recall during a meeting, a senior leader calling them "Cowboys". My thinking was if one of my soldiers became a Green Beret it would benefit the Army.

SSG Locklear was a very levelheaded leader with a Don't Quit Attitude. His squad was the most experienced and this was due to his outstanding leadership ability and having a strong Team Leader in SGT Harris. SSG Locklear later graduated from Ranger School.

SGT Harris was a team leader who was physically fit, a jokester, and a lover of Schlitz Malt Liquor Beer which I called "Shits Malt Liquor Beer". We had a curfew on Ft. Davis and SGT Harris would violate it all the time, but not get caught. When entering the base after curfew, SGT Harris would only be wearing the top half of his uniform and tell the MPs, he was coming from the Pacific Side and they would wave him through the gate. If the MPs had made him exit his car, they would have discovered he was wearing civilian clothes from the waist down.

SGT Harris asked the leadership team if we could ban the use of the word "Hoorah" in the platoon because every time we asked junior soldiers if they had their equipment they would respond with "Hoorah". When we checked their equipment, they would not have it, therefore; we banned the word "Hoorah" in the Platoon. We said the word "Hoorah" means "F_ _ k You" and every time we hear it; we would make the person who said it do 25 push-ups. After a month the soldiers understood the point and started checking their equipment multiple times.

Rangers would come to Panama every year and evaluate squads on Infantry Tactics. SGT Harris was a Team Leader during a training exercise evaluated by a Ranger Sergeant. SGT Harris convinced the other leaders to nominate SSG White as the Squad Leader of 3rd Squad. SSG White was a Sergeant who had 18 years of Military Service and spent 9 years on the M203 Range before arriving in Panama. SSG White knew the M203 better than the Manufacturer, but not a damn thing about Military Tactics. The evaluator asked SSG White for the Squad's location on the map and SSG White responded "Right Here". The leadership team decided to make SSG White the company maintenance person after the field exercise which was right up SSG White's alley because he knew how to build houses, repair cars, and any job involving the use of his hands.

I wanted a Volkswagen in high school, but I could not afford one. I purchased a beat-up Volkswagen in Panama with one headlight shining in the trees, no horn, leaky gas tank, no radio, and water which came up through the floor when the roads were wet. It cost $600 and could only go 60 mph downhill. American vehicles were required to have an inspection sticker by the Panamanian Government, but Panamanians were not. My vehicle failed the inspection and I complained because Panamanian vehicles were operating without a windshield, no brake lights, and no horn. The gentleman responded the rules of the road only apply to Americans. I asked SSG White to fix my vehicle for me, so I could pass the vehicle

137

inspection. SSG White installed a horn under the steering wheel and I put a rock under the front headlight to prevent it from shining in the trees. My vehicle passed the inspection. SSG White was my mechanic in Panama because he installed a new gas tank, fuel filter, windshield wiper motor, and installed a radio in my vehicle.

A Ranger Evaluator who was on a field exercise with the Platoon became nervous when he heard the sound of Howler Monkeys. The Sergeant asked what was that sound and SGT Harris told him it was a 600-pound gorilla and the Evaluator did not sleep the entire night. It was a waste of Army funds to send Rangers from the states to train soldiers from Panama when we had the Jungle School in our backyard.

PFC Burson who graduated from Sniper School with less than a year of being in the Army was an outstanding soldier. The other soldiers were jealous because I thought highly of Burson and they would tell me Burson drinks a 12 pack of beer every night. I told them I don't care if he drank a case of beer every day because when it came to soldiering, he was a performer. He was the second fastest runner in the company, he graduated from Sniper School as a PFC, and he never complained. Burson was severely burned in a plane accident on Green Ramp at Ft. Bragg while preparing for an Airborne Jump. He was discharged from the Army because of his injuries. He would have become a Command Sergeant Major in the Army if it were not for his injuries.

SPC Wright was a college graduate who received a Degree in Ministry and wanted to be a Chaplain. I didn't understand why he wasn't assigned as a Chaplain Assistant. The junior soldiers took him to the Dining Facility and said every curse word they could think of at the table and then they said, "Welcome to the Infantry". The closest curse word which I heard Wright say was "Dag". SPC Wright later graduated from Ranger School.

SFC Tacdol was a former member of the 75th Ranger Battalion at Ft Lewis-McChord, Seattle, Washington would send his new Ranger

138

Soldiers down to the local Infantry unit to beat up their soldiers. The soldiers would return saying a big Black guy beat them up. The Black Soldier ended up in C/Co with Tacdol and told us how he used to beat up Tacdol's Rangers.

Tacdol would go to the club and start a fight, his soldiers would jump in to help him out, he would then escape the melee, and his soldiers would be the ones receiving the punishment.

One day we were jumping off a dive platform into the pool and Tacdol told me to go and do it and I refuse to because I thought I was going to land in the shallow part and become paralyzed. Finally, I decided to do it and as I was entering the platform, I busted my nose on the gate leading to the platform causing me to back out of the situation. Thirty-years later I was diving off a higher platform with ROTC Cadets. While driving his Platoon Leader's Mazda RX-7, someone shot the LT's car. Tacdol said the car was shot by someone who disliked Americans while he was enroute from the Atlantic to the Pacific Side. He was probably shot at by the jealous boyfriend of a girl he was seeing.

SSG Johnson was a big Black Soldier whose face was like SGT Slaughter the wrestler. He ran his platoon because the Platoon Sergeant was getting ready to retire. SSG Johnson would go to the club and say someone called him a name so he could start a fight. Nobody in their right mind called him a name. I was scared of him because he was loud and looked like he was 6'4 and 250 pounds. On a field exercise he was complaining because we were always leaving the base for training while other companies conducted their training outside of the base. He began to complain loudly and CPT Maxwell called him over and chewed his ass out. I don't know what he said to SSG Johnson, but he stopped complaining.

The sergeants and the junior officers lived in family houses four soldiers to a house. SSG Johnson's housemates gave him a going away party. Johnson's going away speech was "I'm going to the NCO

139

Academy so I can get rid of some of you sorry ass NCOs". I shook my head in disbelief at his going away speech. I later saw him in Korea and he was the same height as I was, but I was bigger. He was on his way to the Sergeant Major Academy and said he had a video of me talking with a girl at his party and I told him to get rid of it because I may be President one day.

SGT Wallach who was my best man at my wedding and a very intelligent soldier, married a rich Panamanian girl. We all thought we were rich in Panama, but Wallach's girlfriend put those thoughts to rest. His girlfriend's family was very rich and politically connected. Another soldier had a girlfriend who had two maids growing up, one to cook and the other to clean her room and lay out her clothes. Thank goodness I didn't grow up like her because I would have never left home.

SGT Baker the unit Supply Sergeant was a dancing machine. I would go to the States and bring back RAP videos from BET and MTV. Baker would be at the club practicing his dance moves from the videos. I thought he was going to break his back one night because he was going at it so hard. Anything I wanted, SGT Baker would get for me.

PFC Collins was my radio operator who was told by a judge to join the Army or go to jail. I asked him why and he said he shot someone for sitting on the hood of his car. He said he told him twice to get off of his car and the guy refused, so he shot him in the leg. Thank goodness he didn't have a car in Panama.

SPC Wolf and SPC Hal were soldiers from the 7th ID who had participated in Operation Just Cause. Wolf was reduced in rank by his previous unit for pulling a gun on his Platoon Leader who refused to sign his Leave Papers so he could see his mother in the hospital. I told him he could take leave anytime he wanted to and forge my name if needed so long as he did not pull a gun on me.

Hal was a good soldier who married a Panamanian with four kids. It was a win for her, but a loss for him. I was disappointed when we put him out of the Army for drugs. Cocaine was rampant in Panama. We told soldiers there would be a urinalysis test every month for every soldier and every month someone would come up positive. We knew if someone came up positive for marijuana, they did it in the U.S. because cocaine was cheaper than marijuana in Panama.

Other Officers

Captains and lieutenants stuck together. Battalion leadership treated lieutenants like crap. There were no interactions between Staff Officers and Lieutenants. Lieutenants worked directly for Captains, but it would have been nice if Staff Officers gave career advice.

The Battalion Commander never told us how we were performing and what we needed improvement on. The only time we received counseling was when our evaluations were due. If you arrived to the Battalion Commander's meeting 10 minutes prior, he would make you wait until the exact time of the meeting.

The Commander never put two Black Officers in the same unit together. He had to go against this rule when the Battalion received six Black Lieutenants in a three-month period.

Lindley, Black Captain with a Ranger Tab, had a difficult time obtaining a command. Lindley received a command after obtaining his EIB. The other Captains told Lindley the only reason he received a command was because he obtained his EIB. Lindley was a good Company Commander.

The Battalion Commander had very little social skills. He looked more like a paper pusher than a Commander. I was a gym rat and the commander looked like he couldn't do 10 pushups.

Physical Training was 0600 – 0700 every day and you had to do a minimum of 100 pushups, 100 sit-ups, and run at least 3-miles. We did this and finished at 0650. Captain Maxwell called me into the office and told me the Battalion Commander chewed him out because I finished Physical Training 10 minutes early. I thought he was joking and the next day the Commander came to my Physical Training Session and SGT Harris had us doing drills which entailed us rolling on the ground, push-ups, sit-ups, low and high crawling, and we finished with a four-mile run. SGT Harris said he did all those drills so he could watch the Battalion Commander get dirty. The Commander never returned to another one of my Physical Fitness Sessions.

We were doing the EIB 12-mile Road March and the Battalion Commander drove by and told us to hurry up which made me upset because he should have been walking with us like Colonel Wagner the Brigade Commander. Colonel Wagner later became a Lieutenant General. He was and still is a great leader.

The Battalion Commander's wife would go around asking soldiers if they were Christians and the soldiers would respond sarcastically that they were atheist. There are wild and crazy guys in the Infantry. The Commander would rarely spend time with his companies during Field Training which was good because we did not want him around anyway.

I took Rich, the Battalion S-1, to my hometown during vacation. Rich was from New York. When we arrived in my hometown, he was in disbelief because our electrical meters were located on the outside of our houses. He said in New York; meters were located inside the house to prevent people from stealing them. People whose lights were disconnected would take meters and put them in their houses for free electricity.

My cousin and I took Rich to a bootlegging house and let him taste moonshine for the first time. The house did not have an indoor toilet. Moonshine in my hometown was popular before the show "Moonshine". My cousin gave him Sake, Japanese liquor, before he boarded the airplane. He was feeling so good, the airline stewardess had to wake him up to get off of the plane.

The Company Commanders were strong great leaders who ran the Battalion. Without their leadership the battalion would have failed. There was a company commander who would run into the gym during Battalion Runs and then jump back to the front of his Company

143

Formation. The soldiers would boo him every time he did this. He collapsed on a Field Exercise and the medics intentionally missed his veins seven times while giving him an IV. He told me he was beat up from Ranger School which is why he was out of shape. If that was the case, he should have never taken a Command. He probably would have been a great commander if he was in shape.

Bravo Company Commander, made me do pushups for not having my weapon on safe. We were at a bohea and no one had any live or blank rounds. It was an unwritten rule, officers do not make other officers do pushups, especially in front of another officer. I hesitated and Steve eyes lit up because he thought I was going to refuse his request. I thought about it, but I figured it's best to do what he says. He said his reasoning for making me do pushups was because when he was in the Ranger Battalion, he witnessed soldiers being shot because their weapons were not on safe. The truth is he was flexing his rank. He would not have done it if we were the same rank.

Atlantic to Pacific Travels

Laney Miller, B/Co lieutenant who grew up in Arizona was fluent in Spanish. A policeman gave Laney a ticket for speeding. Policemen in Panama did not have radar guns and would say a car was speeding by looking at it. They never stopped a Panamanian for speeding, only Americans because they knew we had money to pay the fine. Laney elected to go to court instead of paying a fine. Laney won his case. I asked him how did he win the case with a judge who didn't speak English. Laney said the judge was so impressed with his Spanish; he dismissed the case. The judge probably dismissed the case so he could rush and tell his friends a joke about the Gringo in his court speaking Spanish on a 2-year-old level to avoid a $5.00 speeding ticket.

Laney and I dodged a major incident while enroute to a training area. Sergeants Zak Hernandez LaPorte and Ronald Marshal were ambushed by a Panamanian whose father was a high-ranking Panamanian government official. SGT Hernandez was killed in the incident and SGT Marshall was severely injured. I passed by 30 minutes prior to the location where SGT Hernandez was killed. Laney Miller was supposed to be riding with SGT Hernandez, but was told by Lt. Hampton to ride in another vehicle. I don't understand to this day why the United States did not kidnap and bring him to the U.S. for punishment. If we captured Noreiga, we could have captured Hernandez killer. The U.S. and Panamanian governments knew who did it, but refused to prosecute.

Another dangerous occasion occurred while traveling the Panamanian Highway was when my driver suggested we take a short cut to avoid traffic enroute from the Colon to the Pacific side. I knew the road was narrow and he was a weak driver, but took his suggestion anyway. He hit a Panamanian bus while passing it causing the passenger side outside mirror to break. Glass fragments from the

145

mirror struck me in the face. My glasses saved me from seriously being injured. We pulled over and I spoke with the bus driver who demanded $100. I asked my driver how much money he had on him and he told me $60. The bus driver agreed to take $60. I made my driver pay the bus driver because I told him not to pass the bus. Santiago a former Special Forces soldier came out to check on us. Santiago stayed in Panama after he was medically retired by the Army. It was dangerous traveling from the Atlantic Side to the Pacific Side.

Guard Duty

Infantry companies were assigned to guard the Panama Canal, Ammunition Storage Points, and the housing complexes which contained Americans who worked for the Canal who called Zonians.

SFC Bonilla was showing me our assigned housing complexes when I spotted a soldier who worked the same area and shift the day prior. SFC Bonilla told me if a soldier met a girl in their assigned guard duty area, they would pay other soldiers upwards to $50 to pull their guard duty, so they could see their girlfriends. Soldiers did this because we were restricted to the Base. I would have made a mint doing letting them pull my guard duty.

When we were assigned to guard Rodman, an officer would come by and check us to ensure we were pulling duty correctly. There was an unwritten rule that Staff Sergeants and above had to carry live rounds because Operation Just Cause had just ended and there may be some resistant forces in Panama. The S-3 came by to check my platoon. The rumor was the S-3 enjoyed messing with lieutenants. He inspected us and asked me if I had any live rounds and I replied "No" because if I told him "Yes" then he would ask me how many and did I sign for them. There was no right or wrong answer. The S-3 told me to get some the best way I could after I told him we did not have any. The platoon had over 2,000 Live M16 rounds at the location.

There were no showers at our location on Rodman, therefore; the soldiers took a hummer over to Howard Air Force Base for showers. They always took three hours or more for a trip which was only three miles away. When I left the unit Private Christ, told me, they would pick-up working girls at Howard Air Force Base and take them to the beach for sex.

147

I had such a good working relationship with the girls, they would tell me some of their job secrets. The ladies told me about a soldier in my platoon who would treat the girls to dinner and try to convince them to leave the streets. They would not tell me the name of the soldier, but I suspected it was the Preacher in my section.

Sarah who was a very nice looking and bi-lingual working girl told my friend and I; her two biggest customers were a Colonel and Lieutenant Colonel. The Senior Officers would each pay her $100 for a beating. I begged her to give me their names so I could influence them to give me a good job, but she refused because they were paying her handsomely and she did not have to sleep with them. Sarah liked my friend so much; she would give him sex on the house. I told my friend if Sarah is giving him free sex it is because she was hoping he would marry her. I told him if he married her, I was going to take her out the day before their marriage. The thought of me dating his future wife caused him to end the relationship.

I was always asking Service Members from other branches what are their jobs. One day a group of us Army Officers met some Air Force Service Members who served on the AWACS and asked them to give us a tour. They were hesitant at first and when I explained to them everyone had Secret Clearances, they gave us a tour which was nice.

I was in the gym working out on Rodman Naval Base when a Navy Seal approached me and showed me a letter which authorized him to swim the Panama Canal. He was so happy his request was approved. I don't know why swimming in such an oil infested water intrigued him. You could see oil slicks on top of the water. The VA should have given him a 100% Disability Rating for skin cancer and mental issues because no normal person would swim in the Canal and if someone swam in the Canal, they probably developed skin cancer later in life.

Field Exercises

The first field exercise which I attended occurred within two weeks of my arrival. We were deployed for two weeks in the jungle where the Jungle School was held at.

CPT Maxwell told us to get our drinking water and take baths from the streams in our operation areas. He said running streams are safer than stagnant streams because flowing water has less bacteria than stagnant. The rule only worked 20% of the time because there was always someone being sent to hospital after a field exercise from drinking water from streams.

SPC Collins, my radio operator, and I followed CPT Maxwell advice of getting water and taking baths from moving streams. While I was taking a bath in the stream, I noticed fresh cat tracks on the bank behind me. They were huge tracks which I believed belonged to a jaguar. I hurried up, grabbed my weapon, and put my clothes on. We carried live rounds when we went to the jungle for training. CPT Maxwell killed two eight-foot-long bushmaster snakes during a field exercise. Bushmasters are the longest venomous snakes in the Western Hemisphere.

Crowd Control was part of the unit's mission and we conducted a crowd control mission after the field exercise. An Infantry Platoon served as the Opposing Force for the unit. When an Infantry Platoon gets a chance to role play against another Infantry Platoon, the rules go out the door. When they saw us in Riot Control gear, they went crazy and threw fruit, rocks, water bottles, and anything they could pick-up at us. We had to stop the exercise because things were getting out of hand. After the exercise some Panamanian kids approached us and told us they would give us their sisters for MREs. We were stunned at their suggestion and some guys jokingly asked if me if they could give them MREs for a chance to look at their sisters. I denied their request, but I bet their sisters looked like beauty queens.

Two girls approached another platoon and told them they would give them sex for MREs, the Sergeants replied if this was war we would have taken the offer, but it's not so they gave them the MREs for free with no strings attached.

My first Live Fire Exercise could have ended in a disaster. We were assaulting a position when all of sudden, SSG Locklear stopped. I asked why, and he said because the rounds from the support position were ricocheting off rocks and going by their heads. I instructed the support position to shift their fire and then we proceeded to assault the objective.

On Live Fire Exercises the policy was to practice with blanks first and then execute the Live Fire. Captain Maxwell's last month in the command, I briefed him my plan and he said go ahead and execute a Live Fire. I responded "we are supposed to do a Blank Fire first and then a Live Fire", Captain Maxwell responded "if this is combat are you going to ask the enemy for a test run" and I replied "no" and we conducted the live without an incident.

We received reports from higher headquarters stating there were some Panamanian Resistant Soldiers, and we were told to go and investigate the area. CPT Maxwell commandeered the Battalion Commander's helicopter and I asked did we have authorization and he said don't worry. When we returned the Battalion Commander chewed Captain Maxwell's ass out. CPT Maxwell still received a top rating.

On a training exercise which we were conducting boat operations, the driver forgot to put the chalk block on the rear tires and the 2 ½ ton truck began to roll back towards the water where soldiers were training at. I noticed the truck rolling towards the soldiers so I ran to the truck, opened the passenger door, and pressed the brake with my hands to stop the truck. The driver came over and moved the truck to level ground. I asked everyone did they see what happened and I should be put in for a Medal. The soldiers said I probably knocked the truck out of gear for a Medal. That's the Infantry!!!

Most missions were company missions. Once when the Battalion Staff went out, their generator was stolen by some Panamanians in broad daylight. I asked the staff why they didn't give chase and did they know something strange was happening when the lights went out all of sudden. They thought the generator was out of gas in reality the Panamanians cut the cord and took the generator while it was running. I believe the Staff was scared, so they elected not to give chase.

There were some good thieves in Panama. A soldier had his television from his house. The thieves ran through the jungle drinking jungle juice. I bet it was a sight to see, jungle juice containers scattered on the ground.

Garrison Life

Garrison Life in the Infantry consisted of inspections, field preparations and meetings. I was inspecting SPC's Gurney's room when I heard something say "Hello", I was startled and asked him, "What is a parrot doing in your room" when we are not supposed to have pets in the building. Gurney told me when he saw the parrot on a limb by his window, he stuck his arm out and the parrot came to him. I told him could keep it along as it is okay with his roommate and he kept his room clean. I asked Gurney where is his roommate's VCR and he told me his roommate took it to the Working Girl House for the weekend. I said you are telling me he is spending the weekend with a prostitute and he said a lot of guys do it.

Captain Maxwell was an excellent commander who probably should have relieved me after my third month there. There was a PFC who refused to follow the orders of the sergeants and cursed them every day. I heard the sergeants shouting at him to get out of bed and he told them "Fuck You, which infuriated me and I jumped on the bed and began punching him. The sergeants pulled me off him and reported the incident to Captain Maxwell. Captain Maxwell told me not to do it again and he asked me "Did it feel good?" and I replied "Damn great". I gained more respect from the soldiers after the incident.

There were two Black Panamanian brothers who spoke English with a Jamaican Accent. They cleaned our barracks and shined our boots. Every soldier who lived in the barracks had to pay $10 a month for barracks cleaning, the other brother charged $5 to shine two pairs of boots. This was good money because Colon had an over 50% unemployment rate and the minimum wage was 0.76 cents an hour if a business felt like paying their employees that amount. I considered these gentlemen my source of Intel Information. They would inform me when it was safe to go downtown Colon. I would tip them every month for this information which kept me out of trouble.

Entertainment

We went to the base club Thursday to Saturday. We had a curfew which restricted us on base, so the club was our stress reliever. Soldiers would be in such a hurry to get to the club after a field exercise that they would not shower beforehand and it was only a two-minute walk from the barracks to the club.

Infantry soldiers party and train hard. A team leader of mine from Puerto Rico arrived and busted his head open from being drunk on his first night in Panama. He received 10 stiches and the next day when I saw him, I said "Welcome to Panama".

The MPs were always called by the club manager to break up a fight. The club manager called the MPs on a former Ranger in our company for fighting. The MPs told him to leave and he cursed them out, so the MP said he was going to turn his dog on him. The soldier told him not to do it, but the MP did not listen. When the dog went after the soldier, the soldier took off his shirt and almost choked the dog to death. The MP took his dog and left the vicinity quickly.

Girls who worked in the Happy Houses in Colon would attend the club every weekend. One soldier would sign 20 girls on post. The club would be packed on the weekends with working girls. The wives started complaining about their husbands being in the club and the club having working girls in it. The club bowed to the pressure of the wives and said only girls with identification cards could attend the club. No one went to the club for three weeks which forced the club to change their policy because they were losing money. A new policy came out which stated the club manager would sign the Panamanian girls on base. The new policy worked great for us because the club would be responsible for the girls. The only thing the new policy stopped was complaints from the wives.

153

The club reserved a special section for officers because of complaints about officers interacting with Enlisted Soldiers. There were less than a thousand Military Personnel on base and we all knew each other, but someone complained so the club gave officers their own area. Ninety-Eight percent of our time was spent on the Enlisted Side because they had girls and music. The only good thing about the Officer Section is we could bring in exotic dancers without any complaints.

Happy Houses

The bars in Colon were off limits when I first arrived, but the upstairs where the girls lived was on limit. Six months later the Commanding General's Office came up with the bright idea of putting the bars on limit, but the upstairs off limit. The owners of the bars loved this idea and sent the girls downstairs to work the bar. The girls looked better than Jennifer Lopez and were always enticing soldiers to drink more alcohol and go upstairs with them. The did not prevent soldiers from going upstairs. The bar owners would give us a warning when the MPs were coming. It was one of the many crazy rules the military had without much thought put into it. Each Infantry Company had their own special bar. It was funny because the MPs would chase us out of the bars and then they would take over.

We had a curfew and soldiers would find innovative ways to get around the curfew. We would carry our uniform with us to our girlfriend's house in case we stayed past curfew. We would wear the top half of the uniform when we entered the gate past curfew and tell the MPs we were coming from the Pacific side so they would let us on base without punishment. If they made us get out of our vehicles, we would have been in screwed because we never wore the bottom half of our uniform. Senior leaders would hide the prostitutes in the trunk of their cars and bring them on base because the ladies did not have ID cards to enter the base. Some of the leaders hired them as maids. The maids cleaned them and their houses.

I asked my fellow lieutenants why someone would buy sex when women were tripping over themselves to get to us. A lieutenant explained it like this to me "How much money and time do you spend on a girl trying to get her to sleep with you" and I replied three weeks and $50. He then said, "I can go to the bar and in five minutes get a pretty girl for $10 while it took you three dinners, a movie, hotel, and three weeks to get sex". What he said made sense.

155

The first time I went into the bar, I picked up a pretty girl who looked better than Halle Berry. When we were having sex, the bed broke down and she said don't stop and I burst out laughing. We became great friends afterwards. The girls would give you free sex if they liked you and the only thing you had to do was pay $10 for the room.

I was going to the bathroom in the Happy House and noticed there were girls gathered around the entrance laughing at a Zonian man who was bent over, pants down, and playing with himself. I told the girls excuse me and I kicked his ass in the urinal face first, we all had a great laugh afterwards.

The lieutenants gave LT Lenny a bachelor party with girls from the club. Lenny left and we stayed in his room partying. The girls did everything we asked them to do and for payment they asked for $30 and Charmin Toilet Paper. I asked them why Charmin and they said it was because the toilet paper in the Happy House was too rough. I went to the PX and purchased 24 rolls of Charmin for them which was money well spent.

I purchased a four-inch television/radio from a soldier for $50. I became a fan of Seinfeld after watching it for the first time on a training exercise. I asked the soldier how he obtained the television and he told me, he won it on a bet. The guys in his unit bet him he would not sleep with an old fat ugly prostitute. He slept with her and won the bet. When I saw her, she was sitting in a chair with her stomach hanging down to her knees telling me to come and get some. I said "Heck No", but if a free tv was involved I would have done it.

New Leaders

Captain Pettigrew and 1SG Fergurson assumed leadership of the C/Co after the departure of Captain Maxwell and his 1SG. Most of the Company Commanders worked on the Battalion Staff before assuming a Command and the arrival of Captain Pettigrew made other officers suspicious on how an outsider assumed a Command over other officers who were already in the Battalion. Captain Pettigrew came from Ft. Sherman where Jungle School was held. We initially butted heads on how to set up a Defense in the jungle, under Maxwell we used a Circular Formation while Pettigrew preferred a Triangle Formation.

Platoons always kept live rounds in case of an incident because this was after Operation Just Case and soldiers were still getting shot at. I had 900 rounds of M60, 9 Claymore Mines, 2,000 M16 rounds, and 9mm rounds stored in a wall locker in the Platoon area where soldiers were sleeping at which is against regulations in the Regular Army not Panama. Captain Pettigrew, new commander, made us get rid of those rounds. I ended up giving the claymore mines to the MPS on the condition I get to fire one. We just went in the jungle, set up flags for our left and right limits, and shouted "is anybody down range" before we fired them.

He also made us get rid of live rounds in the barracks and the elimination of the cleaning and boot guys. Pettigrew made us fire the cleaning and boot guys because he said we were taking away the soldiers' ownership of the barracks. His actions backfired because the soldiers' rooms were dirtier than when the job performed by the cleaning guy. Sixty soldiers lived in the barracks and they each paid the cleaning guy $5.00 a month. The boot guy earned $2 for each pair of boots. I especially didn't like the idea of firing them because they were good guys, it was their only source of income, and I relied on their Intel when going to Colon. I complained loudly about his decisions

157

and the SSG Duran told me Officers don't complain, only Sergeants complain. I took his advice and shut up.

Pettigrew wasn't as wild as Maxwell. He knew his stuff, but he wasn't as flexible as Maxwell. Soldiers would suggest something to Maxwell and he would take it into consideration while Pettigrew was the complete opposite.

Pettigrew suggested the leaders play the junior soldiers in Tackle Football to relieve some stress. I told him this is a bad idea because the soldiers are waiting to punish us and some of them were very good athletes in high school.

I caught a pass and immediately went down after someone tackled me, when I looked up there were two guys flying over me. They were looking to take my head off. Pettigrew caught a pass and Garrity, who used to rodeo, bulldogged Pettigrew and Pettigrew jumped up ready to fight him. We ended the game after afterwards and the junior soldiers won 14 – 7.

1SG Fergurson, later became a CSM in 10th Mountain, was an outstanding 1SG. We talked about sports and he constantly gave me advice on how to become a better leader. He would play basketball every weekend with the soldiers and he could play. He was the glue which held the company together.

There was a Platoon Sergeant whose wife left him with five children. The Sergeant was depressed and 1SG being the person he was took him out to find a girlfriend. It was funny seeing two White Guys wearing Ray Ban Shades, riding in a tinted car with rims on it. We called them the Blues Brothers.

SFC Picho took over for SFC Bonilla position as the Platoon Sergeant. SFC Picho who was Dominicano came from 101st out of Ft. Campbell. SFC Picho told me a story about his platoon from Ft. Campbell coming to Panama. There were 37 guys in his platoon and they paid $40 each to have sex with a prostitute. I asked him what happened and he told me after the prostitute slept with the last guy,

158

she got dressed, collected her money, and walked past the guys who were passed out drunk in the hallway. I told him, I would have hated to be the 37th guy and he should have made his lieutenant go last.

SFC Picho was a more of "If a leader told you to do something then you did it". I told SFC Picho it sounds good, but you need to do brief backs and spot check soldiers to ensure they are carrying the right equipment. I told him to check the soldiers of 2nd Squad while I was at a meeting because I knew the Squad Leader was weak and his squad had a bad habit of leaving equipment behind. We were going to do a training mission and the Battalion Commander came down for a visit. He checked three soldiers to see if they had water and sure enough the soldiers did not. The Battalion Commander chewed SFC Picho out for this blunder because he considered this a Platoon Sergeant job to check their soldiers before a mission. SFC Picho was furious, but I told him, it was his own fault for not following my instructions. He never made that mistake again. It was very difficult to fire a Sergeant in the Battalion and if you did fire them, they ended up working somewhere in a Staff Position in the Battalion where they screwed the person who fired them. A saying in the battalion was "You screw up and move up" which happened numerous times.

159

Jungle Training

The lieutenants were constantly asking the Battalion Commanders to send us to Jungle School and their reply which was dumb, "we always train in the jungle, so we don't need additional training". We would be the Opposition Force (OPFOR) for Stateside Units attending Jungle School. One training mission it took the company six hours to move 800 meters in the dark and luckily, we stopped because there was a 200-foot drop waiting on us.

We were the OPFOR against a unit from the 82nd Airborne Division. Our mission was to cross the Chagares River in Panama and pass through the unit's defense without being captured. Sharks could be found in the Chagares because it was connected to the Atlantic Ocean.

There were local Panamanians who lived near the Jungle School, who would paddle their wooden canoes across the Chagras with freshly fried fish in exchange for MREs. The locals thought they were getting over on us and we knew we were getting over on them.

I sent a team consisting of SGT Annese, PFC Smith, and another soldier with swim vests to cross the Chagares and find out where the other unit was. Smith made it halfway across then turned around and came back to our location. I asked him why he came back and Smith who was visibly shaken said, "he felt something bump his leg so he came back". I told him since he was halfway across, he should have stayed with the other soldiers and then I told him I could not believe he was scared of a little shark. He swam back to the other side after my motivation speech. Bull sharks were known to swim in the Chagares.

The next day we were preparing to cross the Chagares; I felt mangos whistling by my ears. The monkeys were throwing mangos at us and thank goodness they didn't have good aim. We hurried up and

160

left the area and then most of my unit was killed by a company from the 82nd. The instructors took us to an area where we stayed for two days waiting on our next mission. I became impatient and asked the Jungle Instructor to let Colonel Smith, Jungle School Commander, know what happened and we are out of ammo. The Commander told us to move out and I told the Sergeant we are not going to move until we get resupplied with ammo, the Sergeant being a Smart Ass told Smith exactly what I said. Smith came up to our location and chewed my ass out and made us go back in the fight without any ammo. The only good things about the training were meeting the locals and Annese and Smith made it through the base camp without being captured. Annese said as long as he had his Skoal Tobacco he could make it through anything. Those two survived three days in the jungle on two MREs, a gallon of water, 2 cans of Skoal, and 100 rounds of blank ammunition. Annese graduated from Ranger School and Smith ended up leaving the Army. I met Smith six years later in my hometown at a Fall Festival. He was a good soldier. Once he played a trick on me by putting my lieutenant bar sideways on my hat sideways. I was walking around the post soldiers were laughing at me. Finally, an MP told me to check my hat and I started laughing.

CPT Herniak became the new Company Commander after CPT Pettigrew. CPT Herniak was a CPT Maxwell on steroids. He was a little on the wild side. C/Co acquired some goats from the Special Unit and he grabbed a goat by the horns in front of the formation and told the guys they didn't need to go downtown because the goats can service them. We laughed hysterically. He heard soldiers calling girls sluts and told them to shut up because we want them to be sluts. He was very funny.

When the unit went to Jungle School, CPT Herniak took off his shirt and asked Gurney to camouflage his back. The soldiers loved him and would run through a brick wall on his command.

C/Co hosted a fishing tournament for unit cohesion. When the whistle blew, CPT Herniak's boat took off fast trying to get to the best

161

fishing spots. In his haste, he forgot to secure the boat motor and when the boat hit a stump it dislodged the motor. The motor sank to the bottom of the lake. Soldiers would do anything for him and they went diving for the motor 10 yards from where caiman alligators nested. The motor was never found and no diver was never attacked.

On another fishing occasion CPT Herniak, CPT Reynolds, and I planned a boys' fishing trip together. When we arrived CPT Reynolds wife was present. Herniak and I looked at each other and said "CPT Reynolds must be in trouble and this is going to be a bad day for us". CPT Reynolds hooked a monster fish and as he was reeling it in the boat, CPT Herniak grabbed the line which caused the line to snap. CPT Reynolds was furious, but he didn't curse he just shook his head. It was dry season and then a thunderstorm appeared out of nowhere. We ended up soaking wet and five fish.

A platoon from C/Co was attacked by Killer Bees and dropped all their equipment including weapons and ran. Captain Herniak put on long sleeve shirts and a mosquito head net and went to recover the equipment. Soldiers said the bees stung CPT Herniak so often, he was doing the Humpty Dance while recovering the weapons. One of his soldiers received over 100 stings, but he wasn't allergic to bees.

Wildlife

Panama has excellent wildlife. I enjoyed seeing animals in their native habitat that I don't like going to zoos anymore. I used to wake up to the sounds of Toucans and Parrots in the trees beside my house. A fellow lieutenant in the Boat Company had a Macaw named Dude. It was a young bird which was taken out of the nest too early. The Lieutenant went on a trip and Dude died. I was upset because the lieutenant did not let anyone know he was going out of town. I would have watched Dude for free. I do not understand why people want to purchase animals which can live for more than 50 years. Animals belong in their natural environment, and it is up to us to protect them.

The first weekend we had off, Steve, Dave, and I rented a boat and went fishing in Gatun Lake a man-made lake which contained peacock bass and caiman alligators. 10 yards from where we were goofing off at. We did not see any caimans, so we decided to move closer to where they were and became stuck on an underwater tree. We tried putting the boat in reverse, but it did not work. We decided to get out of the boat and rock it back and forth to get it off the log, as we were doing this, I made a joke saying the headlines in Stars and Stripes Newspaper would be about three lieutenants eaten by alligators in Panama. Eventually, we were able to free ourselves and make it safely to the boat dock. We never saw any alligators, but I'm sure they saw us. Every month we would hear stories of Americans losing their dogs to an alligator.

Field Exercises were enjoyable for me because it gave me a chance to see animals in their environment. The soldiers would watch me staring at the trees and enjoying the scenery. One mission the platoon became upset at me for calling them scaredy cats for stopping

163

their movement in the jungle for an 8-foot-long boa constrictor. The snake would have scared me, but I couldn't let them know. I tried to catch a 5-foot boa and the snake struck at me quickly. Do not believe those TV shows which depict boa constrictors as slow. They move slowly, but strike quickly.

I would run up behind anteaters and make them stand on two feet. I brushed up against a tree on a training exercise causing ants to fall on me. The ants started biting me which caused me to take off my equipment and shirt. Captain Pettigrew asked me" what are you doing" and I told him fire ants were eating me alive which made him laugh hysterically. It was funny to me afterwards.

I had animals run on top of me. We were sleeping on a trail and some animal ran on top of me, I just went back to sleep.

I was bitten by ants which we called 50-caliber ants because they were big. I was grabbing a tree to help me up and down a hill all day and at night when I touched the tree an ant bit my thumb. My thumb was swollen for three days.

I slept in an area full of tarantulas. We stopped in an area for a night it was a placed out of Raiders of the Lost Ark. There were tarantulas everywhere. Soldiers were letting them crawl up their arms. I slept sitting on my rucksack, but they still crawled on my legs.

I slept in an area full of scorpions. It was the last day of a Field Exercise and we stopped in an area to rest before transportation pick-up. I wore spandex shorts on Field Exercises, put insoles in my boots, and wore no socks because the humidity of the jungle caused a rash between my toes. I set up a hammock and took off my boots to let my feet dry out. I went to put on my boots and there were black scorpions in both pairs. I immediately started gathering my things together and noticed a brown spot on my rucksack and began to swat at it and it was a brown scorpion. They told me the bite of a brown scorpion which is smaller than the black scorpions are the worst.

164

We were assigned to guard Clayton Housing area and the Army assigned us to sleep in the top of the hospital which was formerly a morgue. One night I went outside to look at the stars and look for wildlife, I looked down and a Fer-de-lance about 18 inches long crawled right between my feet. It was a juvenile and they can kill a person in less than 45 minutes without anti-venom. I wasn't scared and went to get something to kill it with, but it went into the building. I told the staff the next day about the snake, but they could not find it.

The jungle is a harsh environment and I understand now how it affected soldiers in Vietnam. The jungle is very hot and humid. Malaria is rampant. Some soldiers were hospitalized from drinking untreated water. A couple of soldiers would return sick from every field exercise. CPT Maxwell suggested we wear boxers and no socks because your feet were always wet and you could easily dry them off during breaks. I tried boxers and going commando and neither worked because they created a chaff in the groin area. I suffered no chaff when I started wearing compression shorts/tights. I wore tights every time I went on any field exercise in the Army. The idea of not wearing socks were great, but you needed great foot insoles for it to work. The insoles worked great and I rarely developed blisters by not wearing socks, but I developed a foot fungus.

I was finally able to get rid of bone spurs on my feet after two years with a combination of medical treatment, Hi-Tech boots, and Nike shoes. There was a smart Panamanian doctor who worked in the base medical clinic. He injected something good in my feet once a month and the cysts which he removed on my leg and elbow never returned. The American doctors would remove them and they would return within a month. I believe soldiers in my company were hooked on Motrin. The medic gave them out like candy and we consumed them like a person eating MMs.

I discovered Hi-Tech boots by accident. I saw a Special Forces wearing them and he told me I could buy them in the Military Clothing Store. Soldiers ditched the old jungle boots for Hi-Tech Boots. The

165

Battalion Headquarters sent word down to the companies stating Hi-Tech Boots were banned in the Battalion because they would not dry as quickly as jungle boots. They did not dry quickly, but they felt like tennis shoes when you wore them. I disregarded the rule and wore them for a year. Special Forces soldiers and Air Force personnel could wear them, but not Infantry Soldiers. Another crazy rule put out by leaders. I continued to wear the most expensive Nike Running Shoes sold at the time and I changed them out every six months even if the soles were good to protect my feet. I considered my feet as my most important body part because I was constantly traveling by foot.

End of Platoon Leader Time

I served as a Platoon Leader for 18 months which was the longest tenure of any lieutenant in the Battalion at the time. I thought I was going to get a top rating for all the things which my platoon accomplished, but it was not in the cards.

The Battalion Commander rating comments not the Company Commander's comments determine the career of an Officer. The Battalion Soldier of the Year came from my Platoon, a squad from my platoon won the Best Squad Competition in the Battalion which consisted of marksmanship, 12-mile foot march for time, map reading, assaulting an objective, physical fitness test, and breaking and putting back together different weapon systems blind-folded in a specific time. My platoon had the most Ranger School Graduates. I received Excellent Ratings from Brigade Inspectors on my additional duties and earned the Expert Infantryman's Badge. Despite everything we accomplished, I received a Center of Mass Rating from the Battalion Commander which made me think about leaving the Army.

When the Battalion Commander was leaving, soldiers were booing his speech and turning their backs toward him when he was speaking. I did not attend it because of my Evaluation Rating. CSM Townsend, new Battalion Command Sergeant Major, said never seen such disrespect toward a Commander as he saw that day. I told him why the soldiers did it and how the battalion commander treated his lieutenants. Lieutenants were treated worse than Privates. The Battalion Commander only spoke to lieutenants when their evaluation was due and it was no conversing on what he expected or any feedback from lieutenants on what we needed to do to become successful.

The lieutenants complained to the Inspector General about the Battalion Commander's leadership style and how he never explained to the lieutenants what they were doing right or wrong. The Inspector

167

General told the battalion commander how his lieutenants felt. The battalion commander held a meeting with the lieutenants after the inspection and told us to get out of the Army if we didn't like his leadership style and if we left the Army, we would not find a job which paid as much as the Army. I was making less than $2,000 a month which was during the Dot.com time. I laughed when he said this because I read USA Today every day and I knew what people were making outside of the Army. We lost some great lieutenants because of his lack of concern for the lieutenants.

Lessons Learned

1. *Accept advice from your subordinates* – I was SFC Bonilla supervisor and he took time to mentored me so I could be a successful Officer. He showed me how to conduct training, inspections, what I am supposed to do on Field Exercises, how to run a shooting range, and how to evaluate sergeants assigned to the platoon.

2. *Keep interactions with subordinates professional* – Some Officers would get sloppy drunk while hanging out with their subordinates. This can blur the vision between supervisor and subordinates. You can drink with subordinates, but don't get sloppy drunk.

3. *It's easy to give advice from the sidelines* – If your subordinates are training on equipment jump in and train with them. When my subordinates were training on mortars, I would ask them to show me how to operate it. This action showed I cared and wanted to learn.

4. *How you treat your subordinates determines how hard they work for you* – The Battalion lost some good lieutenants because they were treated like commodities instead of people.

5. *Do brief backs and rehearsals* – Brief backs and rehearsals reduces errors and it ensures everyone knows and understands the mission.

6. *Spot check equipment* – Spot check equipment to ensure everyone is carrying everything to complete the mission.

SFC Bonilla, SGT Harris, SPC Hurley, practicing crowd control during a Field Exercise.

SPC Gomez and the platoon waiting for EOD to arrive and blow-up grenade duds. We had three grenade duds and EOD told us to throw the remaining live grenades or pull guard duty all night on the remaining grenades. I sent the platoon back to Ft. Davis. Myself and two soldiers threw 60 live grenades in five minutes.

170

Hurley, Wolf, Browning, and a fellow soldier enjoying a nice fishing trip on Gatun Lake. Fishing was so good on Gatun Lake that I ate Peacock Bass three times a week. A gentleman on the docks fileted the fish for .10¢ a fish.

171

A/CO

I was assigned to A/Co as the Executive Officer after eighteen months of Platoon Leader time which was a breath of fresh Air. Captain Reynolds and 1SG Prince were the leaders. Captain Reynolds was in Special Forces for over 10 years. The lieutenants were: Shipley, Spencer, Olson, Disney (FSO), Green, and Turner. Shipley graduated from the Air Force Academy and was Commissioned in the Army because he liked the job of an Infantry Officer. I thought he was crazy for not staying in the Air Force because the Air Force treated their Servicemembers better than the Army. Andy Olson was a West Point Graduate, Disney Fire Support Officer, Greg Greene, and Turner who was later replaced by Spencer because his time was up in Panama. SFC Rosario was the Training Room Sergeant. We had two SGT Smiths one was Arms Room Sergeant and the other was the Supply Sergeant who was a Ranger.

A/Co worked like a team. Captain Reynolds turned out to be the best Company Commander the Battalion had during my time in Panama. Captain Reynolds put a lot of trust in me which gave me the opportunity to grow. We connected very well because we were both Prior Service Soldiers and OCS graduates. He told me he runs the company in the field and I run it in Garrison. He would leave every day at 1630hrs except for Thursday to spend time with his third wife. He said he is not going through another divorce. I told him one divorce would have broken me. Thursday was punishment/administration day. Soldiers knew if they screwed up on the weekend, they would see the Commander on Thursday.

1SG Prince was a great 1SG who loved his coffee and cigarettes. I saw him smoking while running in formation. He would tell me to get Lt Spencer out of his office so he could do physical training with his platoon, but 1SG would make him coffee and have a cigarette with him every morning and then turn around and complain to me about Spencer being in his office. Spencer broke his leg trying to prove to his soldiers he was on the same level as Bruce Lee.

Soldiers preferred seeing Captain Reynolds for punishment than 1SG. 1SG would chew them out so bad, I felt sorry for them. One married soldier impregnated a Panamanian girl and signed his name on the birth certificate. 1SG called him a big dummy because there were two other soldiers sleeping with the same girl and he did not have a blood test on the baby. He would threaten to fire Smith, Ranger Supply Sergeant, because Smith thought a Ranger Tab made him better than the other soldiers. 1SG was right, but the supply sergeant always acquired whatever we needed and I wasn't about to lose him. 1SG chewed out Fast Eddie, Puerto Rican Soldier, for running up a $3,000.00 tab in the Working Girls House. I told Eddie he could get any Panamanian he wanted because he spoke Spanish and Eddie replied he was lazy and preferred spending money on the girls than talking to them. I met another soldier at Jungle School and asked why he married a Korean lady with all of the beautiful women in Panama and he said she was the first woman who said "No" to him when he asked for sex. I asked him where did he find all those women who said "Yes" and he told me at the Working Girl's House, I laughed hysterically.

We were leaving Ft. Sherman one day when a driver was speeding and became stuck on a lock which prevented ships from passing through. 1SG chewed him out so badly that no soldier ever sped in a vehicle. 1SG was right to chew him because it delayed our trip back to the base for two hours and it messed up my club time.

1SG kidded me every day for a month because I brought my girlfriend's Cocker Spaniel to work. He said Infantry Soldiers have German Shepherds or Rottweilers not Cocker Spaniels. The Officers, Olson, Greg Greene, Spencer, Disney, and Turner were all great leaders who believed in training their soldiers and leading by example.

173

Turner and Shipley were the leaders for Adventure Training such as Repelling, Helicopter Extraction, and Helocasting. Turner reserved a repel tower and had soldiers Australian Repelling down the tower. Shipley reserved helicopters for soldiers to conduct Helocasting and Extraction missions in Gatun Lake which was fun. Shipley and Turner had soldiers to spread their arms and legs out, then intertwine an arm and a leg, and Turner and Shipley would place a looped rope around both soldiers and hook the rope up to a helicopter, the helicopter would take off and we would be flying around Gatun Lake with only a rope and our arms and legs hooked together. I would be making jokes while flying over Gatun Laker with my partner about falling in the water and being eaten by alligators. When we did helicopter missions, I would ask the National Guard Pilots to give us a Map of the Earth helicopter ride. If there were hills the pilots would go up and down them like we were walking hills and they would lean the plane to the left or right to simulate the way the river was flowing. National Guard Pilots were more risk takers than Regular Army Pilots in my opinion. Regular Army Pilots would not fly in stormy weather and rarely gave us Map of the Earth flights while National Guard Pilots said tell us when and where to go and they would make it happen. I don't know if National Guard Pilots were more skilled or crazier than Army Pilots, but they pushed their helicopters to the limit.

LT Disney, Fire Support Officer, would walk around with his pistol under his uniform while at work. He would find himself in the most compromising positions. He went to Peru with other Battalion Officers and met a Peruvian girl who followed him to Panama trying to get him to marry her. We told Disney if you don't marry her, she would end up in the club and become the girlfriend of the company. She returned to Peru.

I was acting Company Commander and a MP accompanied with a Panamanian Police Officer came to see Disney about a hit and run incident. A Panamanian said Disney hit their car and left the scene of the accident. The Panamanian gave a description of Disney's car along with the license plate. I called Disney into the office and asked him "What in the fuck did you do last night"? Disney said he stayed on post and they had the wrong vehicle. Everyone left the office to check out Disney's vehicle and to our surprise there was not a scratch on the vehicle. If an American had a nice vehicle some Panamanians would say a soldier hit their vehicle so they could get money from the soldier and this is what happened in Disney's case. I advised him not to go to Colon for the next couple of weeks.

Greg came to A/Co from Headquarters Company where he was the TOW Platoon Leader. The soldiers from the TOW Platoon told me they were happy to see him go because he had them doing raids, assaults, and other Light Infantry Tactics instead of TOW Missions. Greg made them get out of their vehicles which they hated doing is the reason why they were happy to see him leave. Greg was put in HHC because the Battalion Command did not want two Black Lieutenants in the same unit. Greg was good and in excellent shape. He competed in two Best Ranger Competitions, with the last one being with Captain Reynolds.

Captain Reynolds gave us plenty of opportunities and guidance to be great soldiers and leaders. His Special Force friends would drop us off 9mm ammo and I would give it to the Platoon Leaders. The Platoon Leaders would use the ammo to practice their drive by skills. A lieutenant would drive a truck and two lieutenants would be in the truck bed. The driver would drive past the targets and the other two lieutenants would rise up and shoot from the pickup bed.

Captain Reynolds Special Forces friends would let us use their shootout houses for training. A/Co did excellent training under Captain Reynold's Command. When soldiers left A/Co they were prepared for anything.

SSG Rosario was the best Training Officer which I ever worked with. His paperwork, which consisted of Awards, Evaluations, Weapon Qualifications, and all other training records were always up to date. He would go off if someone messed with him while he was

175

updating records. He was untouchable and I would get mad if someone disturbed him because he was very important to the unit and made my job easier.

SSG Jeter and SSG Davis were two other soldiers who worked on the company staff for SSG Rosario. SSG Davis was the NBC (Nuclear, Biological, and Chemical) Sergeant. We never wore masks because of the humidity in the jungle so he had an easy job. The first day when I arrived at the company, I walked by and SSG Davis and another sergeant were sitting around bullshitting. I told Rosario what I saw and he told them to get to work. Davis approached me and said if I needed them to do something, all I had to do was ask. He was right and from that day on when I needed something to be done, I would ask that person instead of their supervisor.

Jeter was the Urinalysis Sergeant. Every month the unit conducted a 100% urinalysis test for everyone in the company. We had a SSG with 16 years of service in the Army who came up positive for cocaine on the urinalysis test. SSG Jeter was upset because they were friends and if the sergeant told Jeter he took drugs, Jeter would have told him to self-refer himself to Substance Abuse Counseling. It was hard putting the soldier out because he was a good soldier and it affected his family. There was an Air Force Soldier with three months left to go before retirement who came up positive on a urinalysis test and the Air Force Command was debating to put him out without any benefits because it would affect his wife and two kids. I would have put him out for being stupid. A soldier from another unit who came up positive on the urinalysis test was moved to his company's headquarters section for separation from the Army. The command assigned him as the coffee maker, and he put cocaine in the coffee and the Commander and 1SG came up positive on the urinalysis test. He had to put a lot of cocaine in the coffee for that to happen. The soldier was separated from the Army and nothing happened to the commander and 1SG.

SFC Gonzalez, Dominican, was Olson's Platoon Sergeant and a

176

great teacher who I learned from. PFC Chris who was one of SFC Gonzalez's soldier, asked me to sign off on his marriage papers to a Columbian woman. He told me she was a whore and since we were in the Infantry, I thought he meant she screwed like a whore in bed. He showed me her ID card and she was Columbian. Columbian girls on the Colon side where mostly prostitutes during that time frame. I asked SFC Gonzalez if he talked with Chris about this situation and he said we tried to talk him out of it, but it was his first piece of ass and it drove him crazy. Chris's squad came up with a brilliant idea, for her bachelorette party. They paid for her services that night. Chris married her and divorced her three days later, I guess his buddies' description of his wife's bedroom manners influenced him to get a divorce.

SFC Darby was a soldier who spent 14 years in the same unit at Ft. Bragg, going from E-1 to E-7. He performed well, but hated Panama because he was missing out on his newborn daughter. I saw Darby about 20 years later after his daughter was Commissioned as an Officer at NC A&T State University in Greensboro, NC. We talked about the good times in A/Co.

Jungle Training

Our first field training exercise under Captain Reynolds was a disaster because we started our training on a Monday which gave us no time to inspect the soldiers' equipment. The alcohol which the soldiers consumed over the weekend, clouded their brains. Soldiers forgot their equipment which caused the unit to arrive late on our objective. Captain Reynolds came up with a brilliant idea which was Monday was Prep Day for field exercises, Tuesday – Thursday were Training Days, and Friday was Recovery/Clean-up Day. All training went exceptionally well thereafter and the soldiers enjoyed this concept because it gave the leaders time to inspect their soldiers and resolve any issues before training exercises and clean their gear before the weekend.

Colonel Wagner and his Brigade Staff formulated a training scenario where one company from each battalion had to move over 26 miles through a jungle environment which no soldier had operated in within a week time frame and conduct a live fire scenario with live grenades. A/Co was chosen by the 5/87th Infantry Battalion and the 508th Airborne Infantry Battalion selected a company from their battalion.

The report from the evaluators said the company from the 508th looked like the platoon in the movie Stripes when the soldiers were moving through the obstacle course. The evaluators said the soldiers looked beat down from the jungle movement and during their assault on the objectives some of the soldiers were walking because they were tired.

Captain Reynolds spoke with his Special Forces Buddies and came up with a brilliant idea for completing the mission. He asked his Special Forces friends to recon the route and we were going to navigate through dry stream beds where the vegetation was thin. The company from the 508th made the mistake of trying to move through thick vegetation.

Captain Reynolds stated he was taking everyone on the mission including the soldiers who had been in the unit less than a week. I advised Captain Reynolds not to do this because I witnessed on numerous occasions new soldiers from the states suffering heat injuries when they do not get at least two weeks to get acclimated to the jungle environment. Captain Reynolds said don't worry, they are Infantry Soldiers. Captain Reynolds created Camel Bak water containers for us using sticks attached to a 5-gallon water container instead of us carrying those bulky 2-quart water containers.

We started out strong and the jungle environment began to take a toll on the new soldiers who were E-4s and below. Other soldiers in the company began to carry their equipment to help them keep up with the company. We were going up a steep hill and 1SG noticed a new soldier falling behind his platoon despite having no rucksack. 1SG told him "If he doesn't get up that hill, he was going to kick his ass so hard that he would have toes for teeth". When I heard that, I became scared and ran up the hill.

Captain Reynolds planned worked like a surgeon on an operating table. We completed the mission in three days. Our reward for completing the mission was a real-world assignment. 508th was the battalion on call, but Colonel Wagner (who later became a Three-Star General) selected A/Co for the mission. I was mad and said we are not the unit on call and Captain Reynolds said, "Shut the hell" and I did. I shut the hell up because I was wrong to be complaining in front of the company leadership team. I later found out the 508th Battalion Commander was so mad his battalion did not receive the mission that he began cursing and throwing his phone against the wall. The Infantry is a competitive environment and when a unit which is on call is not selected for a mission, it makes that unit seem weak.

179

Captain Reynolds called the leadership team together to give us the requirements for the mission. He told me to request additional morphine in case someone gets hurt on the mission and we can't get them out then we can give them a lethal dose of morphine. He said this is what Special Forces Soldiers do when someone is injured behind enemy lines. I told him these are not Special Forces Soldiers and the American Public would not accept this. I requested extra body bags instead of extra morphine. A/Co was ready, but the mission was called off.

Ft. Chaffee

A/Co was selected to go to Ft. Chaffee, Arkansas for an Opposing Force Mission. We ran into Captain Simmons who was the previous A/Co Commander. My mission was to keep the supplies going and Captain Reynolds told me if I did not bring him hot coffee every morning, he would have me out there making him coffee. I made sure he had coffee every morning. He told the soldiers they could have two beers when we were not training and the soldiers obeyed. They ordered two beers each the size of a beer pitcher. Captain Reynolds told them two beers, but he did not say the size of the beer. Chris made a commented which said I can't believe it, "we are here in the states and have a curfew earlier than the one in Panama". He was right, but we were on a training mission. The mission went great and we returned to Panama two weeks later.

WW II Airplane

Some Panamanian Hunters found a wreckage of a WW II airplane in the jungle. It was buried in the ground and covered up by the forest. There were no roads leading to the wreckage. SOUTHCOM sent a team to clear a path to the wreckage and assigned us to guard the wreckage. I asked the command can we go see the wreckage so we can determine how many soldiers are needed to guard the message. The Battalion gave us a helicopter to scout the area. The engineers cleared an area just the size for a helicopter to land and the helicopter had to land on some boards to prevent it from sinking. It was a very remote area. We were speaking with soldiers already on the ground when two hunters approached us and one was carrying the head of a wild boar on his back. The boar had the largest tusk which I have ever seen. I thought it was warthog at first. The plane was eventually excavated and the remains of the pilot were returned to the States.

Company Functions

Captain Reynolds asked me to plan a company picnic with a fishing tournament. I coordinated the food and drinks, reserved boats and picnic area, and prizes. Prizes were awarded for the most fish and the biggest fish. I was supposed to be in the boat with Captain Reynolds, but I was late because I was picking up the food. I road in the boat with Olson and Disney. They had never been fishing in Gatun Lake and were without fishing rods, so I gave each one of them one my fishing rods. Captain Reynolds' boat caught the most fish and Olson caught the biggest fish. Olson won the rod and reel. I really wanted that Ugly Stick Rod. Captain Reynolds told me afterwards the rod did not match the reel which I didn't care about because I wanted the Ugly Stick. I am still mad at Olson to this day because he used my equipment to catch the biggest fish and he kept both the rod and reel.

We had a cookout after the fishing tournament and some of the wives were upset because the junior soldiers invited their girlfriends who worked in the clubs to the cookout. I told the wives to be quiet or find the soldiers some girlfriends.

The tournament and picnic were exhausting because I did the majority of the work. SFC Gonzalez approached me and told me, I should have had the NCOs plan it because they know how to do these events. He was right and never planned another event since his comment.

A/Co had a Dining Inn later and I took SFC Gonzalez's advice and let the NCOs plan the event. They planned a great event and if I had planned it like the fishing tournament it would have been a disaster. I was very happy when I heard SFC Gonzalez became a Command Sergeant Major. He was excellent at training officers and enlisted soldiers. He told me he was getting burned out from being a

183

Platoon Sergeant because he was constantly training new lieutenants and enlisted soldiers. He told me soldiers are like professional athletes because we are constantly doing physical training.

End of XO Time

I was going on vacation to the States after serving as an XO (Executive Officer) for 13 months when I met COL Wagner who was returning from the States. COL Wagner asked me to become the Assistant S-4 (Logistics Officer) for the Brigade and I replied I would let him know upon my return from the States. My first choice was to become the XO for Headquarters Company on the Pacific Side and the next choice was TOW Platoon Leader until my departure to the Armor Advance. I enjoyed living on the Atlantic Side and being in the 5/87 despite the challenges.

I returned from the vacation and discovered the battalion sent my evaluation to Washington without my signature and a Center of Mass Rating. I was furious because I busted my ass for the battalion and I served the most time as a Platoon Leader and XO than anyone in the battalion at the time. I had a meeting with the Battalion Commander and asked him why he gave me a Center of Mass Rating and he responded someone told him; I was leaving the Army. I told him it was never said and I did not submit any paperwork for leaving the Army. He heard a rumor and took it and ran with it instead of talking with me face to face. I then asked if I could be the TOW Platoon Leader and he responded the position was only for Junior Lieutenants. He did not know Olson told me the Battalion Commander asked him to be the TOW Platoon Leader. Olson turned down the position because he knew I wanted the position. The battalion commander knew I was going on vacation three months prior and I kept asking about my evaluation which I knew was due and he said it would be ready when I return from vacation. The commander was afraid to tell the Brigade Commander the reason why an Officer's Evaluation was late, so he elected to save his ass by submitting an unsigned OER.

185

The battalion commander who was a West Point grad would offer the more desirable jobs to West Pointers first and then non-West Pointers would get the leftovers. This created tension among the officers. Olson who was a West Pointer and a couple of other officers complained in an Inspector General's meeting about how the battalion commander treated non-West Pointers. The S-1 at the time told the battalion commander what the officers said and who they were. The battalion commander called a meeting with those officers who made those statements. It was eventually swept under the rug. Panama lost some good officers because of bad treatment by senior officers. The Army doesn't look at the write up by an Officer's immediate supervisor, but by the supervisor of their immediate supervisor. An example is Captain Reynolds was my immediate rater, but the battalion commander who was Captain Reynolds rater carries more weight. The battalion commander spent one day with me and it was on a 20-mile foot march in which I was the Company Commander because Captain Reynolds was on a training mission. I do not understand why Senior Raters who know they have people's career in their hands only spend one day with them. I was in 5/87 for almost three years and my Senior Raters only spent 7 hours with me and six of those were on a 20-mile foot march. Lieutenants only received counseling when their evaluations were due and by that time it is too late to correct any mistakes.

I told Captain Reynolds about my evaluation and asked for guidance on filing a complaint. He told me it would be his word against mine and the Army would just sweep it under the rug. I was pissed, but I knew what he said was true. The battalion commander finally offered me the TOW Platoon Leader position because he knew he screwed me over. I contacted the Captain of HHC 193rd Brigade asking about the vacant XO position before making a decision on accepting the TOW Platoon Leader position. He did not grant me an interview for the position for unknown reasons. He received a less experienced XO which ended up costing him 2 months base pay because he was missing a lot of equipment during his change of command.

186

TOW PLATOON

TOW Platoon was good duty because we rode around in vehicles and could bring coolers with us (No beer). One day the Platoon Sergeant and I picked up two young ladies who were walking on a dirt road with no shoes. It was a mile to the end of the road where they had to catch a bus. It was the last day of the field problem, so we decided to help them out because it was hot and they had no shoes on. We stopped and told them to get in the back which had a cover on. When they were getting on, ten more people including women and children jumped in. One of the young girls' feet was perched behind our heads and they smelled like 30 days old cottage cheese. I told him to hurry up because her feet were making me sick. The people thanked us and we laughed about the situation. I told the Platoon Sergeant if anyone finds out what we did, we would be Court Martialed. I did not have a problem helping anyone out in need and we were in their country.

I asked a TOW Squad Leader from Puerto Rico why he joined the Army at 27 years old and told me he did not join the Army after high school because he thought all Army men had ugly wives. He said he joined the Army after his divorce because his wife took everything, but his underwear. I asked him what happened and he told me, he married a Puerto Rican Beauty Queen and the day after his marriage, her older sister started sleeping with him. One day his wife came home early from a trip and found them in bed together. He blamed his wife for the divorce because if she had not come home early, he would have still been married. I asked him what happened when they went to the divorce proceedings and he said his wife's sister gave an Academy Award performance. She was crying in court and told the judge that he seduced her when in fact she was the oldest sister and initiated everything. The judge awarded everything to his wife. He was forced to move back in his parents' house and his father told him he had 30 days to leave the house and began marking an "X" on the calendar to remind him he would be homeless in 30 days, so he joined the Army. Everyone hysterically laughed afterwards.

I hated to leave the 5/87, but I knew I would never receive recognition for the work which accomplished there. CPT Reynolds, CSM Towsend, and SGT Gregory, HHC Supply Sergeant, gave me the best advice for staying in the Army. CPT Reynolds stood up in the Dining In and made a speech which saying I should stay in the Army and the Army would be losing a great officer. CSM Townsend told me to make the Army pay me to get out and not to get out without receiving some type of monetary compensation. He told me some senior leaders make life hard for junior minority soldiers because they don't want them to get that nice retirement money which is financially freedom. SGT Gregory gave me the best advice for staying in the Army when he said I should stay in the Army because Enlisted Soldiers need Officers who care about them.

Other reasons why I hated leaving 5/87 were because I would be missing my friends on post and in Colon. I knew almost everyone on base and I could get things which other Officers could not such as training sites, food, equipment and ammunition rounds for different types of weapons from the relationships I built on the base. If any unit was doing any adventurous training such as repelling or shooting any weapons, I was there. The Battalion was given 14 live anti-tank rounds and I told the Range Officer, one of those rounds is mine and he obliged.

Colon was a small city and did not have all of the entertainment venues as Panama City. What Colon had was people who knew and cared about each other. It was a poor city, but fun. Over half of the people from Colon spoke fluent English and I looked like the local citizens until I opened my mouth and spoke Spanish with a Southern Accent. I was able to move in and around the city with ease because I interacted with a lot of people from Colon who worked on base.

I attended a club which played R&B music from the 60s. It was free to get in because it was a non-payday and the DJ would play any requested music and announce the names of the couple who requested the song. On payday the entrance fee for the club was $5.00.

Soldiers assigned to 5/87 Infantry Battalion were tough. We ran or foot march every day and trained every week in the jungle. It was normal to see guys carrying over 100lbs of gear on their back especially the Scouts and Mortarmen. Scouts operated away from main units and had to carry enough supplies to be self-sufficient. Mortarmen carried such heavy weight because they carried mortar tubes, base plates, and rounds.

Lessons Learned

1. *Learn the language of the country you are living in* – It is a sign of respect when a person learns the language of the country, they are stationed in. I asked a 50-year-old widowed lady to teach me Spanish. She told me her lessons are very expensive and I asked how much and she said $5 an hour which shocked me, but the minimum wage in Panama during those times were .76 cents an hour. I gladly paid her. It was supposed to be an hour for 12 lessons, but she spent 2 hours teaching me. I think she was lonely and teaching me gave her something to do.

2. *Respect Local Customs and Cultures* – I was speaking with Amelia Matthews, about things which would make Panama better and she told me Panamanians like their lifestyles and I should respect their customs and cultures instead of trying to Americanized them. I carried this saying with me to every country which I visited. Every country is different. In government offices of Panama there are no shorts, t-shirts, and sandals allowed. Students wear uniforms to school which reduces bullying and promotes more learning.

3. *Treat others with respect* – If the battalion commanders treated the lieutenants like people, we would not have lost good officers and the unit would have been more cohesive. I never understood in the Military why Senior Raters do not spend more time with their junior officers since they hold their careers in their hands.

4. *Maintain Physical Fitness* – You can't lead if you can't run. We had officers who were fat. One was so fat that he put on a girdle to take his Military Photo. The Military has free gyms so, there is no excuse for any Servicemember to be out of shape, especially an officer.

5. *Your tour of duty is what you make of it* – There are things to do outside of every Military Base and it is up to you to take advantage of them.

190

6. ***Embrace Change*** – I was slow to embrace CPT Pettigrew's leadership style, but everyone is different. I did not like his decisions of making us store ammo in the proper place or getting rid of the cleaning guys. Storing the ammo in its proper place prevented a serious accident. He explained getting rid of the cleaning guys placed more ownership on the soldiers.

7. ***Trust your subordinates*** – SGT Daly a Scout was attached to my platoon for a mission. I asked SGT Daly and another Scout to recon a site and report back to me what they saw. SGT Daly asked if I going was going with them and I told him "No" because he was a Scout and I trusted him to complete the mission. SGT Daly said "Thank You" because his previous leaders always accompanied him on missions. I saw SGT Daly two years later at a swimming pool after he graduated from Special Forces School. I asked him why he wasn't on a team and he said just because you're a Green Beret doesn't mean you're immediately put on a team. You have to earn the trust and respect of other Green Berets first before being on a team. I was extremely proud he achieved his dreams.

8. ***Think outside of the box*** – CPT Reynolds method of training Tuesday – Thursday, navigating using dried stream beds for navigation, and allowing us to plan adventurous training made for a well-trained and motivated unit.

9. ***Think of others before yourself*** – When we had extra food from field exercises, I would give it to the orphanages. I had a chance to go to Rappel School, but I gave my slot to a Corporal because I knew this would be a factor in him re-enlisting.

10. ***Don't let being in a fraternity or sorority go to your head*** – I met several fraternity members especially Junior Black Officers who looked down on their fellow Black Officers who were not members of a fraternity. It does not matter if you are a fraternity

member, a job of an Officer is to lead and help their fellow soldiers.

11. ***Making corrections is part of being a leader*** – SSG Davis was correct in saying, I should have approached him instead of asking his supervisor to make the correction.

A/Co Jaguars – CPT Reynolds, 1SG Prince, and the entire company. The Officers are standing next to CPT Reynolds who was the best Commander I ever had in the Army.

Acting Battalion Commander and Laney was the XO

Parade Field where I was acting Battalion Commander for COL Wagner's Change of Command.

Conducting water crossing operations using our ponchos to float and keep our rucksacks dry at Jungle School. I am the lead soldier.

194

Navigating obstacle course at Jungle School.

195

Soldiers been evaluated on a task for their Expert Field Medical Badge (EFMB).

196

SSG Pruitt evaluating a squad during training. SSG Pruitt retired from the Army.

S5/87 Organizational Day – Companies competed in different competition such as putting weapons back together and relay races. Soldiers had to put different weapons together and do a function check for each weapon such as a M60 machine gun, M240 machine gun, M16, and 9mm pistol while blind folded. The weapons were disassembled and mixed up together in a pile. A soldier from A/CO won the event with a time of 3 minute and 45 seconds.

ASSISTANT BRIGADE S-4

I became the Assistant S-4 with about eight months left before attending the Armor Advance Course date. I rented an apartment in Panama City from a cardiologist who graduated from Duke University. He had opened heart surgery and his students were the doctors who operated on him. I told him he must have been a nice teacher because if he wasn't he sure would not be here today. Apartments cost $900 for Americans and $400 for Panamanians. Every Panamanian knew how much the Government was paying soldiers for housing. Some families would move out of their houses and rent to soldiers.

Major Ira Watkins was the S-4 leader and the shop consisted of myself, MSG (Supply), MSG Nick, a communication MSG from Korea, S-4 Driver (PFC), SSG Calendar, SGT Colon, and PFC Risco who was my driver.

Major Watkins was a very hard-working and dedicated soldier. He would be the first one in and the last one out and he worked seven days a week in the shop. A former soldier in his unit told me Major Watkins was treated like shit in the 82nd which destroyed his career. Major Watkins wife was from the town next to where I grew up and we were JROTC Instructors in the same Brigade after we retired.

The Supply MSG and the driver would party together and then the MSG would try to punish the driver for being late to work. I found this out after the MSG left the unit because I tried to promote the PFC to SPC and it was turned down, so the PFC explained to me what happened.

199

Communication MSG who came from Korea thought he was going to relax in Panama, but it was not the case. We butted heads a couple of times.

MSG Nick, Food Service Sergeant, was a Panamanian and a character. He was overweight and never did Physical Training, but he knew his job and he could get anything you needed. The Army asked MSG Nick if he wanted to be a Sergeant Major or go to Panama, Nick told the Army he can't make any money as a Sergeant Major and asked to be sent to Panama. Nick had a laundromat and apartments in Panama City. We used to joke with Nick and asked if he ever received a blowjob from a woman and Nick would respond with "No he didn't want to fall in love so it is why he never let a woman give him a blowjob", we laughed hysterically. SGT Watson a Cook found himself in some serious trouble. He contacted Nick for help. Nick practiced Santeria, Afro-Caribbean Religion. Watson said the prayer Nick performed, helped get him out of trouble. I told him his commander was doing worse than him which is how he escaped punishment. Nick would give me leftover milk and other food items from field exercise to give to orphanages. Nick retired within six months of my arrival and I hated to see him go.

SSG Calendar, a Panamanian, was a great Supply Sergeant. Nick and Calendar knew a lot of people in Panama City and could me anything I wanted. Calendar reminded me of the Penguin on Batman by the way he walked.

SGT Colon, Puerto Rican, was a partier when he first arrived in Panama. When he arrived in Panama, he said he could not speak English, but when the Supply MSG threatened to send him to Atlantic Side (Colon), he became fluent in English in a week. Soldiers on the Pacific Side thought of Atlantic Side as Stalag 13. The Pacific Side had nice clubs, restaurants, and no curfew while soldiers on the Atlantic Side were restricted to the base and had no good restaurants. SGT Colon ended up marrying a Panamanian girl and leaving her in Panama without telling her. She was pissed until we told her she had a Military

200

ID Card which allowed her on base without an escort and access to free hospital care. Young soldiers would often marry girls so they could get the extra money and live off post.

Risco was a shy and broke PFC when he arrived in the unit. I asked him why he was so broke since he did not have a family. Risco said his previous unit sent him on a thirty-day assignment in Thailand with free stay in a 5-Star hotel and $200 a day of spending money. He said he spent all of his money on prostitutes. I said it only costs $20 a girl in Thailand and he said he paid the girls on how they looked. He gave one girl a $100 and I told him, he was messing the game up for me because I would have to pay that amount. I never went to Thailand.

PFC Risco became a favorite of the Sergeant Major because he knocked a lieutenant out in a boxer smoker. Risco was trained by SFC Mosley, a Gold Glove Champion, in our unit before the boxing match. The Sergeant begged the lieutenant to come and train with the other soldiers, but the lieutenant refused because he said he boxed at West Point. Risco knocked him within 30 seconds of the match. Sergeant Major awarded Risco a Sergeant Major Coin for his accomplishment. The match resulted in Risco getting all sorts of attention from the ladies. He ended up marrying one of them.

The Brigade XO driver was comical. He came in one day and said he slept with his 100th Panamanian Girl in less than a year. The last one he slept with was a stalker and he was afraid to leave the base. I told him that's his punishment. Some Panamanian Girls were racist because they only preferred white soldiers. The girls said marrying a white soldier would help them get ahead in life. I was rejected by a nice-looking Panamanian girl for a Private. I later asked her why and she told me I would sleep with her and not marry her. She said the Private would marry her and she would have a better chance of getting ahead in the world. The Private ended up getting kicked out of the Army and she ended broke in Panama. I met another Panamanian girl who was a Hertz Rental Car Representative and thought the same way until she went to the States and her husband's mom who was on her

201

death bed told him "Never to bring another Nigga to see her". She said the States was crazy and she returned to Panama as divorcee. I met a girl on the Atlantic Side who thought the same way. A fellow white officer told me she was racist, so he took her out, slept with her a couple of times, and then dumped for being racist. She didn't know the lieutenant and I were good friends. The women who rejected me were of the same light-skin complexion as the majority of my family members. The majority of Panamanian women did not have this backward way of thinking.

BRIGADE FIELD PROBLEMS

Brigade Field Exercises were not physically demanding as Battalion Exercises. The first field exercise we were positioned with the Support Element in the rear with bathroom, showers, and staying in an air-conditioned bubble. I told the Communication MSG to set-up communications so we could communicate with the Brigade Staff. The MSG was slow about doing it and was constantly complaining about from being mentally burned out from Korea. I told him the Brigade XO would go ballistic if we are not set-up. MSG kept bullshitting and when the Brigade XO arrived, he made us leave our nice facility and setup a tent outside of the bubble. MSG didn't complain about anything after the incident. I was Lieutenant and I should have sent him back to the rear and asked he be reassigned to another unit instead of being diplomatic. I never experienced an NCO behaving in such a disrespectful way. All soldiers complain, but we know the job must be accomplished. Once I became a Signal Officer, I discovered the Brigade Signal Officer did not do his job. It is the Signal Officer's job to ensure higher headquarters can communicate with their subordinate units and vice-versa. All Signal Sergeants which were under my supervision were in the same office as me. MSG was not in the same room as the Brigade Signal Officer and the Brigade Signal Officer did not evaluate or interact with him.

Brigade Staff

The brigade staff feared the Brigade Commander. They would arrive before him and leave after him even if they finished all their work. They would come in on the weekends to pretend like they were working. I believe in working to standard and not to time and I would leave at 1700hrs. One time the Brigade Commander was leaving and I was going to call the Brigade to "Attention" and the Brigade Commander said "Carry on and it's okay". The S-3 told me I should have called "Attention" anyway because the commander likes hearing it.

Staff members conducted physical fitness every day and after the session was over, the majority of us would play basketball. The games were very competitive because we had staff members who played college basketball. Major Garit, Fire Support Officer played on a college basketball team in Arizona. He was doing the Euro-Step before it became popular in the NBA. Major Garit and a Special Forces Chaplain who played college basketball would go at it like they were getting paid. Drew and I played on unit teams after work. Soldiers in the Infantry are very competitive.

Brigade Sergeant Major was a very funny guy. He found a thousand ways to use the word "Motherfucker". You could tell what kind of mood he was in by the way he used Motherfucker. He would say "it's a good Motherfucking day to be in the Army, that's one tough Motherfucker, or he's a funny Motherfucker". If he was upset, he would say "that's a dumb Motherfucker over there, bring me my Motherfucking vehicle, or this Motherfucking shit is fucked up".

Olson who was the new Headquarters Commander would become upset when the Sergeant Major did not salute him. He said he was going to have a talk to him about this. I told Olson to let it go because I heard the Sergeant Major survived an ambush in Vietnam

204

and you don't want to piss him off because he could screw up your command. Sergeant Majors' control the assignment of Enlisted Soldiers and if you make a Sergeant Major mad, they would assign the worst soldiers to your unit.

Missing Equipment

Brigade HHC lost some two sets of cargo nets which the Army said cost $1,400.00 apiece. I was assigned as the investigating officer to determine who is responsible for the loss. I was a former MP and I knew how to conduct investigations. I interviewed the Supply Sergeant from HHC who told me he instructed his assistant to deliver pallet nets which were not accountable to Howard Airforce Base, but the assistant dropped cargo nets off instead. I asked the assistant if he knew the difference between cargo nets and pallet nets and he said "Yes". I asked him why and he said he made a mistake because he was in hurry. We went to see the Airforce Lieutenant who was in charge of the holding for equipment. She said she noticed the nets at the end of the day and started calling units to see who they belonged to for three days and no claimed them. Soldiers were notoriously dropping off equipment at the unsecure holding area without any signatures which is against Military Protocol. The lieutenant stated she noticed the nets were missing on day four and assumed that the owner picked them up.

I finished my investigation and told the Brigade Commander the assistant supply sergeant should be accountable, but we should write it off because a loss of two months base pay would be devastating to him. The Commander said "the lieutenant should also be held accountable because she did not secure the equipment and what if it was a M16". I responded "if it was a M16, things would have been different". I explained to him, the assistant willingly left the wrong equipment in an unsecure area, and units were constantly dropping things off without receiving a signature. He told me to charge the lieutenant anyway and I said respectfully "Sir you are making a mistake". The commander was going to fire me for not agreeing with him. The commander overruled me and charged the lieutenant for losing the equipment. The lieutenant received a "No Pay Due" on the following month. She called Brigade and asked why she was found guilty and not provided with a chance to rebut those charges. In those days a commander could charge a person without any rebuttal. The lieutenant called her dad who was a Two-Star General and he asked me what was going on and I explained to him that I found her not guilty and the Brigade Commander found her guilty. The General made a couple of calls and the lieutenant received her money back. The unit later found the nets which probably meant they had four nets, but two of them were on the books. When the unit found the nets, I asked CPT Piatt (LTG Piatt) if anyone was going to give me an apology and he told me to shut up and go back downstairs because the commander was going to fire me for not agreeing with him. If I was the XO for Headquarters Company this would have never happened because I had great connections in Panama and a unit would have given me two nets for two cases of Old Milwaukee. Panamanians loved Old Milwaukee because they said it did not give them headache unlike Budweiser. A six-pack of beer was $1.60 in Panama compared to a six-pack of Coke which cost $2.00. We had family members complaining about this and I would tell them to shut up and go back to the States if they didn't like it. Old Milwaukee and Herrano Seco were my negotiation tools.

Donations

Soldiers were constantly getting pulled over by the Panamanian Police for speeding, although; the Panamanian Police had no radar gun. They knew which cars belonged to Military Personnel because Blue Decals identified soldiers as officers and Red Decals identified Enlisted Soldiers. They pulled us over for Donations/Bribes. I was pulled over for speeding near Christmas and the Panamanian Policeman asked me for my Panamanian Driver's License. I handed it to him and in Spanish told him "No hablo Español. He looked at my license and noticed I had been in Panama for eighteen months and told me in perfect English "You speak Spanish". He stuck out his hand and I placed $10 in it for his Children's Christmas Gifts.

A policeman approached me another time at a stop light and I immediately gave him $5.00 because I did not want the hassle. A military family complained to the Military Police bribing the police with their cologne and I told them to shut-up because I was drinking downtown and needed the Police to accept my donations instead of putting me in jail.

We would compare who donated the lowest amount over the weekend to avoid a ticket and a soldier in headquarters company stated he donated $1.00 and I jokingly called him a Cheap Bastard.

I was involved in a vehicle in Panama City in which a car I was traveling in hit the back of a car belonging to two Panamanian women. The women asked for our groceries which contained a ham and I told them heck no, we will pay you $40.00 which they accepted. Our groceries contained two hams which were like gold in Panama and they cost $80 each on the economy and $20 on base. We were restricted to one a month, but I always found someone who was willing to trade liquor for a ham.

208

Clubs

Panama City was like New York City, but less expensive. The clubs were very nice and cheap to enter. The entrance price of most clubs included at least two free drinks. Bacchus was my favorite club because it was small and a lot of good-looking women hung out on Thursday nights which was ladies' night. The entrance price for Bacchus was $5.00, which included two free drinks and the ladies received free admission plus two free drinks. If they looked very nice, they received free drinks the entire night. I always ordered a Cuba Libre, which was rum with a taste of lime. It was the first drink I learned in Spanish and I ordered it for four years every time I entered a bar or club. I stopped going to Bacchus when it became larger because I enjoyed the small atmosphere and you could see all of the nice-looking ladies in a small area compared to the new Bacchus where they could hide. Drew and I would party every Thursday night at Bacchus. I would leave at 4:00 am because we had physical fitness at 6:00 am and Drew would party until 5:30 and change clothes in his car before the start of physical fitness. The Brigade XO knew we partied hard on Thursdays and would do long runs on Fridays to make us vomit, but it never worked. One day I said I was going to show up the XO by beating him on the long run. I finished first and told CPT Piatt I smoked the old man. CPT Piatt replied, "The XO runs an 11-minute two mile-run" which shut me up because my two-mile time was 13 minutes.

Hotel Panama was another favorite club of mine because they had live performances by Salsa Bands. The entrance fee was $10 which included two free drinks. My friends attended Patatus which had an entrance fee of $20 and it included four free drinks. I considered Patatus a rich stuck-up club because the girls were looking for rich white guys. You had to dress nice to get into the clubs in Panama. Button down shirts, slacks, and dress shoes were required, no tennis

209

shoes. We would go to the Mariott and stand at the bottom of the steps to look under girls' dresses because most of them wore no panties.

Thursdays were Bacchus night, Fridays were NCO Club, Saturdays were Hotel Panama, Mariott, or Exotic Clubs, and Sundays were the Yacht club night. We would play basketball Saturday morning to get the alcohol out of our system and then returned to partying. I partied hard, but I always did physical training six days a week twice a day.

Adult Clubs

Panama has some excellent adult clubs. Panamanians called them Pelo Shows because of shaved vaginas. Le Palace, Josephine, and Elite were servicemembers" favorite clubs. The Military made Greta Azul (Blue Goose) off limits because of prostitution, but the truth was all of them had prostitution.

I witnessed the best lap dance in Le Place which I have ever seen. A dancer gave an American Civilian a lap dance so great the guy was leaned back in his chair spread eagle like he had the best sexual experience of his life. The lap dance was so great I gave her $20 for her performance on the guy.

Josephine's, Elite, and Le Palace were considered high class Exotic clubs. I would have a couple of drinks and ask the girls how much for a good time and they would respond $100 and I would say "okay" and put out my hands for them to pay me. They would leave and call me every curse word in the Spanish Dictionary.

I noticed junior enlisted soldiers were coming in for work tired every day. I asked them why and they told me they had been out with the girls from Josephine the night before. I said you guys should be broke because those girls are $100 and they told me the sex with the girls were free. I asked what was their secret and they told me they would set their alarm clocks for 2:00 am because it is when the girls stopped working, pick up the girls, take them to Don Lee's a Chinese restaurant where you could feed a family of 10 off $5.00, and tell the girls sweet things like they were the woman of their dreams and they were going to marry them. The girls knew the guys were lying, but those were things they wanted to hear. Leave it to junior enlisted soldiers to come up with such crazy schemes.

People would take their dates to Push Buttons hotels which are hotels where you drive your car into a garage similar to a storage unit,

211

push a button so the door closes, pay the attendant who gives you a key, and enter the room with your date. They are common in Panama City and you pay by the hour. There was a section in Panama City which had a row of Push Buttons and the Panamanians called the area the Bermuda Triangle because you see a lot of cars entering, but none coming out. One day I was passing by and saw a bus full of couples pulling into the hotel, I said to myself I wonder what if the bus driver was paid in money or sex. Bus and cab drivers had plenty of women because they were the main methods of transportation and women who wanted free rides had to put in a little action.

Restaurants

Panama has excellent restaurants and different types of fruit such mangos, papaya, tamarind, mamey, and pineapple to name a few. My favorite restaurants in Panama were Napoli's Pizza, Las Cascadas, Don Lee's, and an Argentina Steakhouse. A person can order a shrimp, lobster, or seafood pizza at Napoli's. Large pizza cost about $10 and they were made fresh. Las Cascadas was my favorite seafood restaurant and a seafood platter would last two days and cost $10. Lemonade was .75¢ and Cuba Libre (Rum and coke with lime) was .75¢. I ordered Cuba Libre every time I was there. A lot of nice-looking girls worked at Las Cascadas. I think the requirements to be a waitress at Las Cascadas were to be young and beautiful. One day I asked the owner where my previous server was and he told me she quit. He said the problem with keeping good looking waitresses was a lot of servicemembers were coming in there and marrying them.

Argentina Steakhouse had great steaks with reasonable prices. It was my favorite restaurant to carry girls on the first date. Two T-bone steaks with a salad and a drink cost us $20.00. A guy would come and sing for the dates. He thought I was rich because I tipped him $5.00 while other patrons tipped him $1.00.

Las Tablas (Carnaval)

Carnaval occurs at the same time as Mardi Gras, but there is no flashing of breasts for beads. Las Tablas is where a lot of people go to celebrate Carnival. It is a small town, but during Carnaval it feels like the entire county of Panama goes to Las Tablas.

I first went with a group of lieutenants to Las Tablas when I was stationed on the Atlantic Side. We were three lieutenants in a small truck and no one spoke Spanish fluently. We met a family who gave us food and allowed us to sleep in their driveway. I was showing off and boxing with a ten-year old kid and he busted my lip which ended my boxing career. Everyone was laughing at the incident, including myself. We did not pick-up any girls probably because there were too many men in a truck.

When I was the Assistant S-4, I decided to go to Las Tablas again. I asked other officers if they wanted to go with me and they all said "No, because they were having too much fun in Panama City". I asked SSG Calander to go with me to rent a car. I rented a Toyota 4-Runner. I was on cloud nine because it had power steering and air condition compared to my Suzuki Samuri which had none of those amenities.

I purchased a camcorder, 14 cases of Old Milwaukee, 3 gallons of Herrano Seco, a gallon of Vodka, 6 cases of sodas, and 3 cases of MREs. Las Tablas was about a three-hour trip from Panama City.

When I arrived in Las Tablas, I asked a family who I never met before to charge my camcorder. Only an adult and one child out of 20 family members spoke English. The lady allowed me to charge my camcorder. When I returned to my car, the lady approached me and asked where I was staying at, and I responded in my car. She invited me to stay with her family and when I was unloading my car of all the alcohol the men said I could stay the entire week. It was a three-bedroom house and the family made the kids give their room to me. I was shocked at their actions because they allowed an unknown stranger in their house. They fed me and gave me a nice bed. I told them this would never happen in America. The family told me there was no water in the house because the town confiscated all the water to hose down the crowd during Carnival to prevent heat injuries. I only saw drunk people passed out during Carnival. The family kept water in a fifty- five-gallon drum which I used to take a shower with and it was ice cold.

The men packed the cooler and asked me to accompany them to the town square to see the Carnaval Queens and where the crowds were gathered at. When we were carrying the coolers, the men put the coolers on a float to carry it into the town. I asked them if they knew who owned the float and they responded "No, this is what happens during Carnaval". Everyone drinks during Carnaval and we gave some beer to the police officers. There were over 100,000 people in Las Tablas for Carnaval and no crime occurred. Las Tablas only had 10,000 residents during the year. I still do not know why so many people gathered in Las Tablas for Carnaval.

The Carnaval Queens resembled the Brazilian Samba Queens and were paraded around the town square wearing costumes worth over $100,000.00.

I spent three days in Las Tablas. I drunk so much alcohol it caused me to leave a day early to recuperate. The family asked me to stay another day and told them I had to be at work the next day, which was a lie. The truth was they drunk me under the table and I could not last another day. I left six cases of beer and a gallon of liquor with them. Didimo asked me to carry his wife who worked for the Police Department back to Panama City which I did because they were so nice to me during Carnaval. It was a long ride home because she spoke no English and I spoke little Spanish and most of the conversation was about the different types of food in Panama. I could order any food, ask for directions, bargain for things, and carry on a conversation in

215

Spanish on a first-grade level. I liked Salsa and we listened to the radio on the way back. She would sing along with some of the songs which made the ride back not so bad.

I returned home hung over and tired. My girlfriend could not believe I survived in Las Tablas only speaking Basic Spanish with a country accent. We returned later to Las Tablas and the family rolled out the red carpet for us. They took us to a fair, roasted a whole pig, and carried us to a seafood restaurant. The restaurant owner served us fresh fish. He dropped the fish on the floor before cooking, but it did not stop me from eating it.

The family made a big party out of roasting a hog. The men killed a hog early in the morning and the women prepared the other food to go along with the pork. The entire neighborhood gathered for the party. They sang, danced, and drank the night away. It was a very enjoyable time and they made us feel like part of their family. They introduced me to their friends. One of their friends had 100 cows and told me he was poor and I told him he is rich because I could not afford to feed one cow and he laughed. I gave him some clothes and beer. Another gentleman had a 6-year-old son who was a great baseball player. The man and his family lived in a one room house made of mud. We took him home and I gave him some beer and MREs for his hospitality. He told me the only thing he could give me in return was a papaya and I told him, he just made my day because I love papaya. The papaya was bigger than a watermelon and the best papaya I have ever eaten because it was sweet, juicy, and it came from the heart. I ate it in two days.

I spent another weekend with Didimo's family in Cerro Azul which had a lot of pine trees. I never saw pine trees in Panama except for in Cerro Azul. It reminded me of North Carolina.

Brigade Deactivation

I was the Assistant S-4 and the senior officers placed a lot of responsibility on me for the deactivation of the brigade. I was scheduled to attend the Armor Advance Course instead of deactivating the brigade. The brigade leadership team canceled my school date because they said I was needed more in Panama and I could attend the Armor Advance Course anytime. I knew this was a lie and contacted Infantry Branch who told me I lost my Armor Advance Slot because I was involuntarily kept in Panama and I could stay as a Light Infantry Officer or switch Branches. I was mad because my goal was to become a Light Infantry and Armor Officer so, I decided to switch branches. I was only offered Chemical and Signal; therefore, I switched to the Signal Branch. A big mistake because I was only sent to Armor Units and not Signal Units.

I had three months left after turning in the equipment and was sent to the Post Command Center to assist with monitoring the radio. The command group just sent soldiers to different units with no instructions. The Command Center would receive crazy calls especially from Officers' wives which said "I am going to kill that Motherfucker because I caught him sleeping with the maid". Officers' houses contained maid quarters and the wives did not want to clean so they hired these nice looking 18-to-20-year-old girls to be their live-in maids. The wives did not work and the maids only maid $160 a month.

217

Cuban Refugee Crisis

The United States sent a lot of Cuban Refugees to Panama and Suriname to reduce the pressure on Florida. One day the Cubans started a riot in the camp and beat up some soldiers and stole some vehicles which were recovered before they left the compound. The Cubans did not riot in the camps run by Infantry Soldiers. The next day the commander sent the Rangers in to show the rioters who was in charge. There was no more misbehaving afterwards.

The commander in the Command Center wanted me to work for him, but I told him I was leaving Panama in less than a month and I needed time to clear. He said I could work 12-hour shifts and clear during my off time. I looked at him like he was crazy. I was assigned to another organization and I was helping him out of the goodness of my heart. He had two officers working for him and one was a drunk. I was assigned to COL Small's unit. COL Small was an Armor Officer and he told me to take care of everything I needed to do in preparation for departing Panama. I wished I had met him earlier because he would have ensured I attended the Armor Advance Course.

The training which I received in Panama was the basis of my career. I tell everyone the training I received as a MP was like completing Elementary School while the training which I received in Panama was like earning your high school, college, and Masters 'degree in four years.

Panama is a very nice country and history books which I read said Panama is a Third World Country, but it is false. There are more banks in Panama than New York City and their student's graduation rates are at a higher level than those in the United States. There are some remote areas which do not have the same amenities as those found in Panama City. I did not mind sleeping in places which had an outhouse because it was better than constructing your own toilet on

218

field exercises. On field exercises we had to dig a toilet and it provided no protection against the weather and animals. Some people in remote areas of Panama kept their food and drinks cold by placing them in a pond. My motto is "if it doesn't kill the locals then it will not kill me", so I ate everything they ate.

Panamanians are very nice and funny people who knew how to party. They would protest Monday – Friday for the Americans to leave and take the weekend off for partying then return the next Monday and protest for the Americans to stay after realizing how much money we put in the economy I had a lot of great times in Panama, but I had to leave in order to further my career. I enjoyed the culture, people, food, night life, and music. I especially missed listening to the DFJs and the Reggaeton Artist such as El General, Nando Boom, Tony Bull, Chico Man, and others. Panama is the birth place of Reggaeton. Panamanian DJs would rap and mix music on radio stations. I have recordings of Panamanian DJs talking and playing music from when I was stationed there. When people hear my recordings of the DJs, they start laughing because my recordings of the DJs are wishing everyone a Merry Christmas and it's the month of July.

Panama Canal History

We were responsible for guarding the Panama Canal. One day, I asked one of the workers to give us a tour so we would know how to defend it and it was an amazing tour. He took us under the locks and showed us how everything worked. They were using most of the same technology when the lock was built except automation equipment. I became fascinated with the history of Panama after the tour.

The true history of why the United States returned the Panama Canal to Panama was because White Americans tried to establish Jim Crow laws there and the Panamanians refused to allow it. I spoke with people who lived in Panama during the time and they said there were two Commissaries, Golden and Silver, and Black Panamanians could not go to the Golden one. I spoke with the first Black American to be a Policeman in the Canal Zone on several occasions about Panama's History. In the Canal Zone which was run by Americans, Panamanians could only work as maids or lawn care personnel and had to be out of the area by dark. Panamanian police could not arrest Americans.

Panamanian President Torrijos demanded Americans stop mistreating Panamanians. Torrijos died in a mysterious plane crash. He had the same pilot every day except for the day his plane crashed. Noreiga became President afterwards. The Panamanians told me during Noreiga's rule there was very little crime and no drug problem because Noreiga fed the murders, rapist, and child molesters to the shark and he would not let the drug dealers off load their cargo in Panama. The crime rate and drug problem increased significantly after Noreiga was arrested. The History Channel is the only television program which I have seen come close to telling the true history of why America gave up control of the Panama Canal. I became a history buff after those conversations and anywhere I travel to, I speak with the locals to get the true history of their country.

220

Lessons Learned

1. ***When in charge take charge*** – I knew how to setup during the Brigade Exercises, but I listened to the MSG who wanted to relax coming from Korea. I should have ordered him to setup the communication according to Brigade Standards and if he refused then send him home.

2. ***Recognition motivates people*** – When I was promoted to Captain no one in Brigade Headquarters congratulated me nor pinned on my rank, so I read the promotion orders and pinned my rank on in front of a mirror instead of doing in front of a company of soldiers. It means a lot when a person is recognized in front of their peers.

3. ***Lookout for the careers of your subordinates*** – I informed brigade leaders I was scheduled to attend the Armor Advance Course before taking the job. The leaders were more worried about getting out of Panama instead of taking care of their subordinates which costs affected my career. A leader should have sent me on my due date to the Armor Advance Course or contact Armor Branch and request I be placed in the next available school.

4. ***Read*** – I read USA Today every day in Panama. It was quarter more and a day late, but I knew what was going on in the United States and around the World.

5. ***Don't get blinded by the big lights*** – Panama City was the first big city which I lived in and I became too distracted by the women and clubs. I probably could have paid cash for a new corvette if I eased off of the partying.

6. ***Exercise is good for the mind and body*** – I exercised six days a week for a minimum of 90 minutes and I participated on unit sport teams. Exercising so much probably saved my kidneys from alcohol poisoning.

7. *Mentorship* – Senior leaders should find a mentor for their junior officers. The Army saying during those times were junior officers need to find a mentor when it should have said senior leaders need to serve as a mentor or find mentors for junior officers.

8. *Go the opposite where Americans go.* – You meet new people and you learn the culture and customs of local citizens.

9. *Learn the history of the host nation* – I spoke with numerous people about the history of Panama and they gave me a history lesson which could not be found in any book.

10. *Learn the language of the host nation* – Learning the host nation's languages shows you respect the people, their culture, and you will make a new friend. I made and I am still making mistakes when I speak Spanish.

11. *Maintain Accountability of Equipment and Personnel* – Everywhere I have been stationed at in the Military, a commander has lost accountability of their assigned equipment. Do monthly or quarterly inspection and sign things down to subordinates which places responsibility on them and it relieves some of the pressure off of you.

Brigade Staff – CPT Piatt on the left side, is now LTG Piatt

SIGNAL ADVANCE COURSE

Almost a third of the Signal Advance Course consisted of captains from combat arms units. Everyone worked together despite our different Military Backgrounds. We had a couple of Foreign Officers from around the world who were excellent Football Players (Soccer for Americans). We played different sports once a week. The soldiers who came from Korea were great runners and told me being stationed in Korea improved their run times and endurance. The difficult part of about the Signal Advance Course was learning about the capabilities of technical equipment. The only thing I knew about Signal was setting up a PRC-77 which allowed you to talk at almost two miles away in clear even terrain.

The majority of officers lived off post. Daughtery and my wife were pregnant with twins. One doctor at the Augusta Hospital suggested my spouse and I have an abortion because of the expected early arrival of twins and one may be born with brain damage. We said "No" and thank goodness there was another doctor who sent my wife to the main hospital in Augusta which was able to care for underweight babies. My twins were healthy despite the fact my son weighed 4lbs and 10oz and my daughter 3lbs and 4oz. My daughter graduated from UNC-Chapel Hill and obtained the rank of Captain in the Air Force and my son graduated from University of Wilmington and is a Sociologist. Every day I think about what my life would have been like if I had listened to the first doctor and how many times have that doctor told a patient to have an abortion instead of sending them to Augusta Hospital which could handle difficult pregnancies.

Officers are always trying to find ways to save money. Thomas came up with a bright idea of renting an apartment in a crime filled area because the rent was cheap which would allow him to save up more money. We told him his neighbors would steal everything he owned, but the kitchen sink and he refused to listen to us. One weekend Thomas went to his hometown in South Carolina and as soon as he left, an unexpected freeloading roommate moved in for the weekend. When Thomas was returning home, he called his phone to check his messages and his uninvited roommate answered the phone. Thomas began to curse him out and the robber hung up on him. When Thomas arrived home the robber had eaten up all his food, stole his VCR, television, and pictures of his girlfriend. Thomas later moved into a nice apartment complex.

Cheating Scandal

The instructors in the Signal Advance Course told us the final exam is very difficult and if we don't pass it, we would be put out of the Army. There were numerous study groups in the class. There were 25 questions on the test. A couple of soldiers had the exact same answers for each question. The instructors accused them of cheating. A copy of the test was passed around. No student broke into a teacher's room to obtain the test, but soldiers from previous classes assigned each other a question to remember, typed up the questions, and distributed to each class. It was Facebook before it's time.

The Signal Corps assigned all of the former Combat Arm Captains to Combat Units and the officers who wanted to serve overseas they assigned to Stateside units. The assigning of Combat Arm Officers back into Combat Units hurt a lot of officers' careers because they did not have a chance to learn the capabilities and uses of the high-tech Signal Equipment. This was one of the biggest complaints about the Signal Corps at the time which was putting experienced Signal Combat Arms Officers back into Combat Units instead of Signal Units.

Lessons Learned

1. ***Get a second opinion–*** Doctors don't know everything. It is your life not theirs so get more than one opinion.

2. ***Your safety and peace of mind is worth more than a few dollars*** – Thomas saved money initially, but in the end, it cost him more money and time replacing stolen items and moving.

3. ***Change your tests*** – A lazy teacher uses the same test every year. If you don't change your tests then don't complain when students have the same answer for every question.

FT LEONARDWOOD (5TH ENGINEERS)

I arrived at Ft Leonardwood which is better known as "Fort Lost in the Woods" because there is nothing around the base. Springfield, Missouri is almost an hour away from the base. I never received a sponsor letter or any information stating which unit I was assigned to. Someone told me there were a lot of Basic Training Company Commands positions available. I was getting ready to sign into one of those units until the S-1, my neighbor, noticed on her roster I was assigned to 5th Engineers as the Battalion Signal Officer (Sigo).

The Signal Officer Advance Course concentrated more on the heavy signal equipment than the job a Sigo does. I learned more from the Infantry about the duties of a Sigo than in the Advance Course. The Battalion S-3 could not believe the Signal Corps sent a Sigo who had never worked in a Signal Unit before and especially one who had never been in an Armor unit. The S-3 always gave me a look like I didn't belong there and sometimes would shake his head in disbelief when I did not know something He should have coached me along instead of trying to destroy my confidence. I reminded him I was an Infantry Officer and the duty of all Branches is to support the Infantry. He did not like my comment, but it's true.

The Battalion Commander, LTC Holler, was a very calm leader and understood I would make mistakes because this was my first Signal Assignment. I only saw LTC Holler mad one time and it is when someone misplaced a piece of secure signal equipment.

LTC Holler believed in days off for soldiers and battalion functions. Officers were always missing Hail and Farewells. One day I missed one and LTC Holler said during a Staff Meeting that he missed me. I was the only Black Officer in the battalion and me missing a Hail

228

and Farewell stood out like a sore thumb. I felt like I disappointed him and the battalion when I missed the function. It was the first and last time in my Military Career I ever missed a Unit Function.

Ft. Cavazos

The battalion was deployed to Ft. Cavazos (Formerly Ft. Hood) to support a Division Exercise. I asked my Signal NCOIC who was going with me. He said two Privates and I replied" you're crazy and I needed more experienced soldiers with me". Our other Sergeant and Corporal were in a Military School which left us with two Privates. The Signal Sergeant said we would be setup in the TOC (Tactical Operation Center), the Privates did the mission three months prior, and we would not have to go down range. I later found out he did not want to go because he was worried his soon to be ex-girlfriend would trash his house. I was hesitant, but someone in the unit said we would not be going down range and there were only two M113s being deployed which relaxed me.

When we arrived, we setup with the Division TOC. Setup went according to plan except our communication equipment did not work. I tried every method which I learned in the Signal Advance Course on how to correct the error, but to no avail. I was frustrated and the Privates did not know what the error meant and how to correct the problem. After an hour of trouble shooting, I sought help from the Division Signal Officer and he immediately recognized the error which was due to us not having the correct Security Code. He solved the problem in five minutes. The Division worked their Signal Officer like a dog. He probably slept two hours a day for 10 days which made me realize, I don't want to be a Division Signal Officer. Once our equipment was operable, I climbed on top of a tank and read the entire SINGARS (Radio) book. I learned what each error code meant and how to fix them. Our mission went smoothly afterwards. Another thing which I noticed during the exercise was how Senior Officers were afraid of one Major who was a son of General Creighton Abrams. The Major acted like he was in charge. There were signs in the TOC which said "No Smoking" and the Major would walk in smoking a cigar and talking loudly. The Major knew he was going to become a General just based on his father's name. A Colonel was being ridden hard by a General and the Colonel shouted to the General "The only thing separating me from you is $500". The General told him to calm down, but he eased off of the Colonel.

People always say be careful what you ask for and I wanted to be a DAT (Dumbass Tanker) and the Army did not give me my request, but assigned me to a tank unit which was not the same job as a Tanker.

We left our equipment there because we were returning in two weeks. I told the NCOIC he was going this time and he told me again he could not go because he was worried about his girlfriend trashing his house. I told him it sounds like a personal problem to me and he was going on the next mission. He reluctantly went on the next mission. We were operating on all cylinders after the exercise especially when SGT White returned from school.

SGT White was a very professional and quiet leader who knew his job and lead by example. SGT White never cursed. SGT White was extremely overweight before he entered the Army. and had to weigh himself on a feed scale because his weight exceeded that of a regular scale. He lost over 100 pounds in to be eligible to join the Army.

The arrival of LTC Young from the Pentagon brought the battalion someone who knew how to make the battalion automated. I knew the requirements for setting up a Local Area Network (LAN), but I lacked the knowledge of how to purchase the equipment. LTC Young knew how to get funds and used his connections at the Pentagon to obtain the funds quickly. The battalion was automated within six months after his arrival. He once sent me to Post Headquarters to submit requests for computers and other equipment. A civilian lady gave me fits on our requests because she said the equipment had to be purchased through certain vendors for access to the post servers. I explained to her the equipment which she was purchasing costs more than $50k than what I found. She became very upset and called LTC Young telling him I disrespected her by telling her she was wasting taxpayers' money. LTC Young knew I was right and instructed me to leave her alone. The Air Force told her they were not going to use the recommended post vendors and they were going to setup their own network and accessed the post servers despite what the post civilian worker said. Everyone was excited because we moved out of the Stone Age into the Automation Age.

Ft. Carson

Field exercises in the 5th Engineers were not hard compared to those in the Infantry which required us to walk with 50lbs of equipment attached to our bodies. In Panama we walked miles every month and 20-miles twice a year.

We went to Ft. Carson, Colorado to support 4th ID. It brought back memories of when I was a Private in the MP Corps and the 118th left me down range without communication equipment, no map, and no water. A group of us were sent by bus on the advance party for the battalion. There were two bus drivers for the trip. I was asleep on the bus and woke up to a different driver of the bus. I asked another captain when did we stop and he responded we didn't. I looked at him strangely and said "If we didn't stop then how did we end up with a different driver"? He responded the drivers said let's switch and the other responded on my three or your three then they switched drivers doing 70 mph. I told him to contact the bus company once we arrive in Colorado and tell them they cannot do business with the unit anymore because of the actions of their drivers. The drivers' laziness and stupidness could have cost us our lives.

The field exercise in Colorado was not challenging, but it exposed the soldiers' map reading weaknesses. When the soldiers GPS equipment stopped working, they could not use a map to navigate. I would ask soldiers their locations and some of them responded over the radio they did not know their location because their GPS died. I would ask them to identify the nearest the terrain feature they see and I would guide them back to the Operation Center. LTC Holler became upset at the soldiers' lack of knowledge in using a map that he ordered leaders to conduct map reading classes when we returned to Ft. Leonardwood.

End of Sigo Time

I served as a Battalion Signal officer for 18 months. LTC Holler recommended me to the Basic Training Brigade for a Company Commander position. My interview with COL Smith was a total disaster. He asked me what I heard about Basic Training and I told him soldiers from 5th Engineers were told to avoid trainees because we could be charged with Fraternization and the rumor around post is Basic Training was not tough. COL Smith sent me to LTC Redmond's Battalion. I finished inventorying the equipment of the company which I was going to be in charge of and COL Smith sent me back to the 5th Engineers. I believe this was the same COL Smith who I butted heads with in Panama. LTC Redmond was upset with the Brigade Commander's decision, but there was nothing he could do because COL Smith was his boss. LTC Holler asked me what happened and I told him what I said word for word. He went over to visit COL Smith to smooth out the issue. He probably told him I was a dumbass and to give me another chance. I was sent back to the Basic Training and COL Smith assigned me to B/Co 2nd Battalion 47th Infantry Regiment which was led by LTC Zodda. Redmond always joked with me that I was the only commander he knew of who was fired before taking a Command. I met LTC Redmond during a conference after he retired and we laughed about my getting fired before becoming a Company Commander.

Lessons Learned

1. ***Safety short cuts lead to disaster*** – In this case the bus drivers' action on refusing to stop for 5 minutes ended up costing their company future contracts.

2. ***Don't be afraid to make the hard decisions*** – I knew, I lacked the knowledge and training to go to Ft. Cavazos (Ft. Hood), but listened to my NCOIC to take Privates instead of him. I should have told him either he goes on the mission and trains me or look for another job.

3. ***Don't rely on technology for everything*** – If the soldiers maintained their knowledge of map reading, they would not have been lost once their GPS stopped functioning.

4. ***Do what's right*** – We had a Private in our section who everyone thought was slow because one day he forgot to wear his shirt under his jacket and kept his jacket on all day despite temperatures reaching 80 degrees. One day the Brigade Commander was driving in his military vehicle and all the soldiers turned their back in order not to salute him. The Private did not turn his back and rendered a Salute to the Brigade Commander. The Brigade Commander stopped his vehicle and gave the Private a Brigade Coin and a 3-day Pass.

5. ***Speak about facts not rumors*** – When COL Smith asked me what I knew about Basic Training, I should have said nothing. I was making comments about what I heard instead of what I knew.

6. ***A handshake is as good as your word*** – A vehicle transporter gave me a price of transporting my vehicle from Georgia to Missouri. When he arrived and I paid him what he asked for, he looked at me shockingly. I asked him "what's wrong" and he said, "I was the only person who paid him the agreed upon amount and everyone tries to talk his price down once he delivers their vehicle". He called me an honest man for paying the agreed upon

235

price. I told him I was scared he was going to keep my vehicle and I could not afford another vehicle.

Wedding Party

BASIC TRAINING COMMAND

The company which I inherited had great Drill Sergeants, but bad leadership. The commander complained she could not do a lot of the physical requirements due to an injured back. She did not participate in her final Basic Training Company Graduation Ceremony. LTC Zodda asked me to lead the Company's Graduation Ceremony before I assumed command. God works in mysterious ways; I was fired before taking a Command and I became a commander before assuming a Command.

My first day of inventory the commander and SFC Woolery, Drill Sergeant, had an argument in which SFC Woolery said "What have you done for your Country". I was in shock when I heard this. SFC Woolery received a Bronze Star with Valor during the Mogadishu Conflict for manning the Mark 19 Grenade Launcher after he saw the gunner of a Marked 19 Grenade Launcher hit by enemy fire. SFC Woolery could be confrontational because he was a strong leader. I had his respect because we were in the same Battalion in Panama and if you made it through Panama during those times you were tough. He was a straight up Grunt (Infantry Soldier) because his boots were dirty and worn down to the heel.

The Department of the Army came up with crazy ideas stating any E-8 could be a 1SG of a Basic Training Company without ever been a Drill Sergeant and the elimination of the Senior Drill Sergeant Position. The Senior Drill Position was later reinstated and SFC

Burnett was selected for the position. Another crazy idea which the military puts out without doing adequate research.

The Drill Sergeants showed little respect towards the 1SG because he was never a Drill Sergeant and they felt he did not understand what Drill Sergeants go through in order to get trainees to graduate. I noticed their frustration with the 1SG; therefore, I instructed LT Lewis that one of us Officers would be at all training events. This decision kept the peace in the unit.

LT Lewis was a great Executive Officer (XO), but the Army did him wrong by assigning him to a Basic Training Company first instead of a Platoon Leader position in an Engineer Company. LT Lewis was an Officer, but his pay was one of a Specialist because of student loans. I discovered he was eating MREs because of student loan repayments and instructed him I would attend most of the training events so he could eat in the Dining Facility. LT Lewis would leave his Blackberry sitting on his desk and the Drill Sergeants would lock him out of his Blackberry or put on his screen "I eat shit" which was very funny.

Cadre

SFC Burnett was an Infantry Soldier from the 82nd who was always assigned to units which received special pay. He sang in the 82nd Choir and was an Army Recruiter. I learned a lot from him. The other Drill Sergeants would request trainees be put out of the Army or given Disciplinary Action (Article 15) for anything. SFC Burnett told us these are 18 and 19-year-olds and they are supposed to make mistakes and if Drill Sergeants knew how hard it was to get a recruit in the Army, they would not request to put trainees out so quickly. I took his advice and out of 1200 trainees, we only put out 41 and most of them were for injuries. Basic Training Regulation stated trainees get only 3 chances to qualify on the M16. We would give them 6 chances and if they did not make it, we would send them to qualify with another company on the last week of Basic Training. This decision saved the Army a lot of money and it gave the trainees a sense of pride knowing someone cared about them and they could accomplish something when given the opportunity.

Rick, A/Co Commander, had Reddick Bowe's brother in his company. Reddick called to the unit and told Rick he would give him anything if his brother graduated from Basic Training. Rick was strictly by the book and when Reddick's brother failed to qualify after 3 times, he was put out of the Army. I told Rick I would have given him 100 chances to qualify so I could get a Mercedes from Reddick.

SFC Johnson, Drill Sergeant, would make horse sounds when females had extensions in their hair. I made several mistakes as a commander, but the biggest mistake was not submitting SFC Johnson for a MSM (Meritorious Service Medal). The Brigade sent word down they would not approve MSMs (Meritorious Service Medal) for Drill Sergeants because they were not deployed or leading an Active-Duty Platoon, so I submitted him for an ARCOM. The policy was later changed.

SFC Otto was an Engineer and if you looked at him, you would never know he was an excellent runner. He wore Walmart Running Shoes and could easily run 2-miles in 11 minutes. He taught me how to use a Bait Casting Reel for fishing. The first time I used it I tangled up the line because I failed to follow his instructions. He later became a CSM.

SFC Howard could run like a deer. I discovered she was fast runner after running with her platoon one day. She ran three miles without sweating. I was sweating and breathing hard and could not believe her newly hair do was still in place and she was not sweating. I asked her how fast does she runs 2-miles and she said "12-minutes and her 12-mile Foot March time was 2 hours and 20-minutes". Her 12-mile time Foot March was almost 30 minutes faster than mine. She became a CSM.

SFC Herbert was bald guy who had a couple of comical experiences during his time as a Drill Sergeant. His wife noticed a lot of her Kotex pads were missing and asked Herbert was he seeing someone else. Herbert confessed to his wife that he was putting her pads in his Drill Sergeant hat to prevent sweat from getting in his eyes. The pads worked and he should have submitted the idea to Kotex for royalties.

SFC Herbert had another comical experience which occurred at Golden Corral. He was getting food and his 2-year son told him he needed to use the bathroom. SFC Herbert told him to wait, but his son could not wait and urinated in the middle of the restaurant. We told SFC Herbert it was his fault because his son told him he needed to go to the bathroom.

SSG Jackson was from West Virginia and won $80k off a Scratch Off Ticket in Alaska. He brought a 12-pack of beer and spent his last dollar on a Scratch Off Ticket. He is the only lottery winner who I know complained about winning. He complained about paying more taxes because his lottery winnings put him in a higher tax bracket.

He had a room decorated with Army memorabilia and GI-Joes. The other Drills called him grandfather because of his looks. His voice was loud and rough which intimidated a lot of Privates. The Privates later confessed it was all show because he was really a pussycat when he was not in front of other Cadre Members. He cared about his job and the trainees who he trained.

SSG Guzman's wife won Yard of the Month Award using a combination of fake flowers and real flowers. She was a great cook. I despised liver and one day she invited my family over to dinner. She cooked liver and I ate three plates before she told me what it was. I ate two more plates afterward. It was the last time I ate liver.

SSG Ruiz was a hard worker who would take leave to go work in tobacco fields. A private company was tearing down buildings on base and SSG Ruiz was disappointed no one told him the company was hiring. He was prepared to take 30-days of vacation to work with the company.

SSG McCoy would get wound up for the Trainees first day of Basic Training. Her eyes would pop out of her head and she would scream and jump around like a person high on speed. She looked forward to the arrival of new trainees.

SFC Rivera was one of three bulldozer operators in the Army who were Ranger qualified. He was sent to become a Drill Sergeant after one of his soldiers drove a dump truck with the bed raised up on Ft. Bragg knocking down power lines. He would do pushups and sit-ups while watching television.

SFC Westbrook claim to fame as a Drill Instructor was, he shot a 27lb bobcat with a bow on Ft. Leonardwood.

SSG Gurney was a Drill Sergeant who I worked with in Panama. He was leaving when I arrived. When I was inspecting the barracks in Panama, I heard someone say "Hello". I turned and looked up and it was a parrot. I asked SSG Gurney how did a parrot get in his room and he said he saw it on a branch by his window and stuck his arm out

241

and the parrot came to him. I just shook my head and told him he could keep it as long as his roommates did not complain about it. SSG Gurney went into Special Operations after his Drill Instructor time ended.

I worked with some great Drill Sergeants. SSG Friend and SSG Alley were Military Policemen. SSG Welch who I met 20 years later at Ft. Jackson, SC when he was a First Sergeant of a Basic Training Company. Some of the Drill Sergeants came later in my command and others were Drill Sergeants from Army Reserves who helped us in the summer. Overall, I worked with exceptional Drill Sergeants who knew how to train soldiers. The Army did right when it promoted the majority of them to Command Sergeant Major or First Sergeant. I had a great supporting staff which included 1LT Lewis, SSG Franklin, SSG Cronin, SGT McClanahan, PFC Ferrara, Private Lowe, and a host of others who supported the company.

Trainees

Trainees where under a tremendous amount of pressure to succeed because some of them were supporting a family. Some of the females were single parents and they knew they had to graduate to provide a better life for their child. I despised fathers who called the unit requesting their spouse or girlfriend come home because they could not watch the children. Almost all of these fathers were unemployed or had criminal records. I had parents contacting me requesting their child send money home to take care of them.

Senior leaders of the Army came up with a good plan of integrating the training of males and females, but a terrible plan on housing them. Their plan was to house males and females across from each other on the same hallway. We had a lot of sexual activity going on. We spent a lot of time trying to prevent relationships. The day of graduation, I asked a female why we didn't catch more of them in relationships and she told me when the trainees turned on the buffer, it meant a Cadre member was coming on to their floor.

Female Privates viewed male Drill Sergeants as father figures because most of them had no father in their life and would do crazy things to attract the attention of male Drill Sergeants.

There was a female who tried to get a Drill Sergeant's attention by coming to his office with another female dress only in her bra and panties. The Drill Sergeant threw a book at her and told her to get out of his office or she would be Court Martialed. She never did it again.

We had a Hispanic female from New York who was homeless at 16 years old. I don't why her Recruiter put her in the Reserves instead of Active Duty knowing of her situation. She was so excited to be in a warm and safe environment that she told us she was going to marry a soldier for stability.

243

There was a Reservist School Teacher who would chase after the 18 – 19-year-olds males. I told her to stop it because it was going to get her in trouble. I doubted she listened to me after graduation.

Jenkins an overweight trainee from Washington D.C. was one of the most motivated trainees I met because he told us, "No matter what we do to him, he is not going to quit". He was an outstanding soldier and graduated on time. I met Private Rawls ten years later in Korea when I was getting off of the bus. I could not believe she remembered me and I was proud of her because she was a SFC (Sergeant First Class).

The second biggest mistake I made as a Commander was putting Pvt Ala out of the Army. He was a member of SFC Johnson's platoon and was always getting in trouble. I warned him if he does one more thing wrong, I was going to put him out of the Army. He was caught with a female in his room. I took away her pass privileges and started the process of putting him out of the Army. We had to submit the paperwork to the CSM before putting a trainee out of the Army. Other leaders told me the CSM would talk sternly to Trainees who were on the cusp of being put out of the Army and then send them back to the unit. My attempt at scaring Private Ala backfired because CSM immediately signed off on the paperwork. Private Ala did not tell his family about his discharge out of the Army and they attended graduation and sat right behind me. I asked 1SG what should I do and he said tell them I put him out of the Army and the CSM signed the papers. The parents went to see the CSM and he confronted me at the graduation dinner and called me a coward in front of other parents for saying he put their son out of the Army instead of me. I was mad and wanted to curse him out, but I held back because it would have looked bad if there was a confrontation in front of parents. I learned as a commander you cannot be afraid of telling bad things. If the Army did not have a crazy policy of rooming males across from females in the same barracks, then these incidents would not have occurred. The command group later changed the sleeping arrangement of trainees

244

and placed males and females on separate floors. This did not solve the problem, but it reduced a lot of sexual incidents. The next command group which came in, changed the policy to males and females would be housed in different barracks.

SFC Burnett, a former Army Recruiter, told all of us if we knew how hard it was to put a person in the Army then we would not be so easily to put them out and we are dealing with 18-year-olds and they are supposed to mess up. If he was a Senior Drill Sergeant at the beginning of my command, we would have moved Private Ala to another platoon instead of putting him out of the Army.

Basic Training Policy stated if a soldier failed to qualify on their assigned M16 after three times, then they would be put out of the Army. SFC Burnett came up with a brilliant idea when we had soldiers who failed to qualify with their M16 or failed to successfully throw two live hand grenades. We would send those who failed a task to another company for additional training after they passed their End-of-Cycle Test and Final Physical Fitness test. Soldiers spent an additional one to two weeks in Basic Training. We told the soldiers they would graduate from Basic Training, but not with our company after successfully passing the tasks they failed. This additional training motivated the soldiers to pass the tasks which they failed because they completed the other training requirements for graduating Basic Training. We had a 100% passing rate doing this for trainees and it saved the Army money by not discharging trainees. It takes about two weeks to discharge a soldier and the Army is paying the trainee until they are discharged.

When we received any trainees between October – April, we knew they were homeless, unemployed, working for minimum wage, or put out of college. In other words, they were on their last leg. Most of them took the training to heart because they knew if they did not graduate, they would be returning their previous life before the Army.

I was lenient on giving trainees Article 15s because SFC Burnett said we were only taking a $150 of their paychecks when they misbehaved and said taking away their free time was more costly than $150.00. Article 15s received in Basic Training were torn up at the end of graduation. The only time I gave a female an Article 15 is when she lied to me in my face after she was caught having sex with a Black Soldier on the top bed by the Fireguard. The Black Trainee told me the truth and I took away his 4-hour pass. The White Female refused to talk because she thought I was going to tell her parents, so I gave her an Article 15.

I administered an Article 15 and put a male trainee out of the Army for stealing another trainee's debit card and lying to me about it despite being caught on camera. His face and name tag were displayed on the surveillance camera and he still denied it.

1st Class

Our average Basic Training Class consisted of about 120 trainees except for summer classes which was over 200 trainees. Summer classes were larger because they were made up of Reservist and National Guard Soldiers who were in college and high school and had to be back in their school on the first day their school started.

The first week of classes we administered a physical fitness test to determine which run group the trainees would be assigned to. The Command Group warned us if we have a heat injury, Company Leaders could be fired or receive a letter of reprimand. A trainee approached me in a panicky mood and told me another trainee was sweating profusely and laying under a tree. When SFC Rivera saw the trainee talking to me, he ran up to him and said "Private what in the hell are you doing talking to my commander"!!! I was in shock and the Private said there was a trainee sitting under a tree with a heat injury". SFC Rivera loudly said "Don't you ever approach my commander for anything and the other Private was not having a heat stroke and he just needed some water". I was nervous as shit when the Private said heat injury and I saw the Private sweating profusely under the tree. The Private was suffering from heat exhaustion and thanks to SFC Rivera quick thinking of giving the Private water and pouring water on the Private, he prevented a disaster. The Private recovered. When SFC Rivera told the Private not to talk to his commander, it reinforced the idea of using your chain of command and it prevented 200 trainees from overwhelming me with their problems.

SFC Rivera was a prankster who made training enjoyable. The Battalion Commander told us not to use curse words when singing cadences. SFC Rivera would march the company by the Battalion Headquarter singing cadences with curse words. He would be smiling at me the entire time while doing this.

247

Summer Class I

The summer months were the hardest on the staff because of an influx of trainees who had Mandatory Return Dates which means they had to complete Basic Training before the start of their college or high school. The trainees would complete Basic Training one summer and return the next summer to complete their Advanced Individual Training.

My leadership philosophy was to be at every training event and speak with the trainees in a group setting at each training site. This leadership style showed the Drill Sergeants I was willing to work and wanted to learn what they did and the experiences they go through on a daily basis. This also showed the trainees the commander cared about them. I would ask them simple questions such as where they are from and why did they join the Army. The privates reasoning for joining the Army was such as for a better life for themselves and their family, college money, and a challenge.

Trainees were under a lot of pressure to succeed. The ones who joined for their families were under the most pressure. A lot of females were single parents and the sole bread earners because the fathers of their children were unemployed or had a criminal record which prevented them from joining the Army. Some of the husbands were so lost on what to do as a parent that they would call the company and ask us to send their wives home because they can't watch the kids or they would keep their wives' checks and not give them any funds to buy toiletries. A couple of the parents called and told me they need their child to send money home to support them.

Don't Ask, Don't Tell Cycle

The Army had a Don't Ask, Don't Tell Policy which meant you don't ask a soldier their sexual preference and they don't have to tell you their sexual preference. If a soldier told you they were homosexual, you had to put them out of the Army. We had a winter cycle in which six trainees willing told Drill Sergeants they were homosexual without any coercion. This was a training distraction because we had to read them their rights, send them with a Drill Sergeant to JAG for legal assistance, and hold them over for two weeks before releasing them from the Army. A First Sergeant from another company was very frustrated when two trainees told him they were homosexuals that he told them to kiss each other. They never did and he sent them back to training.

I became frustrated when three trainees told me within the same week, they were homosexuals. I told the trainees if they are a homosexual they must call home and tell their family. This backfired on me. A trainee who was in the top 5% of his class and a parent, told me he was a homosexual. I told him to call home and tell his family. He called home and confessed to his sister-in-law who told me her mom knew all along he was gay.

A trainee told me he was a homosexual and his other two partners had AIDs. I immediately sent him to the hospital for testing and he came back negative, but I had to put him out of the Army according to the regulation. A female trainee told SFC Rivera she had something to tell him and SFC Rivera was very suspicious of what she was going to say and asked her not to tell him anything of a personal matter. The trainee who was the granddaughter of a Command Sergeant Major, a parent and spouse, and the best female trainee in the company, told SFC Rivera she lived with her husband and another female. I asked her why did she confess and she said other trainees were making homosexual jokes which made her upset. I hated

249

to put any of the trainees out of the Army because they would have made great soldiers. I had the highest number of homosexuals in the Brigade so the other commanders jokingly called my company the Gay Company. We still graduated over 90% of our trainees. Another way which kept our graduation rate high is because we told trainees they could not leave the Army until after four weeks and it would take two weeks to out process which means they spent six weeks in Basic Training which was eight weeks long. Once trainees made it to week four, they were used to the routine. The company's teamwork and leadership resulted in us graduating over 1200 trainees and losing only 41.

There was one company which discharged 50% of their trainees which I could not believe considering the company commander looked like he was pregnant. When a company puts out such a high number of trainees it is a sign, they do not want to train trainees. Our goal was to provide great training, send Army units outstanding soldiers, and help trainees to become successful and achieve their goals.

Summer Class II

The second Summer Class was one of the best cycles we ever had. The class consisted of college professors, business owners, college students, and high school students. Serving their country and completing Basic Training were on the bucket list for the business owner and college professors. One of the college professors who was 32-years old had a 300-acre farm in France. The other trainees called her grandma because of her age and gray hair. She was one of the top trainees in the cycle. Malone was a college graduate who looked like the cartoon character Mr. Magoo. He was constantly making silly mistakes such as coming to formation in the wrong uniform or leaving equipment behind. I asked him why he joined the Army and he said to be a Commander's Driver like his father was in the Army. Later I asked him how did he graduate from college and his response was his father made a $5 million dollar to the college. I would have become a doctor if my father made a donation in such amount.

Marksmanship Training

The major tasks which trainees had to pass to graduate from Basic Training were qualify on their assigned M16, throw two live grenades, pass the final Physical Fitness Test, and pass the End-of-Cycle Test.

Drill Sergeants did not put too much pressure on trainees during marksmanship training because if the trainees were nervous, they would not qualify. Soldiers had to hit 23 out of 40 targets to qualify on their M16. We had a high qualification pass rate because the Drill Sergeants spent a lot of time training the trainees on marksmanship skills and the trainees could have pizza if we had a 90% or higher qualification rate on the first day of M16 Qualification. This motivated the trainees to pay attention and do well on Qualification Day. We always achieved a 90% or higher goal on Qualification Day. Trainees would eat an entire pizza and become sick because they were not used to eating junk food. If trainees failed to qualify with us after three tries, we would send them to another company for additional training. Every trainee we sent down to another company for additional training qualified and graduated from Basic Training.

Drill Sergeants had competitions with each other on who could achieve the highest score. Drill Sergeants would select a M16 from a trainee who was about the same size and shot from the same size as they did. They all qualified using this technique. The first time I tried it, I selected a M16 from a trainee who shot right-handed and I am a left-handed shooter. I failed to qualify doing this way. The Drill Sergeants roasted me for not qualifying. SFC Woolery told me to choose a left-handed firer the next time and I qualified each cycle using his advice. I participated in all training events except for the Gas Chamber. I refused to go through the Gas Chamber because I didn't want the Trainees laughing at me throwing up and crying. The obstacle course was my favorite training event.

Hand Grenade Course

I take my hat off to the Sergeants who worked the hand grenade course. There would always be a couple of trainees each cycle who could not throw a live grenade far. You would hear the sergeant in the tower saying "short, short" which meant the grenade was going to explode near the bunker. If a trainee failed to throw a grenade over the wall of the bunker, the sergeant had to throw the trainee out of the bunker and jump on top of them to shield them from the explosion. If a grenade was thrown short, the sergeant who was in the bunker with the trainee had to throw the trainee down on the floor and jump on top of them as a human shield. When it was a danger close explosion, about 10 meters outside of the bunker, shrapnel would hit the glass where the next group of trainees were waiting to throw a live grenade. The maximum effective range of a Grenade is about 30 meters.

Final Tests

We only had 10 trainees who were first-time failures on their final Physical Fitness and End-of-Cycle Tests during my command time. The hardest trainee we had to get to pass their Physical Fitness Test was a female with large breasts. Every time she ran her breast would hit her face. The Drill Sergeants came up with an innovative way to stop her breast from hitting her face, they tied ace bandages around her sports bra to hold her breast in place which worked because she passed her Physical Fitness Test. Two of the trainees failed their Physical Fitness on purpose because they wanted to get out of the Army. They completed all of the other requirements and despite us giving them five chances to pass the test, they failed. They were not fat, just lazy.

I thought Basic Training was easy until I became a Basic Training Commander. Trainees received better training than I received in Basic Training. A lot of units said trainees were coming to them out of shape, but they failed to realize the trainees reported to their AIT (Advance Individual Training) units after Basic Training and then to their respective units. Some of the trainees took vacation of two weeks or more before reporting to their units which caused them to be out of shape. I was hesitant at first to becoming a Basic Training Company Commander, but it was the best assignment which I ever had in the Army because I had a chance to watch civilians become soldiers and it improved my soldiering skills because I participated in all of the training which trainees did.

Graduation

Everyone looked forward to graduation. The transformation from civilians to soldiers is a wonderful experience. Soldiers had a four hour pass the day before graduation. We had a chance to meet the families of the soldiers. I met the mom of a soldier who I was thinking about putting out of the Army until SFC Westbrook told me if he had five of those soldiers, he could defeat any enemy force. The mom came to his graduation wearing a white fur coat and several gold necklaces. She told me her son enjoyed Basic Training and it helped him to grow up. Girlfriends of the soldiers would leave their panties in the bathroom.

End of Command

COL Kardos was an outstanding Battalion Commander who did things strictly by Army Regulations. COL Kardos believed in taking care of soldiers. One day he chewed me out because a Drill Sergeant's wife who was in a Post Command Meeting, told the Commanding General I did not give her husband time off to look for a house after arriving from Germany. The only things I remember about the meeting is COL Kardos telling me our goal is to take care of soldiers and pointing his long index finger at me. It looked like he was shooting me with a Desert Eagle Pistol. I told him I gave the soldier 30 days to look for a house, but he came to work on his time off. The soldier wanted to learn his job and prove to his coworkers he was willing to work at all cost. I later ran into the soldier at Ft. Jackson, SC when he was a First Sergeant of a Basic Training Company. The Post Housing Office gave the spouse keys to 15 different houses to choose from. The spouse returned to the next Post Command Meeting and told the Commanding General the Housing Office did not provide her housing. This was a lie and LTC Kardos called me into his office to apologize.

The next time LTC Kardos chewed me out was for not constructing a company's defensive position to his orders on a Field Exercise in which the Brigade Commander was going to visit. I failed to give guidance to the Drill Sergeants on how LTC Kardos wanted Defensive Positions setup. LTC Kardos arrived a day before the Brigade Commander and saw a weak Defense Setup. He told me if I could not follow his direction then he would fire me. I got the message loud and clear and setup the defensive positions according to his orders. I deserved it and the reason he was giving me those orders was to make me look good in front of the Brigade Commander because he knew I only had a short time to make a good impression on him to get a top rating. I did not see this at first.

LTC Kardos assigned my company to star in a short film about Basic Training. I thought he was crazy to assign this to me because of my country accent. It took us about twenty takes to make a 15-minute film because I would look at a Drill Sergeant and start laughing or miss my lines. Acting was a lot harder than I thought.

LTC Kardos conducted weekly runs with his Company Commanders. Once after we ran 4-miles, he asked someone to play racquet ball with him. The other commanders said they didn't know how to play so I took him up on his challenge. I was confident I was going to beat him because I played racquet ball often. He beat me the first game which I considered as lucky. The next game, I made up my mind I was not going to let him score a point. I hit the best shot I ever hit in racquet ball and when the ball bounced off of the opposite wall, LTC Kardos hit the ball between his legs for a point. I was stunned because I have never seen any one hit the ball between their legs. We played another game afterwards. He beat me all three games.

LTC Kardos believed in me and rated me as the top company commander in the battalion. Although I received a high rating, the brigade commander who just arrived did not rate me highly. The Army came out with a crazy policy which stated a senior rater could only give a Top Rating to a certain percentage of their Officers and if they exceeded this percentage, they would receive a call from the Department of the Army about this which could affect the careers of other Officers under their command. This policy forced new senior raters to hold back on giving a Top Rating to a subordinate who was only under their command for a short time period even if the subordinate officer had been in a leadership position for a long time. This policy hurt a lot of good soldiers who were being punished for not working for a senior leader for a long period of time. One of my leaders told me a senior commander came up with this idea after reading one of Jack Welch's philosophy "known as rank and yank or vitality curve in which the bottom 10% of a company got fired". This

257

thinking created a zero tolerance in the Officer Corps because Officers were afraid to make a mistake.

I give credit to the Army and LTC Kardos for doing things right. The Army recognized the hard work and dedication of the Drill Sergeants which I served with and the majority of them were promoted to CSM and 1SG positions. Old Veterans and units consistently complained how Basic Training is not rigorous as the training which they received and trainees are not required to complete all tasks in order to graduate. The truth is Basic Training is just what the first word says "Basic" in which troops receive training on Basic Military Tasks. Majority of trainees are 18- and 19-year-olds and after completing training they are not ready for combat which is why the Army created "AIT" which means "Advance Individual Training" where trainees learn their jobs. Trainees are in shape when they leave Basic Training because they are in a restricted environment where their movement and time is controlled. Problems occur when they are in AIT and go home on vacation. People forget they were once young and young people are going to eat fast food and lay around during their free time. Basic Training does not turn civilians into Special Forces soldiers. It takes time to train a civilian into a seasoned soldier and the military is an environment where a person is constantly training. LTC Kardos knew this and ensured every trainee had to pass every task to graduate. He did not waiver any requirements. I learned from LTC Kardos people join the military to serve their country not to be hazed. LTC Kardos was always teaching us something and another thing which I learned from him, is to train to standard and not to time. Training to standard ensures trainees accomplished the task according to Army Standards and by doing this we produced great soldiers for units.

I enjoyed being of a commander of a Basic Training Company, but I had to leave for my career development. I contacted Signal Branch and the Branch Commander and I graduated from NC A&T State University. I requested an assignment to Korea because I needed to get in a Signal Unit. A classmate from my Signal Advance Course

258

who was serving in Korea told me since I was previous commander, I would be assigned as a Battalion Signal Officer (Sigo). I contacted the Branch Commander and asked if he could guarantee I would be assigned to a Signal Command and he said there is only a 50% chance this would happen. He said the priority for captains who have completed command is to be assigned to AC/RC unit (Active Component/Reserve Component) as an advisor because the Army said too many Reserve Units were not prepared to deploy to Desert Storm. I told the Branch Manager I would take the advisor position because he could not guarantee me an assignment to a Signal Unit.

Soldiers call Ft. Leonardwood Fort Lost in the Woods, but I enjoyed my time there. It had great fishing and hunting spots and it gave me the chance to see another part of the United States. I visited the Bass Pro Shop in Springfield Missouri which has a large collection of stuffed animals, restaurant, and aquariums with freshwater fish. My family rode an elephant in Springfield Missouri. A person doesn't realize how tall an elephant is until you ride one.

On the first day of hunting season, it seemed like the entire population of Missouri descended on Ft. Leonardwood and the deer disappeared. There was not one deer killed on the first day of hunting season, but there was always someone getting shot that day.

Lessons Learned

1. ***Commanders are responsible for the good and the bad things which happens under their command.*** – I should have told Ala parents exactly what happened instead of saying the CSM had final say on who stays and who goes in the Army.

2. ***Don't embarrass a person in public*** – The CSM should have talked to me about the situation in a private setting instead of creating a scene.

3. ***Making mistakes is part of learning and growing*** – SFC Burnett was correct in these are 18- and 19-year-olds new soldiers and they are supposed to make mistakes. Every new person in a new job makes mistakes, it is up to leaders to train them.

4. ***Do not judge a person by looks*** – I did not think Jenkins was going to make it because he was overweight, but he had determination and graduated Basic Training.

5. ***Listen*** – Do not think you know everything and listen to your subordinates. SFC Burnett's brilliant idea of providing additional training for trainees who failed a task increased the company's graduation rate and it save the Army money. SFC Woolery's guidance on how to qualify with a weapon belonging to someone else helped me to become a better marksman.

6. ***Treat people as you want to be treated*** – We were rough on trainees when they first arrived in the unit and we pushed them to do things they never thought they could do, but the trainees knew we really cared about them because we spent countless hours working with them to ensure they graduate.

7. ***Reward achievements*** – Rewarding for achieving goals creates motivation. We rewarded trainees with additional free time for achieving a 90% a or higher on Rifle Qualification. The Trainees normally received 45 minutes of free time to call or write love ones, we gave them an hour and let them have a day of soda and pizza. These rewards may seem small, but when you are restricted

260

to your movement and what you eat these things are highly important. Free time meant Drill Sergeants were not breathing hard on your back.

8. ***Let standards be known*** – When people know the standards they will work to achieve them. Every trainee was told the standards for graduations such as the completions of all foot marches, qualifying on their assigned M16, throwing two live grenades, passing their Physical Fitness and End-of-Cycle Tests, and pass the Battalion Commander Battalion Inspection. If the trainees did not achieve the standards, they were trained until they passed them or recycled to another company until they achieved the standards.

*1ˢᵗ **Row*** – 1LT Lewis, myself, 1SG Hunchberger, SSG Cronin, and kneeling PFC Lowe

*2ⁿᵈ **Row*** – SSG Ruiz, SGT McClanahan, West Point Cadet Meyers, SSG Pernell, West Point Cadet

*3ʳᵈ **Row*** – SSG Westbrook, SFC Burnett, SSG Welch, SSG Jackson

Backrow – SSG Guzman SSG Alley, SFC Otto

1st Row – 1LT Lewis, myself, 1SG Hunchberger, SGT McClanahan, and kneeling PFC Lowe

2nd Row – SSG Jackson, SSG McCoy, SSG Welch, SFC Rivera

Backrow – SSG Friend, SFC Burnett, SFC Otto, SSG Ruiz

LTC Kardos presenting me with my first Meritorious Service Medal at the end of my time as a Basic Training Company Commander.

Captain McQueen
B Company 2-47 Infantry Regiment
August 11, 1998

Captain McQueen:

Please accept both my thanks and my congratulations for your leadership of an incredible group of individuals. I expected basic training to be challenging both mentally and physically. I expected the Drill Sergeants and other NCOs to be serious individuals dedicated to training civilians how to be soldiers. What I did not expect was the Drill Sergeants and other NCOs of B Company 2-47. I have always found it to be the case in life that any group of individuals united to perform a task includes those who are effective, those who are extremely effective, and those with some room for growth, until now. Every single individual working with us privates was very good at their job.

I have been a teacher for six years. For the first year, I was relatively ineffective at my job because no one had taught me how to teach and I had no experience at doing so. Now, because of the patience of my students, colleagues, and mentors, I hope I am effective in exposing young folks to the concepts, terms, and ways of doing business important in agriculture and making sure they have the critical thinking skills they need to succeed at farming or agribusiness. I knew from the very beginning of my career that I was responsible to teach specific information and economic and scientific tools. What I didn't know was that, for the students to learn from me, I had to find a teaching style consistent with my personality. Somehow, the Drill Sergeants in B Company 2-47 figured that out right away. I am confused as to how a group of Drill Sergeants with such varying levels of experience and very different personalities can all be good at their job. Either the army does an extremely good job of training folks to be Drill Sergeants, you and First Sergeant Hunchberger are exceptional leaders, or the company is simply comprised of good folks; I suspect it is the synergy of all three.

Usually in a letter written to compliment someone, I try to point out at least one thing that could be improved to add credibility to the positive experiences I am sharing. In this case, I honestly can not think of anything that could have been done more effectively. Even to me it sounds unrealistically positive to say that every individual under you; First Sergeant Hunchberger, each of the Drill Sergeants, SSG Cronin, SGT McClanahan, and Private Lowe, did an incredible job of training our company and gaining and maintaining the respect of 240 new soldiers but that is what I am saying. There is not one individual in the forementioned list that I would not be proud to work with in any venture. There is also not one individual in the forementioned list that at anytime showed anything but respect for, and commitment to, their job, the company, battalion, and brigade, the U.S. army, this country, and one another. It would seem that an individual faced with the hours and responsibilities of being a Drill Sergeant or serving another role in the training of new soldiers would have a challenging time maintaining such loyalty to the mission. As a civilian, it is incredibly difficult for me to understand but fantastic to see and beautiful to be a part of if only for eight weeks. I am extremely proud to have been part of the company.

In addition to congratulating you on the work of yourself and of these individuals, I would like to thank you personally. I was just one individual among 240 but several times you took the time to help me be a better soldier. You were always kind and spent the time to find out our goals and strengths; this endeared you to us privates. We didn't initially understand the respect that your rank commands; in fact, we didn't begin to get nervous around officers until we were taught, and therefore were responsible to know, how to salute. Quite obviously we had no idea what we were doing and, in fact, saluted incorrectly or at an inappropriate time more often than not. Every time I was wrong, you corrected me; every time. Because you were straightforward and kind in doing so, I became confident enough to salute in many situations where I had no idea if it was appropriate. I knew if I was right,

265

you would respond and, if I was wrong, I would know.

We had lots of practice saluting because you were always there. We always knew that, when it was an important day for us and most of the time even when we didn't know it was an important day for us, you would be there. It got to the point where we could only tell if it was a pivotal day if the chaplain was there because we became used to your presence. It is difficult to explain how much it means to a private in basic training to have the company captain inquire about their family, plans, and performance. I wouldn't need to even attempt to explain if you could have heard the excitement with which my roommates and platoon mates talked about their interactions with you; I suppose you will just need to take my word for it that your presence made an incredible difference in our training and our respect for you and for the rank you represent.

It wasn't just the privates that held a great deal of respect for you, your Drill Sergeants did as well. We were repeatedly told in reception and even at times in basic training that the enlisted are the backbone of the army; in fact, that it is the enlisted who do all the work. I had and have my suspicions about the reality of this but you should know, in the eyes of your NCO's, this perception in no way applies to you. It is an incredible compliment to you that the Drill Sergeants are immensely comfortable with you and, in fact, consider you to be a good friend as well as their commander. Several of them commented that they too could count on you to be there, whatever the reason. This seems to mean as much to them as your presence meant to us. I do not yet understand the roles and responsibilities of commissioned versus noncommissioned officers and the SOPs for interaction but if your relationship with the NCOs at B Company 2-47 is the norm, it is a beautiful system.

I wish I could give back to you and each of the NCOs what you gave to me; I wish I could play the role in your life you played in mine. While I realize it is your job and the best thing I can do is use what I learned to be a good soldier, it will be an honor and a great joy should you ever identify a place or time in your life where I can be of any assistance; you simply need to let me know and I will gladly be there. In the meantime, however, please know that I am a stronger and more patient person because of your efforts and those of the NCOs of B Company 2-47. As such, I can not help but be a better teacher, colleague, and friend. I take with me nothing but great appreciation for the knowledge and skills I gained, all that was provided to me, and the respect that was shown for the job and us privates. Again, thank you and congratulations.

Soldiers were encouraged to write about their experiences in Basic Training. This may seem strange, but the soldiers were honest and their letters would provide us with information on how we can become better leaders. Letter from <u>Professor Wachenheim</u> whom the other Trainees called "Grandma". She was a college professor who graduated from Basic Training.

AC/RC (HOUSTON)

The advisor position was headquartered in Oklahoma with an assignment to Houston. I wanted to stay in Oklahoma, but I was told there was no on post housing and I could not afford to live off post because houses were expensive. Oklahoma had no Black Radio at the time and I loved my Soul Music, so off to Houston I went.

When my family arrived in Houston we went house hunting. We searched for four months before we found a house. Single male homeowners had the cleanest most organized homes which we visited. I could not believe how dirty the homes were for people who had children. There were writings on the walls, holes in the walls, clothes laying on the floor, and dirty dishes.

We stayed in a hotel in downtown Houston near the medical center while looking for a house. It was an eye-opening experience to meet people who were going through cancer treatment. The patient and their families were very nice to my family. We celebrated Halloween at the hotel and they gave my kids candy.

We selected a nice house in Pearland, Texas based on the neighbor. Our house which was 2,100 square feet and costs $107k. I would tell my friends; I lived in the projects because houses on my street were the cheapest in the community. The other houses in the community ranged from $250k to million-dollar plus homes. The neighborhood had seven parks, 5 pools, and a golf course.

Matthew, our neighbor, worked for NASA and was from North Carolina. Houston is the biggest city which I have ever lived in. I hated Houston at first because it was so big. Matthew told me to learn the streets of, Westheimer, Richmond, and Main and the inner and outer

267

loops of Houston. Once I learned those roads, I became more comfortable with Houston.

Matthew loved his nieces, nephews, and other kids in the neighborhood so much he brought them any gift they wanted for Christmas. He was so well known at Toys or Us, they would open the store only for him. When I went TDY, Matthew would cut my grass. I jokingly told him, I don't cut no one's yard without getting paid. Where I was from, we were taught to cut the grass low so we would not have to cut it often. Matthew told me in our community if a person cut their grass too low and the grass dies, the Home Owners Association would send a letter to homeowners for an unkept yard. Matthew told me to invest in the Texas Tomorrow College Fund for my kids which was a great investment tip because it enabled my kids to attend college without having any student loans.

Our other neighbor, Ken, was a Master Chief Petty Officer in the Submarine field and after his retirement he worked for an engineer company. Ken loved his rum and coke. He spilled his drink every day on my car while talking to me. I should have charged him for a paint job.

Unit I

I was assigned to a unit which had twelve Active-Duty Service Members whose job was to train Reservist on Military Tactics. Everyone was very professional, but there was little guidance given which made it hard for us to understand what we were supposed to do. There were no manuals or SOPs (Standard Operating Procedures) to read. We never advised any unit according to the job which the Army assigned us to do.

Fifty-percent of the soldiers were twice divorced. I ask Parker why he married so many times and he said it was an addiction and I told him that's a bad addiction to have. Parker was 6'1 and 260 lbs. He made the Atlanta Falcons football team and they were going to pay him $100k, but he turned it down because it was not guaranteed money. I took Parker to pick-up his Harley Davidson motorcycle which was having new handlebars installed because the old handlebars made him look small. I told Parker no matter which type of handlebars he gets, they could not make him look small.

SFC Danny was a Houston native who grew up in 5th Ward and had been shot before. I asked him why and what did his parents say. Danny said his cousin started a fight in a club and some guys chased them out of the club and shot up his car. I asked him what did his parents say and he said his father told him it was his fault.

I would tell Danny I was going into 5th Ward and beat up someone to establish my reputation. Danny responded you are going to take a "L". He said it would be 2 against 1 or 10 against 1, but I was going to take an "L" and he said we know every car which comes in the neighborhood. I drove in the neighborhood for lunch and everyone was staring at my car, I knew from that moment he was telling the truth. Somedays I would tell Danny I was going to kick his ass and he would say you better increase your life insurance policy. He could bench press over 400lbs.

One day I returned from lunch and noticed a cylinder concrete block thrown through his car window. I thought I was dreaming so I looked at it two more times. I told Danny what happened and he said he knew who did it and he was going to call me to get him out of jail and I told him my phone would be turned off and if I found out he was in jail, I was going to court martial his ass. I did not hear anything of the incident so I guess nothing happened. SFC Danny was a great soldier who I later saw in Korea. He was always talking shit and he picked me up along with a female soldier who was riding with him in Korea and said he was going to beat the bricks off someone's daughter. I just shook my head in disbelief of what he said in front of his passenger. I guess it was true because she sat there quietly.

SSG Gregory was the unit's supply sergeant who drove a Cadillac which was stolen and used in a robbery. I told him I have never seen a 30-year-old white guy with a Cadillac because in my neighborhood only big fat Black men drove Cadillacs. SSG Gregory was a go getter. He was the first person I met who flipped houses. We later completed the Houston to Austin 168-mile bike ride in two days.

SFC Brown was a hard-working soldier. He worked two jobs after he completed his Army job. We asked him, "How did he propose to his third wife" and he answered "can I perform oral sex on you" and she said "I do". We laughed hysterically. It hurt me when I found out he was killed by a jealous ex-husband.

We had a Black Soldier who was one match away from becoming a Chess Grandmaster. He told me after his wife died, he gave up his dream on becoming a Grandmaster. I told him I would have participated in a chest tournament at McDonald's to become a Grandmaster. He beat me in less than 10 moves.

Everyone in the unit had a side hustle because there was very little for us to do. We had soldiers who sold Amway, delivered pizza,

270

worked for Home Depot. I was involved in a Telecommunication Company which wanted people to changed their phone numbers or electrical services to their company. I went to meetings and spent numerous hours on the phone trying to convince people to spend $500 on a kit or change their number or electric services so I could get a portion of their bills. People tried convincing me it was a pyramid scheme, but I was hard headed. You can make money if you are the first one in the group. I would have made more money working ten hours a week than the time I spent working with the Telecommunication Company. I should have followed SSG Gregory's lead in flipping houses. The communication skills which I learned from the telecommunication company helped when I became a Recruiting Company Commander because it gave me salesmanship skill.

Captain Pete worked as pizza deliveryman. One day it was cold and rainy while he was working. People were stiffing him on tips. He delivered pizza to a million-dollar home and the owner left him a .33¢ tip. Pete knocked on the owner's door and told him he needed it more than him.

Augie was a twice divorced captain who claimed he was a ladies' man. He would come to work every day and ask us to smell his finger which he supposedly used during sex. We would say "ewe, get the fuck out of here"! I wanted to find out if he really was a ladies' man, so I went with him to a club. Augie dressed like a man out of GQ Magazine and danced like John Travolta. In spite of the way he dressed and danced he would look for the drunkest and ugliest girl to take home. I asked him why he picked up ugly women and he said because he was scared of women. I found it hard to believe a twice divorcee who dressed like a model, danced like John Travolta, and spoke Spanish although it was bad Spanish was afraid of women. I spoke better Spanish than him and his parents were Mexican. I reported this back to the guys in the unit and we kidded him for months about this.

271

Some of the soldiers enrolled in graduate school. Captain Tonya received $5k from the Bush Family to obtain her Master's Degree from the University of Houston.

I choose to become a physical fitness guru. I participated in the 168-mile Houston to Austin bike ride with SSG Gregory and ran the Houston Marathon.

Houston to Austin Bike Ride

I can't believe rode 168-miles on a mountain bike which I purchased from Greg Greene in Panama for $100. The price of the bike included a fishing rod and reel and a 380 pistol which was only accurate for five feet. I installed shock absorbers, new tires, and a gel seat on the bike in preparation for the ride. I rode the bike twice a day for three months prior to the race. Matthew, my neighbor, told me don't ride on Highway 285 because people threw trash at him, tried to run him off of the road, and called him nigger. I could not believe the ignorance of those people because Matthew is a great guy and he worked for NASA. I took his advice and practiced in the mornings and after work for four months. The manager of the golf course in my neighborhood confronted me about riding on the roads around the golf course. He told me the golfers were upset with me riding on the golf course and I told him if they were any damn good, they would hit me. I continued to ride on the golf trail because I was nowhere near the golfers, the manager was trying to intimidate me and my HOA dues paid for usage of the golf course.

The day of the ride, SSG Gregory and I met a woman who never trained for the bike ride and she told us when she first climbed on her new bike, she fell off of it and the kids in the neighborhood laughed at her. I laughed at her for getting on a new bike for the first time the day of the race. We met some people who were roller blading the race. The last one which I saw was at mile 92.

My butt hurt like crap from the bike ride. I paid $30 dollars for a gel seat and after twenty-five miles, it felt like I was riding on a steel pole. I did not believe in wearing a helmet, but it was required for the bike ride. I haphazardly wore mine. I was traveling 50-mph downhill when a guy passed me and crashed into someone which resulted in his helmet splitting open. That accident made a believer out of me and I fastened my helmet tightly. The guy survived. The ball bearings on my bike broke around mile 80. A repairman fixed the bike as best he could and told me there was a major repair station 30-miles away. I rode the bike 30-miles with a wobbly front tire to the repair station. I was riding down a steep hill at 40 an hour and my tire was wobbling so much; I thought it was going to fall off. I barely made it to the station and a gentlemen repaired it and said the bike may make it to the end which it did. SFC Gregory and I completed 92 miles the first day and the remaining distance the next day. The race wore me out and I never climbed on a bike again for two years.

Houston Marathon

Captain Silerio, my OCS Classmate, and I ran the Houston Marathon. We would run five miles every day. I encouraged SFC Smith (Smitty) every day to run with us in the Marathon and he said "no way". Smitty ran a minimum of four miles every day at lunch in 90 degree or higher weather without a shirt. I could not believe a heavy-set Black guy would be crazy enough to run in such hot weather. We would take bets on which mile he would collapse on, but it never happened. He would return to the unit sweaty and three shades darker. He did not need a tan so I never understood why he was running in the middle of the day without a shirt.

Captain Silerio and I trained in 50-degree weather and we ran 20 miles ten days before the Marathon which is crazy because it doesn't give your body enough time to recover. My reasoning for doing this was because if I could run 20-miles then I could gut out the other 6 miles.

The temperature was 70-degrees with 75 percent humidity at the start of the race which was unusual for January. I knew this would be trouble for me because my run times in hot weather are slow. The professional marathon runners were doing high leg lift sprints before the race. I told one of them there is no need to sprint before the race because we have 26-miles to run. I was tired from watching them. The night before the race I had a dream about finishing in the top ten percent of the race contestants. The sounding of the gun destroyed my dream because when I started the race, the professional runners were a mile ahead of me.

When Captain Silerio and I hit mile 13 at 1 hour and 37 minutes, Smitty came by us saying "Hooah" which shocked us because he refused our request every day to run in the marathon. I advised Smitty to slow down because we had 13 miles left, a mile later we saw Smitty

275

walking and he was thinking about dropping out. Silerio was going strong and I told him to continue on and I was going to bring Smitty in. The heat was starting to get to me and I remembered the advice a 75-year-old runner gave me which is to drink water at every water point. The man was participating in his 79th Marathon. The Houston Marathon's course runs through neighborhoods. Homeless people would tell us to speed up and people whose houses where along the course would give us M&M candy and water. A representative from Gallery Furniture gave me a hat because he said I was looking bad which was true. I wore the hat for four years. A couple was married at mile 13 and Belly Dancing students danced for us around mile 20. It was so hot almost 400 people fell out during the last two miles from heat cramps. I told Smitty I am not quitting and I will crawl the last mile to finish the race. There were four of us from the unit and we all finished the raced. I was so dehydrated, I drunk a 6-pack of Schlitz Malt Liquor Beer in less than five minutes and didn't get drunk.

Seafood Buffet

I exercised three times per day, 5 days a week in Houston. I ran in the mornings, lifted weights during lunch and after work. I believed in the saying "Leaders lead from the front". I worked out with a 73-year-old gentleman who exercised with Joe Weider when he was young. He would always get on me for working my upper body and told me, I need to spend more times on my legs which was true. I told him women preferred arms over legs and I always wore long pants to cover up my skinny legs. He did 50 pull-ups and 50 dips before he started his workout. The guys in the gym said I should have seen him three years ago when he did 100 repetitions of each exercise before starting his workout.

I worked out at a gym in downtown Houston which Professional Dancers belonged to. The dancers were nice looking women who drove corvettes and other expensive cars. They worked out harder than the guys because they wanted the cash flow to continue. The dancers would always invite me to visit their club, but I turned them down because I could not afford to make payments on another vehicle. They were very persistent and one told me to just come at lunch for the seafood buffet. I enjoy seafood and I told my fellow soldiers about the lunch. The rules were no drinking and no lap dances. We went in our uniforms and a married man in line asked us if we are supposed to be here and Danny said "Are you supposed to be here" which quickly shut him up. The club was very nice and it had the best seafood and view of any high-end restaurant I ever attended. The buffet contained shrimp, lobster, crab cakes, crab legs, hard shell crab, scallops, squid, octopus, fish, and seven different types of cake. We slept for two hours at work after returning from the club. It was a well spent $20.00.

277

Unit II

Brigade sent word down to the unit stating only 8 out of 16 Active-Duty soldiers where needed and told the remaining of us to go and find a job since we had been in Houston less than a year and the Army would not approve of us going to another unit outside of Houston. Another case of senior leaders not taking care of subordinates. A couple of us took jobs with a section in the Division thinking we would be evaluating and training Reserve Units. My job ended up helping the Division find its subordinate units. The Brigade told us the Reservists would be our raters and senior raters according to the Commanding General. Every Active-Duty soldier hated this decision. There were two Active-Duty female Majors requesting an Active-Duty soldier be involved in the Rating Chain. They asked an Active-Duty LTC who was an Infantry Officer, to be in our rating chain and he refused. When the LTC arrived in the mornings he would stay in his office until 11:30 am for lunch, returned from lunch at 1:30pm, and stay in his office until 4:30pm. He was overweight, lazy, and retired on Active Duty which means he was riding out his time in the Army before retiring. I never saw him do any exercise. His laziness cost soldiers their careers.

The job which I was assigned to do was to make a spreadsheet and contact over 300 units to tell them they belonged to the 75th Infantry Division. The units never received any guidance and funding from the Division and told me they didn't belong to the Division. I hated the job because I saw people not working and my skills as an Infantry/Signal Officer were not being used. I changed my spreadsheet with units over 30 times because units constantly told me they didn't belong to the 75th. I received a counseling statement because I gave my Reserve supervisor an incorrect spreadsheet. He said I wasn't paying attention when I gave him an old spreadsheet. I asked him, why didn't he give the other soldiers counseling statements one who came in late

278

for work and the other one was drunk on duty and he couldn't answer the question. I signed the counseling statement in the morning and called Signal Branch in the afternoon and told them to get me out of this craziness as soon as possible. When I contacted the Branch Officer, he asked me what was I doing in Houston and I told him Signal Branch sent me here. I could not believe no one from the Signal Branch Office knew I was there. I was assigned as a Recruiting Company Commander in Winston-Salem, North Carolina because the Signal Branch Officer said I needed more Command time to avoid not becoming a Major. I give him credit; he did look out for me.

TDY

I was constantly sent TDY to inform units, the 75th Division was their higher headquarters and to find out if they needed any support. I witnessed the most disciplined unit which I have ever seen in the Army. It was a Transportation Unit in Louisiana which was led by a Black Female 1SG. The unit returned from an Iraq Deployment six-months prior to my visit. 1SG had the unit operating better than a Basic Training Unit. Enlisted soldiers were required to be at Parade Rest when speaking with Senior Non-Commissioned Officers (NCO) and at the Position of Attention when speaking to an Officer. The 1SG made a soldier do pushups after she saw him not standing at Position of Attention while speaking with me. The unit had a high rate of attention. I would follow the 1SG on any mission no matter how dangerous it is. I was so impressed with her leadership skills; I wanted to join the unit after the encounter.

I evaluated a well-disciplined Signal Unit at Ft. Chaffee, Arkansas. The unit set up quicker and better than any Active-Duty Signal Unit. The soldiers knew their job, arrived on time at training sites, and setup their communication equipment in less than 45 minutes. Those two units showed me what a unit looks when it is led by strong and disciplined leaders.

We were sent to Colorado for a meeting to inform units the 75th was their higher headquarters and ask if they needed any support. Some of the units knew 75th was their higher headquarters, but they never received any support from the Division. The Colorado units had great leaders because they were operating on their own without any support from higher headquarters.

A group of us went to eat at a nice restaurant in Colorado Springs and afterwards we walked into the best-looking bar I have ever seen which was a Country and Western. They had a large video screen, a dance floor the size of a gym floor, restaurant, and two bars. It was put together nicely.

A manager of a Gentlemen Club saw us walking downtown Colorado Springs and invited us to come in his club. We were stunned when we walked in because the majority of the people in there were couples. I asked the manager "did we come on couples' night" and he responded "it's like this every night" and I asked him "is it so boring around here that couples have to go to a Gentleman's Club for fun", and he laughed. One of the dancers came up to us and began telling us her life story. She said "her husband is in the Army and she dances because it's easy money and it supports her two young kids. She said, it makes her mad when her husband spends all of her earnings on one girl. She said she preferred him to spend her money on several girls instead of one because if he spent money on one dancer it meant he liked the dancer more than her. I felt like Dr. Phil after hearing her story. We each drunk a beer and gave her some money for her kids' college funds.

Houston Rodeo

Matthew told me in order to be a Texan, I had to attend a rodeo. I went to one and I was amazed at how clean the cows and pigs were for the livestock competition. Livestock owners used buckets and sponges to wipe their livestock. The livestock was cleaner than their owners. I was invited to the barbecue cookoff, but I was unable to attend because of work. If I was there, I would have free range to taste barbecue from all contestants.

One of the Majors, a former member of the 118th MP Company, attended a club held in the Astrodome. She was trying to break up a fight between two women when they turned on her. She asked them to kick and punch her from the neck down because she did not want her $300 cowgirl hat and expensive earrings damaged. She was very funny. She would go on dates and guys would not invite her for a second date because of her salary. She said the only good thing she received out of those dates was a free meal.

Car Accident

People in Houston drive crazy. They constantly were constantly speeding and running red lights. I saw a person driving over 75 mph reading a newspaper with two cell phones to his ears. I said to myself "hopefully his balls were cut off at birth so he could not infect the world with his stupidness".

I started to drive like Houstonians which resulted in me having an accident. I was in a hurry returning from lunch and I pulled in front of a car driven by a guy from India causing him to hit the left front fender of my Isuzu Amigo. I was found guilty by the police officers who were females. The officers told me to show up for court and the judge will throw it out because the other person never shows up to court. I went to court in my military uniform which you are not supposed to do and the judge was a former Military Officer. When I turned around, my jaw dropped to the floor because I saw the person who I hit in court which was the total opposite of what the police officers told me. I spoke with the guy I hit before the judge called us up. The other driver said it was an accident and he was not going to press charges because my insurance company paid for the accident. The judge threw the case out. I was definitely lucky the other driver did not press any charges.

Atlanta Airport

I met a lot of famous people at Atlanta's Airport while returning from a TDY trip. I met Fred Whitfield a calf roping champion. We talked for an hour while waiting on our airplane. When I told co-workers I met Fred Whitfield and they asked why didn't I get his autograph and I told them I didn't know who he was and they kidded me the entire day for not knowing who he was. I met Fred twelve years later in Washington D.C. at an event where he was sponsored by the Army. Fred was wearing his cowboy clothing when a black guy asked him "how much do they pay you brother to wear that" and Fred responded "about $3 million dollars".

We heard girls screaming down the corridor and Fred and I looked at each trying to figure out what the screams where about. I told him I was going to check it out and when I did, I found girls getting Bernie Mac's autograph. He was riding in an airport cart. I approached him to shake his hand. I was nervous and gave him a light hearted handshake and Bernie Mac said "Boy you better shake my hand like a man", I did and we both were laughing afterwards. He asked me where I was from and congratulated me for being in the Army. Bernie was a down to earth man who passed away too early in life.

I met Brigadier General Charles E. McGee a Tuskegee Airman on the same day. He was wearing his Tuskegee Airman Jacket. We talked for about 5 minutes about before the departure of his plane. I wished we had more time to talk so I could hear some of his stories. Meeting three famous people in one location and on the same day was a memorable experience.

Houstonians

There are a lot of famous people in Houston. I drove an Isuzu Amigo which lacked air condition so my coworkers refused to ride with me for lunch, so they were my personal chauffers. We ate lunch at different places because there was not a Dining Facility in the unit. One summer it only dropped under 90 degrees three times between Memorial Day and Labor Day. I met a couple of famous people during my lunches.

I met Haywood Jefferies who was a former professional football player in a grocery store. I knew who Haywood was because he was from Greensboro, North Carolina, he went to high school with my cousin, and I followed his careers at NC State University and Houston Oilers. When I mentioned my cousin's name, he invited me to his house which was in the same community I lived in. Haywood showed me his house, gave me a tour of Houston, and told me about the crazy life of a professional athlete. He gave me great advice which was not to purchase a million-dollar home because it cost $30 thousand or more for up keep not including the payment. He told me he could have lived in a million-dollar home, but chose a $250 thousand home which allowed him to live off of his NFL earnings after his playing days ended. My children played with his children and he invited us to his Christmas party which had a live band. Haywood was contemplating about running for Mayor of Pearland after I left.

Steve McNair and I shared the same barber and he said Steve never asked for a free haircut unlike other professional athlete and gave him $100 tips. I told him, I could only afford to tip him $2. He said Steve was a down to earth country boy who took care of his friends. He was a groomsman at Steve's wedding. Steve flew all of his groomsman to the weeding, gave them $300 each, and then paid for

285

everything at his bachelor's party. His comments about Steve made him my favorite athlete and it was sad about his untimely death.

I saw Charles Barkley at a restaurant and a coworker asked me would it bothering him if she asked for his autograph. I told her the only things he could say was "yes or ok". Barkley happily signed an autograph for her. Barkley was bigger in person than on television which made me understand, how he body slammed Shaquille O'Neal.

I met a DEA Agent at a restaurant who had been shot nine times. He told me there have been plenty of DEA Agents who had been shot before, but the news was kept under wrap. I gained a lot more respect for the dangers which DEA Agents face on a daily basis after the encounter.

The Division had on display a WWII helmet with a dented front from a rifle round. We were hosting an event for WWII Veterans who were members of the 75th Infantry Division and one of them spotted the helmet and told us it was his. He was definitely lucky because if he was not wearing a helmet, he would not be alive today because it was a perfect head shot by an enemy soldier.

We presented Christmas Cards to Veterans at the VA Hospital in Houston where we met a very humbled man. He was a Korean War Veteran and a double amputee who was reading the Bible when we came into his room to present him a Christmas Card. He told us he was the luckiest man in the world because he survived the war and had 13 wonderful children. All of us teared up afterwards.

I met a white Blues singer who had a nice raspy voice. If you never saw her, you would think it was Billie Holiday singing. She had a beautiful voice, but drunk like a fish. I asked her why did she drink so much and she said "the Blues is sad music and drinking made her think of dark thoughts". The way she was drinking I don't think she made it to the age of 50.

My biggest regret in Houston was not joining the Triple Nickel Parachute (555th) organization. The soldiers of the 555th Infantry

Battalion were the first Black Parachutists. I knew very little about them. A former original member of the 555th asked me to join the organization, but I told him I was leaving Houston in three weeks. I should have said "yes" and then offered to buy him lunch to pick his mind. He retired from the Army and the Federal Government.

Importance of Standards

The section of the 75th Division which I worked in could have been a great unit, but too many Senior Officers were focused on their personnel careers instead of training their subordinates. The Army standards for conducting a physical fitness test were never adhered to. Active-Duty soldiers had to take a Physical Fitness test twice a year. There were soldiers in the Division including Officers who went two or more years without taking a Physical Fitness test. Active-Duty soldiers wore the Army Physical Fitness clothes when doing a Physical Fitness Test. Soldiers in the 75th showed up in civilian clothes. It looked like they went shopping at Walmart before the Physical Fitness Test. I told someone LTC Kardos would have fired the entire Chain of Command on the spot if he saw it. Graders counted substandard pushups and sit-ups. I chewed out a former Basic Training Commander for counting a female's incorrect pushups. I told him he knew what the standards were because he was a Basic Training Commander. He was trying to pick up a female Officer who was doing incorrect pushups, but it did not work.

People showed up late or did not show up at all for Reserve Drills. My senior rater would show up for four hours then leave for his civilian job. I told my rater to hold him to the same standard as he holds his subordinates and it is illegal to get paid for three days of work and only work four hours. He told me to be quiet and the boss could do whatever he wants to.

I saw soldiers who worked full-time in the unit and were assigned to a Drill Unit, not drill with their assigned unit on the day their unit was drilling. They would wear civilian clothes and do their civilian job while their units were drilling and then put themselves on Drill Orders on days their units were not working. I complained about this and no one did anything because it was the way things were always done. There were great Junior Officers and Enlisted Soldiers in the

288

unit, but they became frustrated because of a lack of leadership and I was definitely one of them.

Leadership gained more respect for my talents after I trained Division soldiers on the Squad Automatic Weapon (SAW). I was an Infantry Officer for four years and I knew the SAW like the back of my hand.

There were a lot of great soldiers in the unit and half of the unit which I was assigned to consisted of policemen, firemen, and teachers. People knew I wasn't afraid to work and I was offered three great jobs from people whom I worked with. Two of the jobs were with established companies and included stock options. The most lucrative job offer I received, was inspecting newly built houses and receiving $600 – $800 for each house sold. The company built and sold a thousand houses. I had fourteen years in the Army and I was not about to give up those six years.

Houston is a nice city with great people. I learned the importance of establishing standards and enforcing them. The Department of the Army failed the soldiers of the 75th. There were great soldiers in the unit, but senior leaders were not held accountable for their actions. It is mind boggling to believe a Division did not know which units belonged to them. The firing of a couple of commanders would have caught the attention of other leaders. It was shocking to see how units who upheld Army Standards performed compared to those who did not.

Lessons Learned

1. *Hold people accountable* – Department of the Army did not hold leaders accountable for their actions. I believe there was no need for Active-Duty Soldiers to be in the 75th because leaders knew what to do, but they were not held accountable for their inaction.

2. *Use the skills of personnel assigned to your organization* – I was an Infantry and Signal Officer who did spreadsheets instead of training or evaluating units. I only evaluated one unit and trained two units on the Saw machine gun in the 18 months which I was stationed there. It was a waste of Army personnel, time, and money.

3. *Leaders place their subordinates in positions to succeed* – Army leaders should have placed Active-Duty soldiers in jobs to help their careers and there should have been an Active-Duty leader in our rating scheme.

4. *Know your subordinates* – In this scenario know what units belong to you. I was shocked the 75th Division did not know which units belonged to them and the units did not know the 75th were their higher headquarters An Active-Duty Division Commander would have been fired on the spot if they did not which units belonged to him.

5. *Learn your area of operation* – I disliked Houston when I first arrived because of its size, but once I learned the inner and outer loops, Westheimer, Richmond, and Main Street I felt confident to move around Houston without a map.

6. *Participate in your community* – Volunteer or support a Church or other organization in your area. We distributed Christmas Cards to Veterans and I participated in the Houston Marathon and Bike Ride to Austin to raise money for Muscular Dystrophy and Multiple Sclerosis.

7. ***Do your best because others are watching*** – It is hard to do a job which you know is meaningless. I disliked my job, but a lot of people saw me working with a smile which resulted in me receiving three exceptional job offerings.

8. ***Greet everyone you meet*** – I was able to get discounted meals, tickets, and other services just by being respectful. Saying "Hi and How you are doing" which puts people at ease and shows you care about them.

RECRUITING COMMAND

I was assigned as the commander for the Winston-Salem Recruiting Company which was part of the Raleigh Recruiting Command in North Carolina to increase my chances of becoming a Major. Winston-Salem Recruiting Company consisted of six stations: Greensboro, Winston-Salem, Mt. Airy, Wilkesboro, High Point, and Asheboro. I knew the Winston-Salem area like the back of my hand because I grew up in the area. I knew the area so well; I was showing the recruiters short cuts to get to their recruiting areas.

The first person I met as the Winston-Salem Company Commander was retired 1SG Billy Martindale. SSG Martindale could sell shit to flies. He put ten of my family members in the Army. He was such a great recruiter that he put me in the Army twice. He also hired my cousin for a summer job based on my previous work with him. It was a surreal experience to be in charge of someone who put me in the Army twice. He gave me a lot of great advice as a commander. He told me the way you can tell if recruiters are not visiting their schools is to ask students if they know the name of their school recruiter. This was a true statement because if students didn't know the names of their school recruiter, then they would be less likely to join the Military. Most students knew the names of their National Guard Recruiters as compared to the names of their Active-Duty Recruiters. National Guard Recruiters lived in the high schools because their recruits could go to Basic Training after completing their Junior Year in High School and to AIT (Advance Individual Training) after graduating. This meant rising Seniors would be getting paid during their Senior Year of High School. Active-Duty Recruiters were focused on students who were about to graduate. Active-Duty Recruiters can enlist Seniors during their Senior Year of High School, but they will not be getting paid.

292

Seniors would be put in the Delayed Entry Program (DEP). The problem with DEP is the longer a recruit is in DEP the more likely they would not go to Basic Training. When you are dealing with 17- or 18-year-olds, anything can happen such as a relationship break- up, injury, law violation, or buyer's remorse about joining the Military.

Winston-Salem Recruiting Company was the 4th worst recruiting company in 2nd Brigade when I arrived. I was shocked because North Carolina is one of the states which has a plenty of Veterans.

The previous Winston-Salem Company Commander had 14 years of Active-Duty Service and resigned from the Army probably because he didn't want to give his ex-wife half of his retirement pay. The First Sergeant and four of six Station Commanders were relieved in the first month of my Command. The First Sergeant gave the best motivation speeches which I have ever heard. He was relieved because he told the Command Group, they were dumping bad recruiters on the company and he was more concerned with fulfilling the missions of small recruiting stations instead of large recruiting stations.

First Sergeant was correct in telling the Command Group they were giving us bad recruiters. Four Station Commanders were relieved for not making mission and two recruiters were placed in the company despite their previous commanders saying they should return to their units because they were doing illegal things as recruiters. One of the recruiters was constantly being investigated for having relationships with recruits and the other recruiter was using his Government Credit Card for purchasing gas for his personal car and paying for his electric bill.

The Command Group relieved 1SG because of his focus on small stations making missions. The mission of the four stations combined were nine compared to the large stations which had missions of 10 or more. I asked the Command Group to give me six months to work with 1SG, but they refused. 1SG was relieved and worked at the Battalion Headquarters for the last eight months of his Army Career.

293

1SG Richard Armour became the new First Sergeant of Winston-Salem Recruiting Company. He was a big man who easily benched pressed 405lbs three times. He played football for Central State where he was an NAIA All-American and attended the Philadelphia Eagle Training Camp.

1SG Armour brought some heat when he arrived. The second month after his arrival, the company made its mission for the first time in over seven years. We were very excited and the Brigade Commander sent me a letter of congratulations. The next month the company had over ten recruits who did not ship which is called a DEP Loss. The Brigade Commander sent me a letter of concern which stated I would be fired if this happens again. Recruiting is a brutal world because your career is in the hands of mostly 18- and 19-year-olds who may or may not ship for various reasons.

An Army study said every 90 days, someone will have a life changing experience such a relationship break-up, college withdrawal, release from a job, and etc. which is a true statement.

Recruiters

There are plenty of challenges working as a Military Recruiter. Recruiters have plenty of freedom unlike other service members who are stationed on Military bases were their time is more supervised. A commander places a lot of trust in their recruiters because recruiters are operating on their own in colleges, high schools, and the general public. Anything a recruiter does wrong will be magnified 10 times more than other soldiers because recruiters interact more with the community. Most recruiters did the right thing, but some would forget they were in the Army. There were recruiters who were late to work, drunk on duty, overweight, and not visiting assigned schools in their areas.

The worst complaint a commander could receive is a harassment complaint from a school about the actions of a recruiter. A harassment complaint can result in recruiters from all Military Branches being barred from the school. I investigated a case which a high school female accused a recruiter of harassment. The recruiter was doing his job of contacting high school students, but the parents did not like the recruiter contacting their daughter at high school and by phone which recruiters were required to do. Male recruiters have to walk a fine line when recruiting females and some of them refused to recruit females to avoid any potential harassment complaint. Our requirements where you always speak with a female in the presence of another recruiter, never call a recruit past 7:00pm, and never transport a female without a witness.

Recruiters spend a lot of time in their vehicles and eating fast food daily. Putting people in the Army was more important to recruiters in my company than physical fitness. I told them they are required to maintain a level of fitness because it's an Army Standard and they are the face of the Army. Students tend to gravitate towards Service Members who are in shape.

295

The first year of being a Recruiting Commander was hard. We had four new and inexperienced station commanders, a high DEP loss rate, and a couple of new recruiters who should have never been allowed to become full-time recruiters. When we made mission for the first time, I went to a recruiting station and found empty beer bottles in the trash can. I had another recruiter who was upset his former company did not give him an award once he left. I contacted his former unit and they told me the reason he did not receive an award because he was constantly being investigated for sexual harassment and his company commander requested, he not be allowed to become a full-time recruiter, but the Battalion leadership team disregarded their request. I contacted the Battalion CSM about these two individuals and he gave a dumb response which was "We converted 20 recruiters and 10% of them are bad and too bad you got them". I was furious at his dumb statement considering he had a body shaped like Newman from Seinfeld.

I received news from the Battalion Commander I was not selected for Major despite busting my ass in Recruiting working 70 hours or more a week with only Sundays off. My Center of Mass ratings from my previous jobs hurt my chances of making Major the first time. LTC Pederson, new Battalion Commander, told me the command did not take care of me after he found out I did not make Major. He was a physical stud who would give any soldier 4 days off and a Battalion Coin of Excellence if they beat him in a 2-mile race. The only person who beat him was a Body Building Supply Sergeant. He also said the Battalion did not send the best recruiters to the Winston-Salem Company. This confirmed what the previous First Sergeant said was true.

The second year of being a commander, was better because I learned from the mistakes made during the first year. 1SG and I realized that we had to cover more recruiting stations if we were going to turn around the company. Normally, the Commander and 1SG ride together because it shows the recruiters we are on the same page.

296

Recruiters would play mom against dad with the leadership team which meant if Company Commander said "no", the recruiters would go to the 1SG with their problems and convince him to say "yes". 1SG and I disregarded this policy of riding in separate cars, but we constantly communicated with each other before, during, and after work. I developed a bad attitude after not making Major and being chewed out by the Battalion Commander for DEP losses that I began to ride hard the recruiters who I felt were not pulling their weight. I would show up at three different Recruiting Stations a day when most Commanders would only visit one. At the end of the day, I would stay in stations who were not on track to make mission and help make telephone calls to potential soldiers. Majority of the time people would hang up on me, but this did not deter me. The recruiters complained to 1SG about me hanging around their stations for long time periods of time and he asked me to play the good guy while he played the bad guy. 1SG was a big teddy bear. The company was beginning to turn around when 1SG left because his time was up in the position.

1SG Robinson was a great First Sergeant who believed in physical fitness. He ran and lifted weights every day at 5:30am. I told 1SG my run time in two-miles was arounds 14-minutes and he told me I was not running to my potential. 1SG advised me to incorporate more sprints in my runs and I took LT Parks advice of sprinting on the straight aways and jogging on the curves. My run time only improved by 30 seconds. 1SG later made CSM and I saw him on the back of a financial magazine working for a Fortune 500 Company.

Recruiting is a very difficult job. Your career is in the hands of people who are not in the Army. You can't take things personal in Recruiting because people are going to say no to you. A famous rejection quote which I liked is "My brother served for the family and it is why I nor my child is joining the Military". Only 1 out of 10 persons may be qualified to join the Army, the others may be disqualified because of test scores, medical reasons, or law violations.

297

We had a stripper who achieved a high score on the ASVAB, but we could not enlist her because she was pending the trial date of a case involving the overdose death of her boyfriend. I said to myself, if we put her in the Army, every soldier would be calling to thank me because she was better looking than most models.

Recruiters have to be creative. They have to convince teachers to let students make up work or inform judges a recruit is joining the military so the recruit can pay for a law violation on the spot instead of going to court for the offense.

I negotiated a deal with a lawyer which allowed my cousin to join the Army in exchange for him signing over his $9k Signing Bonus for child support. We all reached an agreement and my cousin served four-years in the Army.

A high school classmate requested my help in getting his son in the Army. When I went to speak with his son, his mom told me I could not talk to her son unless I brought her a six-pack of beer. I went next door and purchased her a six-pack of beer. You have to do certain things to make mission.

DEP Losses

Recruits would not go in the Army for many different reasons such as medical, relationship breakup, injury, and law violations despite signing a contract to join. If a recruit stayed in the DEP pool for over 90 days or their recruiter did not check up on them often, there was a high probability they were not shipping.

Sometimes it felt like the Military Entrance Processing Station (MEPS) was working against recruiters. I had a recruit rejected because the doctor said he had too much acne on his back. Almost every teenager going through puberty has acne. I advised him to see a dermatologist. The dermatologist prescribed him medication for his acne problem which enabled him to ship to Basic Training. The crazy thing is he could not use the medicine in Basic Training.

I asked the Battalion Commander for a 30-day ship extension for a recruit who needed time to get his family a place to stay before entering the Army. The commander was hesitant because this sounded like a recruit who was not going to ship. The recruit told a doctor at MEPS, he smoked 2,000 joints in 30 days which resulted in the doctor saying he was an addict and rejecting his admission in the Army. I told the doctor, there is no way a person can smoke 2,000 joints in 30 days, heck Willie Nelson and Snoop Dogg can't do that. His recruiter called me with the news of his disqualification and I told her to put him out of the car immediately which was 60 miles from his home. She told me he became nervous after what I said and she could not in good conscious put out a person so far from his home. The Battalion's policy stated we do not have to transport a recruit back home who made untrue statements or refused to join for no reason at all.

A recruit asked his recruiters to be part of his marriage ceremony. He was scheduled to ship the next day and when the recruiters arrived the next day, his wife said he was not home. The recruiters saw his feet sticking out from under the bed and told him to come out. He refused to ship and we had to release him from his Army commitment.

Recruits would get a law violation or have a positive reading on a urinalysis test which prevented them from joining the Army.

Our policy for female recruits was to ship them to the Army in 30 days or less because they either became pregnant or their boyfriends would hold them back by threatening to break up with them if they joined the Army. I went with a recruiter to pick up a female for shipment and she was living with three other girls who had kids and I told the recruiter I would not be surprised if she was pregnant and he assured me she was not. When she arrived at the Charlotte processing station, they gave her a pregnancy test and the results came back positive.

We put a former UNC linebacker in the Army and when it came time to ship, he refused. 1SG went over to his apartment on his shipping day and gave him some forceful words of motivation in front of his girlfriend. He shipped to the Army as scheduled. I would have paid anything to hear that conversation. I guess 1SG's 20-inch biceps scared him.

One day the Battalion Commander called the company commanders to his location for a meeting because the Battalion suffered a lot of DEP losses. I had to drive three hours to his location for an ass chewing. The only benefits I received were a free hotel stay and food.

SFC Burnett was correct when he stated if Drill Sergeants knew how much time and effort it takes to get a person to join the Army, they would not be easily to dismiss them. It is deflating to recruiters to lose a recruit because recruiters put a lot of time and effort in getting a person to join the military. It is a waste of money for any Branch of Service when a recruit does not join.

300

Community Leaders

North Carolina has a lot of Veterans and a recruiting company cannot be successful without knowing the important Veterans in their area of operation. We had to work with judges. Judge McSwain, former Paratrooper, helped us get recruits in the Army. He did not say "Join the Army or Go to Jail", he worked with recruits in resolving their case in a timely manner so they could join the Army. Judge McSwain was once a judge for Child Support and every morning before work, he would stop at McDonald's and a local Grocery Store to pick-up Job Applications so when someone said they can't find a job to pay for child support, Judge McSwain would hand them an application and say "McDonald's and the grocery store are hiring".

I spoke with COL Bull Simons a Special Forces Soldier about getting a friend's son in the Army. I told COL Simons no branch of Service will take his friend's son because he had two DUIs under the age of 21 and a host of other charges. COL Simons said back in the old days the Army would take soldiers like him and I responded "Yes Sir, but today's Army does not take civilians with so many law violations". Once he found out all the charges the student had, he agreed with the Army's decision of not letting him join.

MG Leonard, Mayor of Thomasville, NC, was a strong supporter of the Military and we participated yearly in the Thomasville Memorial Day Parade which is known as the largest Memorial Day Parade in the Southeastern United States. If we had problems getting into any high schools, we would contact MG Leonard for assistance in getting into schools.

People think of drug dealers as uncaring people. A recruiter and myself met some drug dealers in a housing area where the recruiter was picking up a recruit. A drug dealer asked my help in getting a 16-year-

301

old on the right path. The drug dealer said "we have messed up our lives can you please do something to save this kid from messing his life up". I was impressed by what he asked of me. The 16-year-old was a high school dropout who I advised to return to school and graduate which will open up plenty of doors for him. I did not see him the following week selling drugs, so hopefully he took my advice and graduated.

Recruiters often work with Law Enforcement Agencies on finding potential recruits who need someone to show them the different options which can lead them to a successful life. I met a plenty of smart teenagers who just needed someone to tell them there is a better life waiting for them because they came from a dysfunctional home where no one cared about them.

Travel

There is a lot of traveling involved when one is working as a Recruiter. Recruiters traveled to the MEPs station in Raleigh or Charlotte to prepare recruits for the Military. Traveling to and from those MEPs stations were all-day events. If the Recruiters knew which MEPs doctors were difficult to process a recruit for induction in the Military, they would avoid that station and send the Recruit to another MEPs station.

Recruiting Stations are very spread out from the battalion and company headquarters, so the Battalion Commander would authorize Company Commanders to stay in hotels. Thank goodness, my first Battalion Commander made me join the clubs of Hertz, Hilton, Mariott, and etc. I traveled so often; I had free stays at major hotels.

On one occasion the Brigade held a conference at Myrtle Beach for the Battalions. The conference was held in the winter when rates were less expensive. I met some of my buddies from Panama and we decided to go out and have a few drinks. We saw a bar called Derrière and went to check it out and the bouncer said we don't sell beer, but you can go to the store across the street to buy beer and we will give you a cooler with ice for free. The bouncer said when you get to the counter ask for a $3 discount ticket. We did as the bouncer said and entered the bar with 4 cases of beer. When we entered the bar, the women were totally naked. We all started high-fiving each other like we hit the lottery. It was a fun experience which I paid for the next day. I almost missed the next day meeting because I was hung over.

Sometimes the Army set Recruiters up for failure. The Army would send Black Recruiters to remote areas where there were no Black People. Recruiting Command reasoning was Americans are color-blind when it came time to serve their country. I met a Black Recruiter who was sent to an area where no Black People had ever

303

lived in. The Recruiter only put one person in the Army in 14 months and the Recruiter was told by the locals he was not wanted there. He was finally moved to a more diverse area. I blamed his failure on his Command because they are supplied with a vast amount of information on the demographics of a Recruitment Area and the Command has the power to move recruiters to areas where the recruiter will be successful.

End of Recruiting

I visited over 80 high schools in two years. Most of the schools were receptive of Recruiters because we talked to students about different career options and we gave teachers gifts such as coffee mugs, key chains, and calendars. Recruiters have to talk to everyone to be successful. The recruiters would be upset with me because I would speak to any class if a teacher requested regardless of grade level. The Army's mission is graduating students and recruiters cannot put in anyone under 16. The reason why I spoke to students no matter what grade they were in was because the students may have an older family member who is eligible to join the Army or they could become a future soldier. Magaret Workman, my former fifth grade teacher, allowed me to speak with her class. She was a great teacher who influenced me to become a teacher after retiring from the Army.

I met some great recruiters who loved their jobs and did everything to ensure the Army received outstanding recruits such as CSM Robinson, CSM Godwin, CSM Burton, CSM Clay, CSM Crenshaw, 1SG Armour, SFC Martindale and 1SG Hudson who I served with at Ft. Stewart. I especially thank 1SG Armour and SSG Greer for their mentorship. They passed away too early. There are others who made my time successful as a Recruiting Commander. I tell people I can sell anything after working as an Army Recruiter because if I can convince people to give their life for $1,000 a month then I can convince them to buy anything I am selling.

I worked in two of the most thankless jobs in the Army which are Recruiting and Basic Training. Recruiters go through many people to get two people in the Army each month. They work 6 days a week and over 14 hours each day trying to find two recruits a month for the military

Drill Sergeants work over 14 hours a day, seven days a week turning civilians into soldiers in 9 weeks. Drill Sergeants have to play psychologist because trainees bring their problems in the military such as financial and family issues.

Lessons Learned

1. ***Your reputation goes a long way*** – 1SG Martindale hired a family member of mine based on my reputation of being a hard worker and he mentored me as a Recruiting Company Commander. Classmates sought my assistance in putting their children in the Army.

2. ***Every job is important*** – Every job in the military is important and intertwined with other jobs. I thought Recruiting was an easy job until I had to put a person in the Army. Recruiters are an integral part of the Military. If the Military had no recruiters, then there would be no soldiers. It is a thankless, but important job for the Military to have recruiters.

3. ***If you want to learn about Americans, become a traveling Salesman/Recruiter or a teacher*** – CSM Clay enlisted a rich high school kid and his mom asked how he was going to live off of a $1,000.00 a month. I visited some houses were high school students lived with their friends because they were kicked out of their parents' house or their family was homeless. Rich kids join the Military for adventure and less unfortunate kids join for a skill or educational benefits.

4. ***It is easier to get out of shape than to stay in shape*** – The American Public expects a soldier to look like a soldier. Potential recruits gravitate to soldiers who look like a soldier than one who does not. CSMs Burton, Godwin, and Robinson always worked out and lead by example.

5. ***Enroll in the rewards program offered by companies*** – You can achieve free hotel stays and other perks for enrolling in a company's reward program.

307

August 2, 2001

Winston-Salem Recruiting Station
Attn: Captain Lee McQueen
616 Hanes Mall Blvd Suite D
Winston-Salem, North Carolina 27103

Dear Captain McQueen:

Thank you so much for agreeing to present the Korean War Medal to my father, Veteran
Billy H. Smith. He was thrilled to accept the recognition and he's still talking about it
every day! Your kindness and patience were greatly appreciated. Most people are in a
hurry these days, yet you took the time to visit with him and look through his Korean
War scrapbook as well as agreeing to speak on behalf of my father and present him the
award. It was a truly successful day and again, my father and I are grateful for your time
and generosity. I am enclosing copies of the newspaper articles regarding this special
day for you to keep. The presentation was also recognized on WXII television newscast
that evening. I hope you had a chance to see it! I am also forwarding a copy of this
letter to Lieutenant Colonel Pederson so he can see our appreciation for you, your time,
and your service to the United States Army.

Again, thank you for helping make the day one of the proudest and happiest I've ever
seen my father.

Sincerely,

Debbie Hauser

Anytime someone asked for a Military person to present an award to a
Veteran, I would volunteer for it. Above is a copy of a letter which a Korean
War Veteran's daughter sent to me. Her father was in a nursing home when
I presented a medal to him. He showed me his pictures from when he was in
the Army.

308

2ID KOREA

I requested to be reassigned to a Signal Unit in Korea after Recruiting Command because I wanted to learn the job a Signal Officer in does in a Signal Unit and I knew Signal Officers in Korea were involved in real world missions. The Branch Officer, a Lieutenant Colonel, told me there were no positions for Signal Captains in Korea. I called Korea and the Assignment Officer in Korea told me there were plenty of available positions for Signal Officers in Signal Units. I informed the Branch Officer about the information which I received and asked if could I be assigned to a Signal Unit. The Branch Officer chewed me out for contacting Korea and told me to stay in my lane and quit telling him how to do his job. As an Officer you are told you are responsible for your career and if there is a position out there to help your career then pursue it.

The Branch Manager called me two weeks later and told me he found a position for me in Korea. A former Advanced Officer Classmate contacted me and told me I was his replacement as a Brigade Signal Officer in 1st Brigade, 2ID. I contacted the Branch Manager and informed him of the information which I received and he told me all Officers are assigned to 8th Army and I was going to a Signal Unit. I knew he was lying because my former classmate and I were good friends.

Raleigh Recruiting Battalion assigned me to the NC A&T ROTC Department for four months because my report date to Korea was four months away. I worked with LTC Burnett, the Primary Military Instructor (PMS) for A&T and took Spanish Classes in the afternoon. I assisted with training ROTC students to becoming an Officer. LTC Burnett used my skills to train the Cadets because I was an Infantry Officer and a Basic Training Commander. The job was rewarding because I was preparing them for real world situations and I was

309

working with CPT Hines who was a college and Infantry Officer Basic Course classmate.

I arrived at the reception station in Korea in August 2002 and a Sergeant was calling out the names for soldiers going to 2ID and told them to stand to his left. I was the second name which he called and I told him you don't have to tell me where I am going because I already know and I immediately walked over to his left which caused him to laugh. I was pissed off for being lied to.

I arrived at 1st Brigade on Wednesday and ran with the Staff Section the next day. I considered myself in good shape, but the day of the run I was the last Officer on the Staff Run. Those hills in Korea kicked my behind and a Major told me to get my ass up there with the rest of the formation. The hills which we ran up were so steep, I could touch the road while running up them. I was embarrassed at my performance. We had off for four days because of Labor Day. I said to myself this would be the last time I finish last on a run. I ran every day during those four days off. I had no problems with the runs from then on during my time in Korea.

Field Exercise I

The first field exercise was brutal for me. There was no overlap time between the outgoing Signal Officer and myself. The Brigade assigned a captain from one of the companies as the acting Brigade Signal Officer only because he had been in Korea the longest out of every Signal Officer. There was not a Standard Operation Procedure (SOP) Book available. I found some old Operation Orders which told me the Call-Signs of the Brigade Units, but not the setup of the Brigade Communication Network. MSG Jones and I were lost. We had a SSG who was excellent source of information. MSG Jones had not been in a Signal Position in four years and I haven't worked as a Sigo in four years. This is not an excuse, but it is easy to forget things if you haven't worked on them in a while. MSG Jones was a nice and easy- going guy.

The Battalion Signal Officers for the other units were new except for the one who was the acting Brigade Signal Officer and he didn't have knowledge on how the communication operations worked on the Brigade level. I developed a plan for setting up a Brigade Network which I felt was excellent. The Brigade S-3 was one of the most out of shape and laziest officer I ever worked with. He told me, we were not allowed to setup our communication sites on the second tallest hill in Korea because a Military Intelligence Unit said it messed with their operations.

The day of deployment to our area of operations, the Brigade Communication equipment failed while COL Ierardi was talking with the Division General. He was mad, but he solved the problem by using his vehicle radio.

The Brigade TOC was setup in an area surrounded by hills and the brigade was operating outside of the setup area which made communication difficult. I came up with a plan for using the smallest

311

hills around us and using single channel retransmissions stations for the Brigade to communicate with the Battalions. The Brigade constantly lost communications with the Battalions. We had 14 retransmission sites in our area of operations. I only slept three hours a day because of we had so many communication issues. It was the worst field problem I have ever experienced. I was struggling so much; COL Ierardi requested the Division Signal Officer to come down and give me so training. It did not work because we were setup in an area surrounded by hills and the tallest hill in the area was supposedly off limits to us.

When we returned from the field exercise, the Brigade Executive Officer said I should have told the Brigade not to setup in that area because the surrounding hills would cause communication issues. I was a new officer to the unit and the Brigade XO and the Brigade S-3 had been in the unit for a while and Korea previously. I could not believe what he said. I took the heat round because I was the one in charge.

The only good thing I enjoyed out of the field problem was the food provided by Ajumma which is a respectful way to address an older Korean woman. I ate hot fries and drank ice-cold bottled Cokes every day. I spent $14 dollars on her food in those two weeks while some of the soldiers had tabs over $100. I asked some of the soldiers how can you have a high tab when we have a Dining Facility on site which served two hot meals a day. They told me Ajumma's coffee was hotter than the Dining Facility and she had hot fresh beef (Bulgogi), rice, and fries. She would let you eat on credit.

The Brigade had a Brigade Run the following Friday after our return from the field exercise. The XO asked me to play "Iron Man by Black Sabbath" when the Brigade Commander entered the track after the run. I was thinking why is the XO brown-nosing so much and what in the hell is a Black man doing listening to Black Sabbath. My driver who was very computer savvy said he had the song and he would play it on the entrance of the Brigade Commander. The Brigade Commander entered the area and when I instructed my driver to play

312

the song, he said he did not have it after telling me the night before he had it. The XO chewed my ass out and I chewed my driver's ass out (Shit rolls down hill). MSG Jones and the SSG said I should have told them of the XO's request and they would have made it happen.

I took some heat rounds that first month and I promised myself I would not take anymore. I was promoted to Major the next month. I had the SSG to pin my rank on. CSM Washington told me it was the first time he had ever witnessed a Sergeant pinning on the rank of an Officer. I did this to show how much Enlisted Soldiers meant to me and as a sign of respect to the SSG for his mentorship.

I was a Major now and I was determined not to experience the same crap as I experienced before. When I made Major, another Black Major who did not talk to me when I was a Captain approached me and said "Welcome to the Club and look around and see how many other Black Majors are in the Division". There were only 5 Black Officers in 2nd ID, 3 Majors and 2 Captains, which I found disturbing.

Field Exercise II

I met with the Battalion Signal Officers and told them we were going to set up our retransmission communication sites on the tall hill which the S-3 said we could use. I gave them the operating frequencies which we would be using and told them if they change their frequency or settings without my knowledge, I was going to kick their asses. I worked out every day and they saw me bench press over 315lbs, so they knew I wasn't kidding.

When the S-3 found out I was setting up my communication networks on the hill which the Military Intelligence unit said we could not setup on, he became upset. I told him to speak with the Brigade Commander if he has an issue with it. He didn't think highly of me and I definitely didn't think highly of a no running, sloppy looking Officer. I was told he was promoted to LTC and if it is true, it was only because he was one of the few Officers who spent significant time in 2ID. If you spent over three years in 2nd ID, you know every training location blind folded.

The Brigade and Battalion units set up their communication networks as I instructed them to do. There were no communication issues. The Military Intelligence Unit contacted me and told me, we could not use that hill and I told her to come and tell the Commanding General, she is the reason he can't talk with his subordinate units. She never showed up and the crazy thing was the Military Intelligence Unit was operating on a hill over 20-miles away and there was a Korean Unit operating on the same hill we were using.

The Brigade Commander and XO congratulated me on the success of our communication network. The Brigade Commander asked me why did everything work so smoothly this time and I said we put new batteries in the radios. I did not tell him we setup on the tall hill in case he received an ass chewing from the Commanding General for us using the hill. CSM Washington told me he was worried about MSG Jones and myself after the first field exercise because of our struggles and it was nice seeing us working like together as a team. The field exercise went so smoothly, I became tired from sleeping too much.

Field Exercise III

Major B the new S-3 was a great addition to the Brigade. We clicked from the beginning. He did not care where we set up at, just as long as we could talk. We set up our communication retransmission sites on the same hill as the last exercise and experienced no communication issues.

The Brigade was preparing to brief BG Coker when I turned around and spotted Major Russell who was now a Green Beret. We were in the same Officer Basic Course. We joked and talked for a while. Major Russell said in a loud voice "Korea sucks and I want to be sent to Iraq for some real action". A Battalion Commander asked him was he serious and Russell said "Hell Yeah". I thought he was going to chew Russell out, but Russell's size, 6'5 and 250lbs, intimidated the shit out of him. Russell calmed down right before BG Coker arrived. BG Coker asked a question about communication setup and all of the Senior Officers in the tent froze up. I spoke up and told him the location of our retransmission sites and the frequencies we were set on and he said "okay". COL Ierardi said great job. Officers in the Division were intimidated by General Coker because of the thorough questions he asked. He was very knowledgeable and he knew if you were bullshitting him. I didn't appreciate his thoroughness and knowledge at the time until I briefed him at Ft. Monroe, Virginia.

316

Field Exercise IV

We conducted our 4th Field Exercise in the winter. In 2nd ID you were constantly training which was a good thing because the DMZ was about 14-miles away. I was in Korea when it was a warm winter and the temperature was $-14°F$. The year before, I was told temperatures reached $-30°F$ and when the snow melted it flooded some buildings on post.

We set up our communication retransmission sites on the same hill, but this time the hill was covered with snow. I instructed all Signal Personnel to put chains on their vehicles. Specialist Tom, my driver, was a great driver with a sense of direction. If he drove a route once, he would remember it. The hill seemed steeper than before because of the snow. When we reached the top, we saw ROK Soldiers, South Korean Soldiers, wearing wooden rucksacks and sweeping the snow packed road with brooms. I don't know the reason why they swept the snow instead of shoveling it to this day.

ROK Soldiers are tough. When we began our descent down the hill, I told Tom to take off his seat belt and if we begin to slide to jump out of the vehicle and let the vehicle go off the cliff. Our lives where worth more than a hummer. We made it down the hill safely. I told everyone to be careful descending down the hill and keep those chains on their vehicle. The second day as we were approaching down the hill, I told Tom, I was surprised no one has skidded off the cliff. On the third day as we were descending, I noticed a hummer in a tree.

We drove a little further down and I asked one of the Battalion Signal Officer what happened and he said "as his hummer was sliding down the hill, he looked over at his driver and noticed his driver was not there so he jumped out also". They asked me what to do and I instructed them to call their Battalion and request someone bring some chains to pull the vehicle out of the tree. It looked like something out of a Mission Impossible movie to see a military vehicle stuck in a tree. The tree was the only thing which prevented the hummer from falling 700 feet down. The unit recovered the vehicle.

Brigade Inspection

The Brigade conducted an inspection of the battalion units to assess their combat readiness. My section inspected the Battalion Signal Units. You can always find something wrong in any organization if you look hard enough. We inspected a Battalion Signal Unit belonging to LTC Queen. I found something major which would have caused them to fail the inspection, so I allowed them to correct it on the spot. I wrote on the inspection checklist that I only found dirty wire in which was a minor deficiency. LTC Queen approached me after the inspection and said "Dirty wire, is that all you found", I just laughed. Every time he would see me, he would say "Dirty wire" and shake his head.

Christmas

Christmas is hard for soldiers in Korea because we were away from our families and only 50% of the unit could take vacation during the holiday period. The soldiers who had been in Korea for 6-months or longer were given priority for vacation over other soldiers. I had only been there for 4-months. The soldiers who stayed in Korea were assigned duty during the holidays. I was assigned as a Staff Duty Officer for Christmas and a Major paid me $300 to pull his duty on New Year's Day so he could spend time with his wife who flew in from the States which I gladly accepted.

I accompanied Chris who was fluent in Russian for an adventure downtown on Christmas Day. Chris dressed like Santa and gave gifts to all the girls who worked in the bars. I served as his unofficial elf. The girls were very surprised and thanked us. I guess everyone knows who Santa is no matter where they are from.

Seoul

I contacted my friend Rick from Basic Training and he allowed me to stay with him for a weekend. I thought I went to Heaven when I saw how soldiers were living in Seoul. Rick had a car which he paid $700 for and an apartment with heated floors which I never knew existed. Used cars were cheap and if you arrived early to relieve the person whom you were replacing, they would give you their car free of charge. We went to a Military Ball and I ran into a Signal CSM who I used to play basketball with in Panama. I could not believe how many Black Signal Officers were in Seoul. CSM said if he knew I was coming he would have ensured I was assigned to a Signal Unit.

I asked a cab driver to take me to Hooker Hill so I could see why soldiers were always talking about it. My 70-year-old grandmother looked better than most of the women up there.

Manchu Mile

Two weeks after I returned from vacation, 2nd Brigade was conducting the Manchu Mile which is a 25-mile foot march to commemorate the 9th Infantry Regiment's 85-mile march during the 1900 Boxer Rebellion in China where they fought against Manchu forces. I spoke to two CSMs about their train up plan for tackling the Manch Mile and they said the only plan they have is to put one foot in front of the other which reminded me of a song in Santa Claus is Coming to Town. I told them I needed to train or I would not make it. I had two weeks of preparation time before the Manchu Mile. My plan was to do a six, nine, and twelve-mile foot march before the Manchu Mile.

2nd Brigade was conducting the Manchu Mile close to the DMZ. 1st Brigade conducted their Manchu Mile in December. Soldiers marched around Camp Casey for eight plus hours. They passed our barracks at least six times and I knew right then and there that I could not do it on Camp Casey because if I passed my barracks three times, I would have gone up stairs and went to sleep. I selected to do the Manchu March with 2nd Brigade who were marching near the DMZ.

2nd Brigade weighed the rucksack of every soldier who was participating in the Manchu Mile to ensure their rucksack weighed 35 lbs. or more. The brigade checked the weight of everyone's rucksack and placed guards at the entrance of the barracks so no soldiers could not take out anything in their rucksack. I packed my rucksack according to 2nd Brigade's guidance and it weighed 25 lbs., so I put two 10 lb. weights in my rucksack to ensure I made weight.

We marched from Camp Casey to near the DMZ. The Brigade said if you fall more than 10 feet behind the group, they were going to put you on the back of the truck because North Koreans were always

322

looking for an American Soldier to kidnap. That was all the motivation which I needed to complete the march.

The march did not become hard until mile 23. I learned from being in Panama to drink plenty of water and change socks often to avoid blisters. Soldiers developed bad attitudes at mile 23 because they were tired and someone kept saying "One more mile". When we stopped at mile 23, I noticed a lot of junior soldiers were slow to standing up after a 10-minute break and constantly complaining about the length of the march. I knew I was going to make it after hearing them talk. I gained my second wind from their complaints.

When the march ended, everyone said "Hoorah"! The Manchu Mile was the furthest I ever walked. I completed three 20-mile foot marches in Panama which mentally prepared me for the Manchu Mile.

The next week, 2nd Brigade presented belt buckles to acknowledge those of us who completed the Manchu Mile. I was very happy when the Brigade Commander presented me with my belt buckle. My enthusiasm soon died down when I met a Captain who completed 5 Manchu Mile Miles in a year. He should have received an Army Achievement Medal for doing such craziness. If you completed two Manchu Mile Foot Marches in a one-year period, you received a large belt buckle. Heck, I barely completed one march.

Entrances

There are two entrances to enter Camp Casey. Rear gate is located near 2nd Brigade. There was a bar located outside of 2nd Brigade and anytime we visited it, we called it going over to the Dark Side. The bar reminded me of the bar in Star Wars. It was dingy, dark, and full of characters. They had a stripper who was a midget and supposedly if you slept with her, you received a t-shirt saying "I Fuck the Midget".

The best bars and stores were located at the front entrance of Camp Casey. The first week I was in country fellow soldiers asked me to accompany them downtown for drinks. We went to a bar and the soldiers were giving me drinks containing different colors like those found in Kool-Aid. I later found out it was Soju, a rice liquor. It tastes good, but you pay for it later and I paid for it. The base had a curfew and we waited for the last bus to our barracks. We did not want to miss the bus because if we did, we had a long walk back to the barracks. I wanted to get something to eat, but Popeye's Chicken was closed and I knew this spelled trouble for me. An hour later while lying in bed, I saw the ceiling spinning and began to throw up. I was sick and promised myself I would never drink Soju again which I failed to do, but the next times I drunk Soju, I ate before and after drinking it.

A tv show did a special on how soldiers were contributing to prostitution in Korea. This was totally untrue. There were Russian girls working in the clubs, but their mission was to get service members to buy them drinks. Beer for soldiers cost $1 and $12 for the Russian girls. Soldiers would buy a Russian girl 12 beers and the girl would not be drunk. One girl told me she drunk 26 beers in a night. I suspect the girls' drinks were water. We would be sitting at a table and a Russian girl would approach us and asked us to buy her a drink. I would joke around with Ajumma, Korean Bar owner, and buy two beers; one for me and one for the Russian girl. Ajumma would take back one of my

324

beers and say I needed to pay $12 for the girl's drink and I would laugh and say "I don't have $12" and she would kick me out of the bar for not paying for the girl's drink. I enjoyed getting kicked out of her bar every week. It was the first time I was kicked out of a bar for not being drunk. I would go to the bar and ask Ajumma's "where are the Korean girls" and she would say "No Korean girls work here" and I would say "you are discriminating against Korean girls" and she would kick me out of the bar. Somedays she wouldn't let me come into her bar.

Some of the guys became lonely and proposed to the Russian girls. My driver wanted me to sign his vacation papers to go with a bar girl to Uzbekistan and I refused his request because he just met the girl and did not speak the language. He was mad at me, but it was for his own good.

Some soldiers found out a captain was planning on marrying a Russian girl so they went downtown and brought her several drinks. She was falling all over the place sloppy drunk. I don't know if he married her, but the rumor was the commander was not going to give him a company command position if he married her.

We were restricted to the base almost every month because of young Koreans protesting American Soldiers presence in Korea. Once we were restricted on base for 2 months and the liquor store almost ran out of beer. One day a Military Policeman noticed a group of soldiers standing by the tree line and walked up to them, the soldiers were lined up getting sex from their girlfriends through the fence. Those ladies were backing their ass up. The next day, the trees were cut down 15 feet from the fence.

Shopping

The front gate of Camp Casey provided the best shopping experience in Korea. Soldiers would come from Seoul to shop at Camp Casey. I purchased over 25 suits, 25 sweatsuits, 20 blankets, and a host of other items. I gave away the majority of the items to friends and family members. The key method I used for shopping was not to shop on paydays, 1st and 15th of the month. I shopped on non-paydays because soldiers were broke which allowed me to get things cheaply. I was able to get ten suits for a total of $400. I purchased some of the suits off of layaway because soldiers would order them and not pick them up. Korea has good tailors. I purchased a pair of pants from "Q's Tailor and the pants were short. I asked Q for an exchange or my money back, Q told me to leave the pants with him and come back in two days. I returned and the length of the pants were corrected. I asked Q where did he find another pair from and he said he added a section onto to the legs of the pants. I asked him where is the place where he sewed the extension and he pointed to it and I could not see it. I wore those pants for 10 years. Q loved Popeye's Chicken and I would bring him some for a discount. I had sweatsuits of professional and college teams. Friends would send me the colors of their school teams and I would have a sweatsuit made for them. The key for getting quality goods was to buy from stores close to the street. Items from stores in the alley were of less quality than those near up front. The other places to shop at were Osan Air Force Base and Seoul. Items in Seoul were more expensive because it was a tourist area, but you could find great quality goods. I purchased a Gortex Timberland Jacket for $40 and it is warmer than any jacket found in the States. Soldiers preferred Korean Cold Weather Gear over Military Issue Gear. I have cold weather clothing items which are almost 25-years-old which I still wear this day

326

I made $3k from selling suits, baseball caps, jackets, and gloves. I thought I was making money until I met a servicemember who made $100k selling basketball and football jerseys.

Physical Fitness

I give the XO credit; he developed an outstanding physical fitness program. We ran three miles on Mondays, four miles on Tuesdays, 9-mile foot marches on Wednesdays, sprints on Thursdays, and 70-minute runs on Fridays at an 8-minute pace.

I worked out twice a day in Korea. I did physical fitness with the staff in the morning, lifted weights after work, and played basketball on the weekends. Ken, S-4, was my workout partner. His wife told me "Thank You" for getting her husband bulked up. I should have charged him for my training services.

Enlisted soldiers challenged the Officers to a game of football. I told an Enlisted Soldier they need to be careful of what they are asking for because our Officers are no slouch potatoes. There were some athletic studs in the Staff Section. I saw CPT Powers, Brigade S-1, throw a football 60 yards with ease. I played basketball with him and other Officers on the weekends. CPT Powers had game in football and basketball. We beat the crap out of the Enlisted Soldiers in football unlike the game in Panama. The Enlisted Soldiers went back to the barracks with their heads hanging down.

In Korea you are either a drinker or work out king. One day a Puerto Rican bet some of his friends $63 that he could drink a bottle of Bacardi 151 straight. He did and passed out in the middle of a field. I asked his friends what did they do and they said they carried him to the medical clinic, knocked on the door, and ran. I said to them "you guys are some sorry friends". The guy recovered.

I hung out with the Latinos in Korea despite speaking broken Spanish. They prepared Spanish dinners every month and we watched Banco de Popular Spanish music videos of Latin Singers. They were surprised by my knowledge of their customs and Latin singers. They gave me several CDs of Latin Singers. The Hispanic Lieutenant was the second soldier I met who was an Enlisted Soldier, Warrant Officer, and an Officer. He was a Demolition Specialist who had a car tag which said "KABOOM".

Taekwondo

Some of the Battalions had a Taekwondo Instructor to train their soldiers on self-defense tactics for two weeks during their physical fitness hours. I took Taekwondo after hearing all ROK Soldiers have Black Belts in Taekwondo and the story about three soldiers who tried to rob a pizza delivery driver and he beat their asses because he had a Black Belt in Taekwondo. I figured if ROK soldiers have Black Belts then the North Korean soldiers have Black Belts, so I better take some Taekwondo classes. My motto was if North Korean soldiers crossed the DMZ, they were going to get one of heck of fight from me.

Mr. Li (pronounced Lee), Taekwondo Instructor, was a 55-year-old chain-smoking man who had forearms hard like steal. Koreans loved my name "Lee" because almost everyone had someone in their family named "Lee". It is spelled different, but sounds the same. Mr. Li told me there were over 5 million kids who died during the Korean War. He said if a kid made it out of that War, they were tough and he made it out of the Korean War. One day he told me to hit him, I hit him and he said harder and I struck his forearm which was so hard it felt like I broke my hand. He could knock a person out delivering a kick. I regretted not taking up Taekwondo earlier.

330

Barbershops

Korea had outstanding barbers. I would get my haircut every week because we had an excellent female barber on Camp Casey who was in her 50s. Haircuts cost $6 and she would give her customers back massages, head massages, and pop their necks and fingers. I would leave her $4 tip because of the way she treated me. The other officers would tell me I was tipping too much and driving up the price of a haircut. They only tipped her a dollar. I told them in the States it costs $10 for a haircut, so I didn't have a problem leaving her a $4 tip for the outstanding treatment I was receiving. I enjoyed it when she popped my neck and fingers. The other officers complained she caused a permanent crook in their neck from the popping. I had no such problem. She would laugh at me constantly because I would go to sleep every time I sat in the chair. I could have 10 hours of sleep before getting a haircut and still go to sleep in her chair. She gave me a hug when I left. I definitely miss her and I will gladly pay her a $100 for one more haircut.

There were some female barbers in Seoul who had a line of male customers. They would give haircuts, massage the chests, and massage between the legs. The command found out about this and made them stop. I wonder how much tip they received for their extra services.

I was about to leave Korea when Signal Branch sent a female who had a medical profile due to injuries to 2nd Brigade which was an Infantry Unit. I have no issues with females in the Infantry, but to send an injured soldier to a forward deployed unit made no sense to me. This really showed how little Signal Branch cared about soldiers and units. The unit deployed to Iraq without their Signal Officer which is unusual. The former Branch Manager could not believe what Signal Branch did. I don't know why he was shocked because he screwed me over.

331

End of Korea

COL Ierardi was a great commander. I sucked so bad my first month in the Brigade, I thought I was going to be fired. He probably knew if he fired me there would be no one to take my place. He never chewed me out, but he did holler at me for messing with the radio while he was talking to the Division Commander. He apologized, but I felt there was no need to because I was in the wrong for messing with the radio while he was talking. I setup the radio correctly, but I was overthinking things and changed a setting trying to get a better signal. There was nothing wrong with the radio. I was in COL Ierardi's office fixing his computer when I noticed on his desk that he had a copy of "I have a Dream" speech by Dr. Martin Luther King Jr. I was surprised to see the speech on an Italian's desk.

There is a lot of history in Korea. We studied and walked the land where the Battle of Chosin Reservoir took place in the Korean War. When you study any War, you become amazed at the heroic actions of servicemembers and the obstacles which they overcome to be successful. Korean Veterans had to overcome poor weather, insufficient cold weather gear, weapon issues, and a large Enemy force to be successful. The weather in the Chosin was $-40°F$ and when I was in Korea the low was $-14°F$. The river was frozen when we walked it and I can't imagine American Forces fighting in such cold weather wearing shoddy cold weather gear. I trained in a jungle environment which is hard, but nothing compares to a cold weather environment where you are wet and cold. Servicemembers had to be mentally and physically tough to survive the Korean War.

If people do not believe the War in Korea is tough then they need to visit Korea and see all of the Crosses of deceased people scattered throughout the Country. There are a plenty of hills in Korea and the weather can be frightening cold. When you study history, it makes you realize the importance of taking and holding high ground. High ground gives you the advantage for observing and engaging enemy forces from long distances. It is easier to shoot downwards than upwards.

I contacted Signal Branch asking what assignments are available after I leave Korea. I wanted to go to Alaska after my Korea assignment, but Branch told me there were four available positions with ten people fighting for them. The other positions were all Brigade Sigo Positions which I definitely did not want. I saw a position where Joint Task Force Bravo in Honduras was requesting a Signal Officer. I immediately applied for it because it was a one-year assignment, I could improve my Spanish, and I was hoping it would increase my chance of being assigned to a Signal Unit.

Lessons Learned

1. ***Be truthful to your subordinates*** – I would have happily taken the Korea assignment if the Branch Manager told me I would be sent to a Signal Unit afterwards. I never understood the Branch manager reasoning for lying to me when he was a LTC and I was a Captain. He may have fulfilled an Army requirement, but he failed on his responsibility of taking care of soldiers.

2. ***Strive for improvement*** – I initially struggled as a Brigade Signal Officer. I read Signal Manuals, and listened to the advice of more experienced soldiers regardless of their rank to improve my understanding of Signal Equipment which enabled us to have successful Field Exercises.

3. ***When you get knocked down, get back up*** – I got my ass kicked on the first field problem. Junior Signal Officers were looking up to me for guidance after the first field exercise and I was not about to let them down, so I was willing to take an ass-chewing for putting Retransmission sites on a supposedly off-limits hilltop.

4. ***Disseminate information*** – I should have informed my Senior Sergeants of the XO music request instead of trusting a Specialists. The Sergeants would have insured we met the XO's request.

5. ***Do your own research*** – The Military Intelligence Unit put out a crazy order stating units could not use a hill 20-miles away without knowing the ramification of their actions. I looked on the map and noticed they were setup far away from us and a Korean unit was using the same hill which they tried to banish the American Units from using.

6. ***Take care of your body*** – I looked at Korea as a time to get into the best shape of my life. I walked everywhere I went and exercised twice a day.

334

7. ***Treat others respectfully regardless of their job*** – Chris taking Christmas gifts to the girls showed someone cared about them.

8. ***Take advantage of what the Military Offers*** – The Military has great offers such as discounted travel programs. Some of the soldiers traveled to Japan, Australia, and different parts of Korea for a discounted rate. Units enrolled their units in free Taekwondo classes.

Communication briefing on 2nd Field Exercise. The first field exercise was a dud because we were supposedly not allowed to use the biggest hilltop in our area for communication retransmission. I disregarded the S-3's advice on the next exercise which enabled us to have no communication issues.

Korean Temple where I was representing NC A&T State University, my Alma Mater.

336

Japan

I traveled to Japan to visit my cousin during my tour in Korea. Tokyo is the cleanest big city which I have ever visited. I went to use the airport bathroom and an old lady walked in the Man's Bathroom. I went outside to make sure I was in the correct bathroom, which I was. I walked back in the bathroom and the old lady was cleaning the bathroom and said "go ahead" which made me so scared I couldn't use the bathroom. The only time I ever saw a woman in a men's bathroom was at a club and the woman was drunk. The lady cleaned the bathroom so well you could eat off the floor.

My cousin and I drunk a 12-pack of beer as we rode the train back to his home. He told me as long as we don't make a scene and pick-up our trash the police would not bother us. We had a great time on the train.

The next day we ate at McDonald's. The McDonald's in Japan taste better than in the United States. I was taken back on how friendly the cashier was and she smiled when I ordered my food. I never experienced such kindness from a fast-food restaurant employee so I took a picture with her.

We took the train to the Hard Rock Cafe in Tokyo. My cousin gave me some coins to pay for my seat. I started putting in coins like I do for a parking meter. He looked at me laughing and said "what are doing" I told him I was paying for my ticket with these quarters. He told me I used $100 in coins to pay for a $5 ticket. We did not get a refund for my ignorance. Our meal of a grill chicken sandwich, fries, and a beer costs us $40 each. We spent $400 on beer, food, and train tickets that night. We had such a good time that I missed my flight the next day. The stewardess was very nice and put me on the next flight to Korea.

337

My cousin Kim and I on the subway.

Kim and I enjoying Tokyo, the
world's most populated city.

Hard Rock Cafe Japan – Hamburger, fries, and a beer cost $40 during the time period.

McDonald's Japan – Cashier was so nice that I had to take a picture with her.

339

Lessons Learned

1. *You are a representation of your company* – The employees at McDonald's gave the sense of someone loving their job which made me feel like I was important.

2. *Travel Overseas* – There are vast amounts of history lessons and customs which one will learn when they travel overseas. Tokyo is the largest city in the world and the cleanest city which I have visited. Japanese take pride in cleaning and I never saw one piece of trash on the ground in Roppongi which is the entertainment center of Tokyo.

3. *Get involved in the culture* – Eat what the local citizens eat. I never ate Sushi until I visited Japan and now, I enjoy it.

Hawaii

The Army gave soldiers leaving Korea up to two weeks stay in Hawaii in the Hale Koa hotel. Only three soldiers in the Brigade took advantage of this. I needed the rest because I was mentally burned out. The hotel representative asked me if I wanted to pay $80 for a non-ocean view room or $85 for an ocean view room and I looked at her like she was crazy and told her if I am staying at an ocean front hotel, I expect to see and smell the ocean. I mostly stayed around the hotel except for one day when I went to Bubba Gump for dinner. When I was walking back to the hotel, a nice-looking young lady approached me and said do you want to have a good time for $100. The first thought which came to my mind was what a Hawaiian Pimp said in the movie "American Pimp". He said Hawaiian working girls must dress nice to get clients because Hawaii is a tourist area. I told her she should be paying me and I take cash only. She gave me a stun look and began cursing at me. I told her I was worth $200 hour, but I would give her a Military Discount and she proceeded to curse me out more and walked away. I was laughing the entire time she was cussing me out.

I left Hawaii after a week. A stewardess asked passengers if they wanted to pay $100 for an upgrade to First Class. The plane was almost empty and no one took her up on the offer. I was almost going to take her up on the offer until I asked her is anyone sitting beside me on the exit row and do I get free drinks, she said you have an entire row to yourself and because it is an international flight all drinks are free and you get the same food as First Class. I told her, I am staying right where I am at. I was watching the movie "Daredevil" on the plane and I asked the stewardess why is it so dark in here, she began to laugh historically and removed my sunglasses and I laughed afterwards. I was drunk before the plane took off. I watched the movie "Daredevil seven times on the trip from Hawaii to Atlanta.

341

JTF-BRAVO
(HONDURAS)

I reported to Honduras about three months before my due date. I met with COL Phelps, JTF-B Commander, who told me his expectations were for me to maintain constant communication with higher headquarters in the states, with our forward deployed units, and maintain accountability of equipment. I told him it was not a problem because I had been in Korea and if I survived 2ID then I could do any job Signal job.

I was expecting Honduras to be like Panama, but it was the opposite. It was located in Comayagua a small town outside of the base. The minimum wage in 2003 for Hondurans was .33¢ an hour. Hooches were on two feet high wooden stilts and made out of wood. They had a kitchen, bed, electricity, AC, tv, geckos, and ducks which lived underneath them. There was no bathroom just a sink with running water.

The bathrooms were communal and at night you could find mosquitos, geckos, frogs, gnats, flies, and all types of insects. I despised going to the bathroom at night because of the animal life. I was fortunate to have a short walking distance to the bathroom.

Geckos were always in the hooches because of the numerous openings in them. I don't know where the ugly ducks came from, but they lived under our hooches. When my kids arrived, they named the ducks and fed them every day. One of the ducks was named Mr. Snaggles who was always the first in line for feeding.

JTF-B is a joint base which has servicemembers from the Army, Air Force, Navy, and Marines. When servicemembers got drunk, the Marines would put the ducks in their hooches. It was a sight to see

342

because the ducks crapped all over the place. I can't imagine someone waking up looking face to face with a duck. It was the main reason; I kept my doors locked at all times.

The Air Force is viewed for having the smartest servicemembers, but the least physical. In Honduras the Air Force had the strongest servicemembers. We had a competition between each Branch of Service. Army personnel thought the Air Force would place last. The Air Force kicked everyone's behind and would have won the contest if they had four personnel on the swim relay team which included boat rowing and swimming with the boat. The Air Force had a Black Captain who did the race by himself and finished first. The judge disqualified the team for not having four personnel. The Air Force had the most servicemembers who benched pressed over 300lbs.

There were three Air Force pilots on base and they were in excellent shape. I could not believe the Air Force sent a F-16 pilot to the J-6 Section (Communication). He was transitioning from Active-Duty to the Reserves. He was wild. He flipped a golf cart which was our main transportation around post by pretending it was a jet. Soldiers would always take another section golf cart because they did not want to walk. Taking another unit's golf cart was easy because the golf cart keys were universal. The pilot went to a Honduran Club in Tegucigalpa and the club kicked him out for being White. When he told me this, I said now you understand how Black People felt in the 60s". I went to the same club the next weekend and entered without any issue.

A National Guard unit from Puerto Rico served as the base security team. They were very professional and we talked about everything from their culture to their food. They were surprised I knew a lot of Latin Singers.

A Honduran came on post selling paintings. I was speaking Spanish to him, but he was not understanding me. I asked a Puerto

343

Rican National Guardsman to come and listen to me speak Spanish to see if I was speaking correctly and he said yes. I thought my country accent was difficult for the seller to understand so I asked the sergeant to speak with him. The sergeant was speaking to him in Spanish and he did not answer back. Then the sergeant wrote down the price I was going to pay on paper and the painter responded. That is when we found out the painter was deaf. I could not believe I did not recognize the painter was deaf. I purchased the painting for $45. The painting was a person followed by a donkey crossing the Andes Mountain with a condor flying above them. It is not a Picasso, but it is a Picasso to me. I still cherish the painting till this day.

A Puerto Rican soldier was hanging out downtown wearing his Mr. T Start-up Kit when he was robbed of his gold chains. The Puerto Rican soldiers told the Honduran General about the incident and the Honduran General sent some troops downtown to recover it. They recovered the stolen jewelry and the young soldier learned a valuable lesson of keeping a low profile.

There was a Puerto Rican Sergeant who made Sangria from scratch. It was the best tasting Sangria which I have ever had. I asked for the recipe and he told me could not do it because he promised the person who taught him how to make it not to share his recipe.

The number one racquetball player in the Army was a Puerto Rican who was assigned to my shop. He carried his racquetball in a case everywhere he went. The Safety Officer who was a Puerto Rican and a good racquetball player challenged him to a match. I told the Safety Officer he was stepping out of his league. He disregarded my message and the sergeant beat the crap out of him. In three games the Safety Officer may have scored a total of two points and it was because the sergeant was feeling sad for him.

Clubs

My first week in Honduras was comical. The soldiers invited me to Church on Thursday night, but we had to meet at the bar first. I'm thinking what kind of Church requires it parishioners to drink before attending. The bar was for E-7s and above. We met at the bar and we started drinking tequila. I am not a liquor drinker and it showed because I passed out on my floor with one pant leg on. I never made it to Church.

I made it to Church the following week and it was not what I expected. We met in the E-7 and above bar and had two beers each when someone suggested we go to Church. I am following the guys and we go to a club on the backside of the base which they called Church. I asked them how in the heck did they associate a bar with Church and someone said during a previous command a Colonel's driver wanted to meet his girlfriend early at the club, so he asked the Colonel for permission to leave work early and the Colonel replied "you can only leave early for Church". The driver returned the next Thursday and asked the Colonel if he could leave early for Church and the Colonel replied "Sure", so that is how Thursdays is associated with Church.

The club was only open on Thursdays and considered on base. Servicemembers accessed the club through a hole in the fence behind the club because it was easier than walking almost a mile around to the front entrance of the club. All drinks were $1 regardless if it was beer or liquor. The club played mostly Latin Music. Hondurans had a line dance for Michael Jackson's Billie Jean Song which I thought was interesting because I never heard of a Michael Jackson song being a line dance song. SFC Castro conducted free Salsa Lessons for those of us with two left feet. I think I was the only one who went to the club to put his lessons to use. There were young girls sitting around waiting for someone to ask them to dance. I encouraged the young soldiers to dance with the girls and they refused so us old guys danced with them. One night I took $50 to the club and brought drinks for all the ladies sitting down. They all thanked me and we danced the night away. People dance at a Latin Party and drink at an American Party.

A group of soldiers from Miami arrived for two weeks. I took them to the club and they all found girlfriends that night. The soldiers had a good time and told me they were going to miss their flight so they could spend more time in Honduras. I told them if they missed their flight, I was going to Court Martial them for being AWOL. They burst out laughing and invited me to Luke Campbell's club in Miami for Happy Hour which had Lap Dances for $5.00. I never went.

There were three clubs on post which opened only on the weekends except for the E-7 and up club which was opened on Thursdays. Each club raised money to support an orphanage. One unit's way of raising money for their orphanage was every soldier who arrived or left the unit made a donation to the orphanage. It was not mandatory, but soldiers took pride in helping the children. The unit raised $3,000 in one night. The soldiers entering and leaving the unit would buy rounds for the entire bar. I had one soldier who tried to drink every time someone brought a round and he was drunk for two days.

The bar for senior ranking servicemembers raised only $300 a month because we were cheap. I would buy a five-pound bag of candy containing jawbreakers, bubble gum, and lollipops every other week. I would only eat the jawbreakers and give the rest to the kids in the orphanage. The nuns who were in charge of the orphanage asked me not send any more gum because the kids would leave the gum under their desk. I would send them more anyway. The kids did not know how to eat ice cream on a cone and this was in 2004. We take for granted a lot of things we have in the States. I stopped eating jawbreakers because I was breaking a crown every month and helping my dentist with his monthly Porsche car payment. A ten-dollar bag of candy cost me $300 in dental care.

346

Comayagua

Comayagua is a city outside of the base. There were three restaurants which servicemembers visited. There was a restaurant which most servicemembers visited. The food was good and they served Huevos de Toros (Bull Testicles). There was only one person which I know of who ate them and he claimed they tasted like octopus. I was going to order some until I saw his facial expression.

The last time I ate at the restaurant there was a dead body at the bar next door. The guy killed a policeman and another officer killed him. We were in the restaurant for almost an hour and the body was still uncovered.

Another restaurant served Chinese food and the rumor was whatever you did not eat or take with you; the restaurant reheated it and served to new customers. The rumor made me always ask for a carryout and then I would give it to the teenagers plus $5 for calling a cab.

The other restaurant which servicemembers visited was owned by an American. He was killed while being robbed by three men. He killed one of the robbers.

A Master Sergeant opened up a bar called Blue Moon which closed after the second robbery. We warned him not to open a bar in a high crime area, but the Master Sergeant rank went to his head. He hired a policeman, but it didn't help because he did not pay off the local area gangs.

A Wendy's restaurant opened and there were 400 plus people in line every day for two weeks. I went there a month later and the cashier asked me if I wanted Cocoa to drink and I said "What" and she said it again, but this time she pointed to the menu and I said "Coca Cola". In Panama if someone said "Cocoa" it means Cocaine.

347

Shopping

Honduras was known for making mahogany furniture. They have some of the best carpenters in the world. There were two carpenters who worked on base, one of them was named Arturo. The carpenters made me a bar, tables, picture frames, entertainment center, rocking chairs, and storage chest. They could carve any design which you wanted. They made me a table with the carvings of the Mayan Ruins in the center and a storage chest with Snow White and the Seven Dwarfs. I should have listened to them when they advised me to make my entertainment center into sections. I was hard headed and had it made in one piece which almost prevented it from fitting in the shipping box plus it was heavy to move. It took six people to move it and I had to take the crown off the top to put it in the shipping container.

I enjoyed buying fruits in Honduras. Watermelon cost .25¢, pineapple .10¢, and mangoes were 3 for .5¢. There were cart vendors who sold fresh pineapple drinks on the street for a .10¢. The drinks were sold in zip lock like bags. The base had lemon trees with lemons the size of your palms. The only clothes which I purchased were jerseys of soccer teams which costs $14 each. Large were the largest sizes which they had and I quickly out grew them.

The saddest thing which I encountered while shopping, was a woman who lost a child to drowning asking for money. She lost a child during a hurricane. She and her two children were swept away in a flood, her two kids were holding onto her and the flood swept her oldest child from her. When I saw her on the street asking for money, I gave her $20 and I told her I will be back the following Saturday. I took $100 downtown to give to her, but she was gone. A personal rule of mine is to only carry enough money which you can stand to lose and I rarely carried over $40 with me in Honduras.

Easter

Christmas and Easter are the biggest holidays in the Hispanic Culture. Panamanians would visit different churches on Christmas Eve and have dinner at midnight. I learned the true meaning of Christmas when I was in Panama and Honduras. People in Panama and Honduras who had little or nothing, worshiped more on Christmas and Easter than most Americans. Some Hondurans reminded me of the story my great-grandmother told me which was her mom did not have money to give her children toys, but told them she was going to give them a Christmas Gift which would last a life time and it was the gift of learning how to read.

Hondurans visited Comayagua to celebrate Holy Week and view the art work by local artisans. SFC Castro, a very talented artist, assisted local citizens with decorating the streets. Hondurans would lay patches of sawdust on the street, wet it, and then paint it with scenes leading up to the Easter.

Easter Art Work

353

NO TENGAN MIEDO

Comayagua Church

People were always asking me to take their picture. Unknown man in front of the Church.

Honduran ladies posing by Church's door

360

Trips

I carried my family to Valle de Ángeles, La Ceiba, and Copan Mayan Ruins. Valle de Ángeles is a touristic area located about two hours from Comayagua which sold local handmade gifts and craft shops.

We visited a resort in La Ceiba which was very nice. All drinks were included in the price of the resort. I ordered a rum and coke and tipped the bartender $5 because I did not have any change, the bartender thought I was a big fish and brought me another drink before I finished the first one. I told him to slow down because I'm poor and he just smiled. He probably earned his monthly salary during the three days I was there.

The employees of the resort worked numerous jobs on site. I saw the bartender serving morning breakfast, bartending in the afternoon, and acting in a play at night.

We toured the Copán Ruins which were very interesting. We saw areas where the Mayans played sports, worshiped, and socialized. I learned more about the Mayan Society from that visit than any history class which I took. I made my kids do a report on their visit so they could tell their classmates about their experiences.

We were leaving the Mayan site and saw a group of kids holding a rope across the road to make vehicles stop and give them candy. The rope was so thin, it looked invisible. Our driver chastised the kids and told them how dangerous the thing they were doing. We gave them what little candy we had.

Scuba Diving

I always wanted to learn on how to scuba dive because I thought it would be neat to see whales and sharks in their natural environment. I had a dive instructor in my platoon in Panama, but I felt I wasn't a strong enough swimmer for the ocean. I finally took a dive class in Honduras for $135. The instructor supplied everything except pen and paper. We did the swim test and book work on base. The final phase of scuba certification was held at Bay Island (Roatan). We had to complete three daytime dives and one night dive.

We took the bus to Tegucigalpa Airport and boarded a plane to the Roatan. The flight is about an hour long. I felt like I was in the movie "Indiana Jones and the Temple of Doom" because I could touch the pilot. There was no door or barrier separating us. Some of the passengers had live chickens on the plane. I received a headache from smelling the fumes on the plane. We made it safely to Roatan and the cab drivers charged us $14 for a three-mile ride. A person could take a cab from Comayagua to Tegucigalpa for $10 and it was a 2-hour trip each way.

My first dive was rough because I had difficulty putting on and taking off my scuba tanks in the ocean due to choppy water. On my first dive I saw a stone fish which are poisonous, but no sharks. We dove down 40-feet and the instructor made us take off our mask and put it back on and take it out our regulator, clear it, and put it back in to breath normally. I started breathing heavily and began to panic when I took off my mask and took out my regulator. I put my regulator back in and inhaled sea water which caused me to panic while putting back on my mask. I gave the signal for returning to the surface and the instructor said "no" and he began to calm me down. I probably scared the crap out of him because we were 40-feet down. The water was so clear at that dept, you could see the sky.

It was a full moon when we dived at night which made it easier for us to keep track of each other and see wildlife. The next dives went smoothly compared to the first dive. Some of the servicemembers were certified as Master Divers and could go down past 80-feet. We had a few people who went swimming with whale sharks in Tela.

The second day in Roatan we heard African Descendants from the slave trade singing in their Parent's Language. The third day we walked the beach in the evening looking for a place to eat. We saw a place which advertised fresh lobster and rice for $5. The restaurant was a wooden building with banana leaves for the roof and it was about 11x11 square feet in size. We sat on a wooden bench and ordered 4 lobster tails. The owner was taking a long time to bring us our food which caused the gnats to have a buffet party on us despite our use of insect repellent. We turned around and noticed the owner returning from the ocean with four lobsters. He did not tell us he had to go diving for the lobsters, but he did tell us fresh lobster and our lobsters were fresh from the ocean. He cooked the lobster and rice in front of us and the food was great. We dined on fresh seafood and the gnats dined on us.

The trip back to Tegucigalpa was better than going to Roatan. I was still able to touch the pilot, but there were no chickens and no gas smell on the plane. I received my Scuba Diving Certificate after a 12-year wait.

Transportation

Tegucigalpa is the only airplane trip which I have been on where the passengers clapped when the plane landed. The plane had to make a sharp turn and drop suddenly before approaching the runway which was a little over 6,000 feet long. I was told six months prior to my arrival an airplane slid off the runway. There is a sharp drop off when the plane is departing the airport which makes it scary arriving and leaving the airport. Honduran Government Officials moved the airport to Soto Cano after I left.

When servicemembers arrive, there were numerous people asking to carry our bags. One Honduran who spoke good English made a living off of carrying servicemembers bags to and from taxicabs. I would give him $5 for carrying my bags. My friend Hank gave him $20 for two bags and I told Hank he gave the baggage handler his monthly salary.

The bus driver who took us to and from the airport only made $5 a day and once he dropped us off in the morning, he had to wait six hours for the next group of soldiers to arrive in Honduras and bring them to the base. I would buy him lunch and give him a tip for driving us to and from the airport.

The Honduran bus was called the Chicken Bus because people were stuffed in there like chickens. People would be hanging outside the door while the bus was moving. It costs .25¢ – .50¢ to ride depending on where you were riding to. There was no such thing as a safety inspection so you rode at your own risk.

364

Golf

There was a country club near the base which had a golf course. I only played golf once before arriving to Honduras and it was in Missouri which resembled a cow pasture converted into a golf course. When we entered the road leading to the golf course, about 15 children ran to our van requesting to be our caddie for $1. We each had three caddies because we didn't want any kids to be left out from earning money. Some of the kids were pretty good golfers. One of the holes was over a tall hill. A kid told me which club to use, how to hold it, and the distance to the next hole. It took me four swings to reach the top of the hill. The kid took my club and with one swing hit the ball three feet from the hole which was 160 yards away. We played nine holes and afterwards we told all of the kids we were going to buy them lunch and pay for their entrance into the club swimming pool. The club would not allow the kids to swim so we brought them hamburgers, fries, and soda for lunch. Some of those kids could have played on the collegiate level with a little coaching.

365

TDY Miami

JTF-B higher headquarters, SOUTHCOM, was in Miami and the command also worked with USARSO in San Antonio, Texas. I went to Miami often. On a trip to Miami there was a bar near the hotel I was staying at. A gentleman who was driving an $80k Mercedes, wearing a Rolex watch, and an expensive looking gold chain sat beside me. I told him I was in the Army and he said order anything you want, it's on him. I ordered $20 worth of food and beer and then we had a

shot of liquor together. We were talking and the man asked me to watch his plate while he goes to the bathroom. He was gone for 30 minutes and I went to check on him and no one is in the bathroom. I told the bartender the man skipped out on his bill and I would pay for mine not his because he had a tab over $100. The bartender told me not to worry about it and it happens a lot. I could not believe someone wearing a Rolex and driving a Mercedes would walk out on their tab without paying. It shows you can't judge people by how they look and talk.

Puerto Rico

JTF-B sent a group of us to Puerto Rico for conferences. We were staying near the casino and a Puerto Rican soldier asked us to accompany him to a less expensive bar than the one in the casino. There were few people in the bar which had a nice atmosphere. I noticed an old lady with big breast looking at me. She walks over to me and pulls down her shirt and told me to feel because they were real. They felt like ballons and if I stuck a pin in them, they probably would have deflated to a size A. The other soldiers fell out laughing and teased me about a grandma hitting on me. I could not believe what she did.

The next night we went to a Gentleman's Club for drinks. We were drinking and the bar was boring. A dancer saw a guy in our group nodding off and told him to lean his head back, close his eyes, and open his mouth then she put one of her breasts in his mouth. We fell out laughing and gave her $100 for the entertainment which she gladly took and left with her boyfriend.

367

Physical Fitness

Soto Cano has a nice gym for a small post. They had free weights, weight machines, and different types of cardio machines. My daily workouts consisted of 3 – 5 mile runs, 100 pushups, and 100 sit-ups in the mornings, weight lifting in the afternoons, and 45 minutes on the elliptical or the stationary bike on Sundays reading a Spanish Dictionary or other Spanish learning book. When I arrived, I lifted weights every day after work, but stopped because I was out growing out of my clothes so I changed Thursdays to rest days.

I ran 5 miles on Friday to run Thursday night alcohol out of my system. My motto is "If you hang out then you run it out". You would think I would have changed my drinking habits, but I didn't because Church/Club on Thursdays were fun. Fridays runs were very interesting because the 5-mile run took you around the airfield, by a neighborhood across from the airfield, and the old Ollie North Compound. I always waved to the neighborhood people when I was running. On one run a bull came out of the wood line and scared the crap out of me. It weighed over a ton. I only had a knife on me and began to look for a tree to climb up. The bull just looked at me and continued eating. I reported what I saw and everyone laughed because they could not believe I did not know there were cows on base. I saw ducks and goats on base every day, but seeing a bull was something out of the Twilight Zone. Ducks were out in the daytime and goats at night.

A female was robbed as she was running by a group of people from the neighborhood across from the runway. They took her shoes and gold necklace. The command put the run route off limits, but I continued to run without any problems except for seeing the bull.

368

Spanish

My Spanish definitely improved while in Honduras. I conversed with the Hondurans and asked them to speak Spanish to me. I listened to Spanish Tapes daily in preparation for the Army Defense Language Aptitude Battery (DLAB) Test. A passing score is a 2 for listening and 2 for math and you must pass both to receive credit. I scored a 1 for listening and 2 for reading the first time I took the test. I retook the test a month later and scored a 1+ and a 2+. The listening part of the test did not use words which you converse with people in the community. When I retired, I discovered the Defense Language Institute had CDs for all languages. This knowledge was not shared at any installation which I was stationed at.

The people who I worked with would let me answer the phone so they could get a laugh from me speaking Spanish with a country accent. I wasn't discouraged by their laughter. There was a coworker who took a history class at a local college. I wasn't ready for the challenge of taking college level classes at the local college because all of the lessons were in Spanish.

I am intrigued how different the sounds of Salsa (Spanish Music) in each Spanish Speaking Country. Hispanics were coming to me for Salsa because I had over 20 gigabytes of Salsa Music.

Servicemembers

LTC Wiley, S-3, was a great leader who kept things in perspective. He loved golf and Captain Morgan. A Honduran Soldier was injured on an Airborne jump and the Hondurans contacted the base for medical assistance. The S-3 shop was celebrating someone's birthday at the time when the Assistant S-3 came running in the shop requesting our ambulance crew to take care of the soldier. LTC Wiley told him "Not one damn minute and go tell the Honduran Military to contact their Emergency Services" and we continued on with the birthday celebration. It was some good cake. The soldier suffered a sprained ankle.

I used to cross my arms a lot when talking with others. LTC Wiley told me it was a defensive position and I immediately stopped crossing my arms when speaking to others. We talked about worldly situations and he asked me why "Black Americans and Africans do not like each other" and I did not have an answer for him. I don't have a problem speaking to anyone. When Wiley asked me for something, I always did it without asking why. I had great respect for him and I told him if no one is shooting at me, I would do anything for any soldier. He asked me why didn't I join Special Forces and I told him I was not initially planning on making the Army Career. LTC Wiley would have made an outstanding Brigade Commander because he cared about soldiers and was very knowledgeable tactically.

The Airforce leadership team provided a different leadership style to the unit. Senior leaders in the Airforce were more receptive to junior Airmen bringing their issues with them directly. The Army encourages soldiers to report their issues to their direct leader, who in turn reports it to their leader. The Army's way is to allow issues to be resolved at the lowest level which provides senior leaders more time to concentrate on the mission.

The J-8 and I served together in Panama. Anything the base needed, he acquired it. Staff Officers and Senior Sergeants worked together and mentored junior servicemembers. There were disagreements on certain situations, but everyone put their egos to the side and resolved their issues in a professional manner. Deployments outside of the U.S. create logistical issues and if servicemembers are not working together, the mission is not accomplished.

General Colin Powell, who was Secretary of State at the time, arrived in Honduras for a meeting with their government. He visited the base and gave us a great speech on his time at JTF-B. I did not know he served in Honduras. General Powell was a down to earth person who greeted and shook hands with every one present.

Secretaries

The base secretaries looked like models out of Vogue Magazine. They dressed to the nines, hardworking, very professionals, and bi-lingual without an accent. The secretaries were a wealth of knowledge because they were there permanently and we were there from six-months to a year.

Raymie, my secretary, was one of the kindest, smartest, humblest, and hardworking persons which I have ever met. She kept me out of trouble. She covered for me on Fridays because I would arrive late after being hungover from Thursday night.

Raymie got on me in a subtle way. I was typing up memorandums for logistical requests when Raymie noticed what I was doing and said "Major I have been here 19 years and you don't have to do this because it is my job to type memorandums and she already had some on file which only required the date and signature to be changed". I received the message loud and clear which said she is the boss. All the secretaries were great. Yami, Janet, Sandra, and Mercedes were the ones who interacted the most with.

You did not want to mess with Yami, Commander's Secretary, because she kept track of all awards and would let you know if the commander was in a good or bad mood. One day I told her the cable director gave me a drink called Noni and Yami fell out laughing. I asked her why she was laughing so hard and she said 'it is a drink for guys having problems in bed". I began to laugh afterwards. She kept it real.

Janet a good friend of Raymie and J-4 Secretary, had a very outgoing personality. She helped me a lot with transportation and supply requests.

Mercedes, Engineer Secretary, would have been a top model if she lived in the States. She was very beautiful and dressed like she was

372

going to a VIP Dinner every day. One day she wore a beautiful mini-skirt and the entire base drooled over her. She told me she had five proposals that day and I told her if she wears that dress again, she would have six. The secretaries did not date soldiers which kept everything very professional.

Base Secretaries.

Raymie, my secretary, talking to other Servicemembers after General Colin Powell's Speech.

Base Support

Tony, Special Forces Retiree, worked for a civilian company which provided communication support from JTF-B to the States. Tony gave me a history on the Ollie North Compound. We had a communication tower on a steep hill which could not be reached by vehicle. Tony contracted with local Hondurans on helping the base to service the towers. The Hondurans used donkeys to carry soldiers and equipment to and from the tower for servicing.

A very humble and nice cleaning lady worked for the J-6 Shop. She would come to work nicely dressed and wearing her gold chains. She cleaned like she was getting paid a $1 million. She asked me to buy her a camping chair. She gave me the money and I turned it down and said it would be her birthday gift. I purchased a green chair and she asked me if I could exchange it for a red, white, and blue chair. I was surprised she wanted a chair with the colors of the Flag. I guess it was in remembrance of a former boyfriend.

Maid jobs were considered respectful jobs. When servicemembers left Honduras they gave the Maids their money, food, and clothes. Maids on post cleaned four to five hooches monthly for $50 each. The maids made $200 - $250 a month and school teachers in Honduras at the time made $120 a month. When I arrived in Honduras, the school teachers were protesting because they had not been paid in a month.

Martha, my maid, spoke excellent English and would have been a model if she was in America. She was a single parent with a son and daughter to support. The maids cleaned the hooches and washed their servicemembers clothes every day. I was told in the 80s the maids washed the servicemembers clothes in the retaining pond on post. Martha thought I was going to fire her or reduce her salary when I asked her to come every other day and wash my clothes twice a week

375

instead of every day. She was over cleaning considering I only used one glass and wore one uniform a day. I changed running shoes every six-months and would give my old pair to Martha's son. One day a gang cornered her son and demanded money because he was wearing Nike shoes which I gave him. He told the gang leader a soldier gave them to him which foiled the gang's robbery. I gave him another pair for good luck.

The shoe shine man was also an avid tailor who worked with his son on maintaining uniforms and boots. He had a great job until the Military changed to boots which didn't need shinning. When I carried my boots to him, he would always say "Chekeleke" which means everything is okay or cool "only in Honduras. Chekeleke is not in the dictionary. His son would record Reggaeton Music for me. Central and South Americans have the best DJs in the world because they are good at mixing different styles of Hispanic Music.

The ladies in the barbershop were very kind and professional. They did not do massages or pop the neck and fingers like the Koreans, but they washed your hair after a haircut. They did pedicures and manicures for $10 and $6.00 for haircuts.

My barber made me feel relaxed like my barber in Korea. One day she was late so I went to another barber for a haircut. When my barber arrived and saw me sitting in another barber's chair, she respectfully told the other barber I was her client and the other barber asked me to change chairs which I did gladly did. She would not let no other lady cut my hair and would always give me her schedule because I was the only one who would leave a $4 tip. If I paid $10 in the States then I could pay $10 overseas. One day I went to sleep and woke up with trimmed eyebrows. I was the laughing stock of the post for two weeks.

The cable director negotiated a cable contract the year before I arrive which included the Playboy Channel. We ended the contract because servicemembers were coming to work late and tired. I renegotiated a better contract which included free HBO, Cinemax,

376

Showtime, and a sports package consisting of all the professional and college football and basketball game.

JTF-B has an excellent MWR Program. Sandra an employee of MWR scheduled trips for servicemembers to the Bay Islands, Lake Yojoa, Guatemala, shopping trips, and a host of other activities for people to do around the country. There was always something to do every weekend we were off.

Bay Islands provided servicemembers a chance to scuba dive. Servicemembers could fish, operate jet skis, or get certified to operate a pontoon boat. Another servicemember and myself took a pontoon boat out for fishing. We did not catch anything. We should have paid a local to show us around the lake.

The guys who went to Guatemala visited Hooters every day for lunch and said they had the best-looking women of any Hooters Bar in the World. I did not go because I was getting my Diving Certification. There were trips to resorts, Mayan Ruins, beaches, golf courses, horseback riding, and fishing trips for Servicemembers every week. If servicemembers did not take advantage of these programs it was because they did not want to participate.

The dining facility had outstanding employees who were great cooks. Each time I entered the dining facility; I spoke Spanish to the employees which showed them I respected their culture. They served rice every day and my son who loves rice thought he died and went to Heaven because he could eat rice twice a day for lunch and dinner. I interacted with every person who worked on post. I spoke Spanish to them and I gave them a good laugh with my accent.

Servicemembers received 300 minutes a month free phone calls to family members back in the States. Phone service was intermittent because of limited bandwidth from the satellite. The operators were young girls who each made about $300 a month. A Warrant Officer was drunk and began to harass the operators because he could not reach his family. The operators called me crying and I asked them to

377

put me in contact with the Warrant Officer. I told the Warrant Officer the next time he cusses out my operators, I was going to come down to his location and kick his ass. He never cursed at them again and I suspended his phone privileges afterwards.

Haiti

We were tasked of providing food, water, and other items to Haiti because the country was having civil unrest. Haiti's government said they did not need the items and the command said they would send the items back to the states for destruction. I could not believe what I heard considering we were living in a country with a minimum wage of .33¢ an hour. I spread the word throughout the base for servicemembers to go and pick up some items for themselves and Hondurans. I picked up toothpaste, deodorant, Pop Tarts, cereal, water, juice, and other items and gave them to every Hondurans who worked on base.

MAC FLIGHTS

MAC flights known also as Space-A flights are free or low-cost flights for Military personnel and their dependents. A MAC Flight would bring servicemembers and equipment to and from the States weekly. It was only four-hour flight from Honduras to Charleston.

A MAC Flight carrying family members was having problems with its landing gear. We began to prepare for an emergency by having emergency vehicles in place. Thank goodness nothing happened. Military planes have experienced pilots and go through a thorough inspection. I was on a MAC Flight and there was water dripping on me and then I noticed what look like transmission fluid on the wall. I told a crew member about I saw and he said not to worry and that I only needed to worry if I don't see any leaky fluids. He gave me a blanket for water protection and told me to enjoy my flight. I normally go to sleep on an airplane, but after what he said, I stayed awake the entire flight.

Change of Command

COL Phelps was an outstanding Brigade Commander and who gave me a top rating. He knew I put a lot of work in improving the communication network in Honduras. He told me when I arrived, do not let his communication network fail and I did not. My boss in Panama was his boss at Ft. Campbell, Kentucky. He was relinquishing his command to COL Bassett.

COL Bassett and I served together in Panama. He was a Company Commander on the Pacific Side and I was a lieutenant on the Atlantic Side. The only thing which I felt COL Phelps could have been stricter about was the lateness of some staff officers to his training meetings. Training meetings were held once a week at 1100hrs every Friday which provided plenty of time to recover from Thursday night Church meetings. I told the staff COL Bassett is not going to play that crap of his staff being late.

The first training meeting which COL Bassett held there were four Officers who were late. COL Bassett walked out of the meeting and told us to let him know when everyone is present. He chewed out those Officers who were late. There were no one late for his training meetings anymore. COL Bassett and I talked about our time in Panama. I served under him in Honduras for four months because my assignment time was finished. He asked me to stay another year and work in the S-3 shop, but I told him I needed to leave because I only saw my kids 70 days in two years. He understood and gave me an excellent rating when I left.

The Army is a small force and you will run into a person whom you have previously served with. I ran into the Signal Branch Manager, a Colonel now, who assigned me as a Brigade Signal Officer in Korea. I asked him why did he do it knowing that I never previously served in a Signal Unit and he said "It was the best assignment for me". I wanted to call him an asshole, but I held back because I needed an XO or S-3 job after the Honduras Assignment in order to make LTC.

I was leaving Honduras and asked him if I could serve on his S-3 Staff to gain experience in a Signal Unit. He told me "No" because I haven't finished CGSC (Command and General Staff) school. He found out after he made the statement to me that over half of his staff had not finished CGSC. It was a Distant Learning Course and I would have finished once I was in the States.

I contacted Signal Branch to inquire about available follow-on assignments and the Branch Manager told me there was no record of me in the Army. I said, "What" and he repeated the statement. I had to fax a copy of my orders and pay voucher to prove I was in the Army. I had been in the Army for 18 years when this occurred. I told my friends I am the "Black Rodney Dangerfield" because I get no respect. This was the second time the Army lost accountability of me. The first time was in Houston.

Signal Branch offered me an assignment to Ft. Monroe, Virginia, or Ft. Meade Maryland. When I told the former Branch Manager about my choices, he said I can't believe those are your only choices and I gave him "you are an asshole look" because he could have stepped in and did something. I choose Ft. Monroe because I was leaning towards retirement and wanted to become a JROTC Instructor at my old high school to give back to my community.

End of Tour

Work in Honduras was not as intense as in Korea, but it was a real-world mission. I was responsible for communications throughout Central and South America. I renegotiated the base communication contract which saved the Army $5 million dollars over a 5-year period. In spite of me writing the contract and saving the Army money, I was not hired for the civilian position after I retired. I guess it was because I saved the Army too much money.

Soto Cano Air Base was a great duty station with outstanding leaders. It was out in the middle of nowhere, two hours from Tegucigalpa and two hours from San Pedro Sula. Honduras is the only assignment I served in which had a combination of great leaders and a great duty station. I either had great Duty Stations and bad leaders or Great Leaders and bad Duty Stations during my previous assignments. I learned a lot about people in Honduras because I interacted with everyone from the maids to the Honduran Soldiers. Honduras will always have a special place in my heart and it is the only Duty Station which I served in twice.

Lesson Learned

1. ***Respect the customs and courtesies of the host nation*** – I spoke to Hondurans in Spanish and I ate what they ate. Remember we are guests in their country.

2. ***Speak nicely to everyone you meet*** – Greeting people cordially helped me to acquire anything I needed and probably prevented me from being robbed while running.

3. ***Travel*** – When in a foreign country go visit the sites which the country has to offer.

4. ***Exercise*** – Do not wait until you are old to exercise, do it now.

5. ***Arrive 15 minutes early for meetings***

6. ***Do not judge others on what they have*** – Honduras is a poor country with nice people. When a Honduran invited me to their house for dinner, I went regardless of their income or size of their house. I showed them respect and kindness by bringing them a house warming gift and eating what they placed before me which made it an enjoyable experience.

Sleeping quarters. Ducks lived under our quarters and gecko lizards lived inside. Hooches had running water, but no bathroom. My kids gave names to the ducks when they visited. We used communal bathrooms which frogs, mosquitos, geckos, and other wildlife took over at night.

The only ducklings that I know of which start as cute and become ugly ducks.

Hail and Farewells

Major Johnson (Right side) and CPT Beard receiving their end of tour awards

Major Johnson with his pre-iPhone Camera.

MSG Steele is cheating Chief Fields, CSM and Major Johnson out of their money in a Dominoes game.

Janet (J-4) and Raymie (J-6)

Janet smiling after a nice meal.

388

Relaxing after a nice meal.

CPT Beard and his assistant sharing a Mountain Dew.

389

Food must have been really great!!!

CPT Medina, the Assistant J-6. CPT Medina, West Point Graduate, left the Army to get his Master's Degree in Engineering from Georgia Tech University.

Tony and Freddy. Tony, right side, was our go to guy for maintaining the communication between Honduras and all of the countries in Central and South America.

J-6 Staff enjoying their meal at a local steakhouse. No one ate Juevos de Toro that day.

Honduran Furniture

393

Mahogany Furniture – Honduras has a lot of skilled carpenters.

394

Painting which I purchased from a deaf guy. I paid $40 for the picture and $50 for the frame.

FT. MONROE, VIRGINIA

I arrived at Ft. Monroe in December 2004 and was assigned as a Team Chief in a Combat Development Unit. I was a fish out of water. Most of the Active-Duty Officers were Acquisition Officers. I worked for a Colonel who was excited he received a Signal Officer. We sat down for our initial meeting and he explained the job which was for a Signal Officer who had been in a Signal Unit. I told him I have never served in a Signal Unit. I could not believe Signal Branch set the unit and me up for failure. Most leaders think all Signal Officers have the same qualifications which is not true. I was experienced with tactical and satellite radios and not with Warfighter Information Network-Tactical which the Colonel thought he was getting. His facial expression changed when I told him my background and I was retiring in 18 months. He said he never had a soldier retire on him; I told him there is always a first time for everything. I later requested to attend the Acquisition Course because but it was denied and the Colonel told me I was a Major and I could learn the job. If I attended the course, I had a two-year commitment after completing the course which I would have gladly accepted.

The good things about Ft. Monroe are it's on the beach, has great history, nice gym, small post, and within 30 miles of 5 other bases. There were more Generals on the post than Majors. Majors were like Privates in the Army. I met Jerry a good friend of mine from Panama and our families spent a lot of time together. A civilian told me only 20% of the people actually do work on Ft. Monroe and too bad you are in the 20% group.

The Colonel was sharp because he knew how to get money for projects. He could have become a General, but he turned it down because he wanted to spend more time with his family. Companies were offering him $200k plus for his services. He was so good in acquiring money, the Army told him he had to wait six months before working for any company doing business with the Army.

There was another Retired Colonel who worked in the office for another company. He turned down a chance to become a General because he only saw his second wife 30 days in two years and he said he wasn't going through another divorce. The company which hired him had to pay for his airplane fuel and hanger space. He flew from Columbus, Georgia to Ft. Monroe every week. When the price of gas went up, the company told him they had a job for him in Columbus, Georgia.

The first year I was there we had a $5 million dollar budget for a section of nine people. The second year our budget was $20 million dollars. Our job was to find new equipment such as protective armor, protective gear, and communication equipment for units in Iraq and get it to them in 90 days. The Colonel sent me to different installations asking them what equipment they needed for deployment.

The funniest mission which I went on was to Yuma Proving Grounds. A coworker told me Ft. Bliss was the closest base to Yuma Proving Grounds. I took his word without looking on a map. I landed in Ft. Bliss, picked up a rental car, and proceeded to the guest house. I asked the clerk how far Yuma was from here and she said eight hours and I almost fell out. I repeated in a loud voices eight hours. I doubted her and looked on a map and sure enough I was eight hours away. I had to be there the next day at 8:30am. I drove all through the night. Thank goodness there was no traffic in Phoenix. When I arrived in Yuma, I had another 30 miles on dirt trails to reach my location. I arrived at 8:20 am. The meeting was a waste of time because we thought there was going to be equipment testing, but instead it was a meeting about the design of the equipment and its capabilities. The information could have been emailed to us.

397

Yuma was one of the crossing points for immigrants entering the States. Anyone who entered the States through Yuma has to be tough because it is a hot and desolate place. I stayed overnight at the Marine Corps Air Station in Yuma and drove back to Ft. Bliss the next morning. When I arrived at the car rental place, the representative was in shock on how many miles I put on the car in three days. He asked me did I go to California and I just smiled. Thank goodness my rental contract came with unlimited miles.

The Colonel sent Daryl and I to the Pentagon for a meeting. Daryl was a retired Marine who served in Marine Force Recon. Everyone is required to go through a strenuous background before entering the Pentagon. Guest must be escorted to the section which they cleared for. When Daryl and I arrived, we discovered Daryl was not on the list of names for the meeting, so the Pentagon denied his entrance to the meeting. We saw a group of elementary school kids entering the Pentagon and I said to security guard if they can enter why can't a guy who spent twenty plus years in Force Recon and has a Top-Secret Security Clearance can't enter and the security guard said they are on the list and Daryl is not. I said "damn Daryl those kids have a higher security clearance than you". On our way back to the hotel it took us over three hours to drive 10 miles because of traffic. I promised myself I would never live in the D.C. area afterwards.

The next day, I was going a second meeting when a Hispanic girl reported to the front desk that she was raped. The ladies at the counter did not speak Spanish and I was the Spanish Interpreter. I asked her the basic questions in Spanish such as her name, where did it happen at, who did it, the description of the guy, and the name of a family member who she could contact. I translated for the police until their Spanish Interpreter arrived. Those Spanish lessons came in handy.

398

Senior Officers

I thought I was escaping from General Coker and General Ierardi when I left Korea, but the Army had other ideas. They ended up being my bosses at Ft. Monroe which I could not believe. I gained a lot of respect of General Coker's attention to detail when I prepared a brief for him. The first thing which he noticed on my Power Point briefing was missing page numbers. The slides were in order, but I did not list the page numbers on each of them. He accepted my briefing after the corrections.

I had conversations with General Officers in the gym. Ft. Monroe had one of the nicest gyms in the Army. It was small and had more modern equipment than larger gyms. I worked out five days a week and lifted weights with General Turner, General Bray, and General Winfield. Ft. Monroe had more General Black Officers than any post which I have ever been on. They were down to earth Generals who were willing to share information with anyone who requested it. The conversations were kept respectful and professional and they made you feel like you could talk about anything without any repercussions.

Major General Crutchfield was another down to earth General Officer who I had many great conversations with. He was from North Carolina also. When I retired, he provided guidance to an Army 2LT who was a student of mine at NC A&T State University.

COL Johnson, LTC Jenkins, and LTC Evans were a great source of advice. Another officer told me, COL Johnson could have been a professional golfer because he shoots a 70 every time he plays. COL Johnson asked me to bring him my assignment record and evaluations and when he saw them, he said "Damn you were screwed over". That is a hard pill to swallow. If I had him as mentor, I would have been at least a Colonel.

399

LTC Evans and I attended the NC A&T State University at the same time. She discussed with me her up and downs in the Army and how she overcame them. One day a Captain from our college took a picture of me wearing a sweatshirt from our cross-city rival, UNC-Greensboro and emailed it to her. Everyone hysterically laughed about the photo.

LTC Jenkins a Hampton Graduate and LTC (Retired) Al Mattheson of NC A&T were other officers who provided me with guidance on future assignments and careers outside of the Army.

IRAQ

All soldiers were required to attend a week training session in El Paso before deploying overseas. Part of the training required servicemembers to qualify on the weapon which they were deploying with. I went to the 9mm range to qualify and after I finished shooting, the Range Sergeant asked "who was on lane 19" and I nervously said my name. The Range Sergeant said good shooting because I only missed one target. I rarely qualify on the 9mm the first time because I don't practice with it often. I guess going to Iraq made me focus on my shooting.

There was a soldier who was going back to Iraq for his second tour. He shook nervously when he talked to anyone and he could not put two words together without shaking. He had the most severe case of PTSD I ever seen in a soldier. I could not sleep the first night because I was worried about him returning to Iraq. I remembered what Chris told me in Korea which was a lot of soldiers were killed in Iraq because no one spoke up about their safety. I went to the Ft. Bliss Company Leadership Group and told them; they cannot send the soldier back to Iraq because of his PTSD. The Company Leadership Group called him into a meeting and noticed his severe case of PTSD. They called his unit and told them the situation and the unit said to send him anyway and he would not leave the base. I could not believe the unit wanted him to return to Iraq considering his severe case of PTSD. I did not like the unit's decision, but I felt relieved because I spoke up.

We were at a range qualifying with Navy Sailors. The Sailors told the Army Instructors they have their own weapons and asked them to hurry up so they could deploy to Iraq quickly. I said "What person is trying to hurry up and deploy to Iraq" and the sailors said they were in a hurry to get there for the extra pay. When they told me the amount they would be getting, I asked them could I join their unit.

The Command told us we were restricted to base and a group of us said we are not staying on base and we were going to El Paso for what could possibly be our last drink. We ended up at a Gentleman's Club. The manager gave us a case of Coronas because we were soldiers. There were very nice-looking girls working in the club. Thirty-one out of thirty-two of them could have been models.

I deployed to Iraq to meet with units to see what equipment they need to be successful on the battle field. It was like a reunion with friends and former Servicemembers who I worked with. I met a lady from my hometown who managed the gym, a cousin working out in the gym, a LTC who was from my hometown, a LTC who was a college classmate, a Major who I served with at Ft. Leonardwood, and SFC Asher a former soldier of my platoon in Panama.

I met a soldier who returned from Germany after been shot in the rear end in Iraq. I asked him why was he not sent back to the States for his injury and his unit told him they were short soldiers and that he had a non-life-threatening injury. I told him if he was in the Air Force they would have sent him home with a Bronze Star.

The first base I arrived on; a soldier showed me the area where a contractor was killed by a mortar shell which landed in the food court. The Iraqis would shell the area daily and stopped three days before I arrived and directed their attention to the second base I was going to. I flew on helicopters to different bases in the mornings and attended meetings in the evening. I was working with a LTC from Puerto Rico and he could not believe how many Salsa Artists I knew. The Hispanic Soldiers choose Thursday night as their Salsa night because the Iraqis did not shell on that night, but shelled the base on Friday Nights which was Country Music night.

Soldiers were getting trapped in their vehicles after an IED (Improvised Explosive Device) attack which resulted in more injuries for soldiers. A message from higher headquarters told soldiers to work

402

on their upper body strength more so they could easily open up a stuck door on a Hummer. I don't know which commander said such dumb crap, but I bench pressed over 315lbs at the time and I could not open my door when it became stuck. My driver had to get out of the vehicle and open the door. Those doors weighed almost a ton from the armor plating on them.

I went to the second base which the Iraqis were shelling daily. The day prior a captain was walking from his shower when a mortar round came flying onto the base. The only thing which saved the captain's life was the mortar round hit the top of the concrete movie screen which was about 20 feet high. CSM Wright who served with me in Korea survived a mortar attack because his coworker persuaded him to go to the Dining Facility for dinner. A mortar round landed in the door of the building which he slept in and didn't explode. I am surprised we did not lose more soldiers in Iraq. I compared being a soldier in Iraq to being a uniformed soldier in New York City where every New Yorker has an AK-47 Assault Rifle.

SFC Asher my former Squad Leader in Panama. Asher was always wired tight from drinking coffee and Mountain Dew daily in Panama.

Every night when this vehicle went outside of the gate, it would return with gun shots.

404

Home away from home. The connexes contained two beds, electricity, and AC, but no bathrooms. Iraqis would shell the compound daily with mortars.

Saddam's Castles

Saddam had numerous castles which were more extravagant than Biltmore House in North Carolina. The castle contained marble, gold, crystals, and numerous other expensive pieces. I visited one of Saddam's castles built near the Tigris River. It was very immaculate and visitors could take a picture in one of Saddam's chairs.

The one thing which frustrated me about our responsibility for units in Iraq was the denial of radios which units requested. The Army sent units radios which had limited operational capabilities, therefore; the units refused to use them and placed 25,000 of them in connexes. The radios the units requested cost $1,400 each while the other radios cost $800 each. We purchased 50,000 more of the radios which the units refused to use and sent a team to train them on it. They probably put those 50,000 radios in connexes.

Saddam's Chair

S-3 OFFICER

I was sent to Ft. Leavenworth, Kansas to be the S-3 Officer on a computer exercise. I never worked in an S-3 shop before, but I learned what an S-3 Officer does from being in Korea. One of the evaluators were Retired COL Holler who was my Battalion Commander at Ft. Leonardwood. I was surprised he remembered me. I guess he could not forget such a lost Signal Officer.

The job was intense and being an Infantry Officer and being in Korea gave me the skills to handle all scenarios which we encountered. My chest was sticking out because an evaluator said I did a good job. I learned from the experience and I felt I short changed my career by avoiding working in an S-3 shop as a Junior Officer. I believe the S-3 and S-4 sections provide the most learning experiences for a Junior Officer to have a successful career. An officer learns about planning and mission execution in an S-3 shop and, in an S-4 shop an officer learns about equipment accountability and supply requirements for missions. I worked in the S-4 section in Panama for a year.

I met Ken who I served with at Ft. Leonardwood. Ken was attending CGSC at Ft. Leavenworth. He told me and I saw for myself one of the most embarrassing things which I ever seen in the Army. There were more Foreign Officers than Black Officers in CGSC. I could not believe it. Attending CGSC in person almost guarantees an Officer a Battalion Command Position which increases their chances of becoming a General Officer.

The Commanding General for Cadet Command was looking for an Aid. I interviewed for it and one of the requirements was an officer had to get permission from their Branch to serve in the position. Signal Branch refused to release me because they said they did not have another Signal Officer to fill the current position I was in. I explained

410

to them I was not doing anything associated with Signal, but when a unit request a certain branch specified position, it must be filled no matter if they are doing something in that officer's career field or not.

A friend told me there was six-month tour opening in Honduras as an Assistant S-3. I applied for the position, although; I was retiring in three months. The clerk asked me did I want to retire in three months or go to Honduras for six months. I told her going to Honduras was more enjoyable than retiring. She looked at me like I was crazy. Honduras is the only base in my military career which I was stationed at twice.

HONDURAS II

The secretaries were excited when they found out, I was returning to Honduras to work in the S-3 shop. The reason why they were so excited was because the S-3 Director was giving all the staff secretaries a hard time especially the one who worked in the S-3 shop. They were in tears because of his actions.

When I arrived in Honduras the personnel dynamics had changed. In 2004 most of the servicemembers were Army soldiers. In 2006 the Air Force made up most of the servicemembers on base. I was assigned as the Assistant S-3 which I felt prepared for because I was in Honduras previously and the I was an S-3 Officer for a computer exercise.

Airshow

We worked with the Honduras Military which was located on the base. A Honduran Major, whose nickname "El Lobo" (The Wolf), approached me on a Tuesday requesting a Joint Airshow with American and Honduran Soldiers. I asked him when did he want it and he replied on Saturday which was Memorial Day Weekend and soldiers were off for four days. I reported this to the Brigade Commander and he gave me guidance on how to make this happen in a short period of time. I contacted every unit on base requesting support and I told every servicemembers who participated in the Airshow they would get a day off. The servicemembers liked my proposal because it meant they would have five days compared to other soldiers' four days off.

Honduran citizens were allowed on base during the Airshow, so it required us to have extra security measures on base. The units provided the requested support without any complaints because I always supported them on their needs. The Airshow went on without any problems. The Honduran Major and I became good friends after the Airshow and anything I requested from the Honduran Military, I received.

New Leaders

LTC Dempsey arrived as the S-3 Officer in charge. We hit it right off the bat because we knew the same Officers and he was a former Military Policeman. We developed a friendly competition of who was the better Spanish Interpreter for servicemembers who had Honduran girlfriends. I guess it was a tie because no one was smacked because of our interpreting.

COL Hughes became the Brigade Commander. I was retiring in three months when he asked me to become his ROCKS Leader. The ROCKS is an organization which provide mentorships to junior minority officers. COL Hughes had attended a ROCKS meeting and wanted to start a chapter in Honduras. I was impressed because he was a White Officer who saw a need for minority officers to have mentors. I declined the officer because I was retiring and frustrated with dealing with Signal Branch. I wanted to serve as a Battalion Commander even if it was a canine battalion, but I knew my past assignments prevented this.

Honduras is a beautiful country with beautiful people. Soto Cano is a small base which I thoroughly enjoyed because it gave me the opportunity to learn more about the country, culture, and improve my Spanish. I would go back a third time if the Army asked me.

Lesson Learned

1. ***Treat people with respect*** – The first S-3 Officer treated the secretaries so bad they cried at work. You are not going to get good production out of a person if you establish a hostile environment. I felt like a superstar when the secretaries told me they were waiting for my return so they could enjoy their work.

2. ***Become a mentor*** – COL Dempsey understood the importance of mentorship and how it affects the Army and Minority Soldiers which was why he wanted to establish a ROCKS Mentorship Program in Honduras.

3. ***"Yes" goes a lot further than "No"*** – I could have easily said "No" to the Honduran COL's request for conducting an Airshow. The Airshow established a good relationship between the U.S. Honduran Military, and local citizens.

4. ***Not everyone will recognize your work*** – The Honduran Military Colonel and secretaries knew I worked hard and took care of people, so they always brought me food and other special gifts.

5. ***Don't be afraid to step out of your comfort zone*** – I avoided working in an S-3 Section like the plague. Stepping out of one's comfort zone increases a person's knowledge.

6. ***There is no such thing as a natural born leader*** – Leaders are developed through education and training. I have never seen a baby in charge of a company.

RETIREMENT

When I returned from Honduras, I had knee surgery three months before retiring. I called the 118th MP Company, my first unit in the Army, and spoke with CSM Rivera. CSM Rivera was a Sergeant the last time I saw him and I told him about the time he chewed my ass out for having unsecured ammunition in Grenada, of course he did not remember it. We reminisced about the old times. He was the last Active Duty Soldier from the 118th who went to Grenada and he was retiring within a year. He told me there was an open Signal Officer position in the Brigade. I thought to myself this would be a storybook ending to retire from the first unit which I served in. I was on crutches and asked Signal Branch if I could be assigned to the Wounded Warrior Program at Ft. Bragg to heal up and then I would go on any assignment where the Army needed a Signal Officer and course it was denied.

The Colonel and I had our last conversation the day before I was retiring. He told me he did me wrong by assigning me as a Team Chief of an Acquisition Section. This confirmed what I already knew that I was in the wrong job. There was no need to argue about it because I was retiring. Retiring from the Army, felt like a ton of bricks were lifted off of my chest because it opened up new opportunities. I knew what I wanted to do after retirement unlike some of my former coworkers.

My daughter cried when I retired because she enjoyed all perks which we received from being in the Military. We went to Disney World, Carowinds, Busch Gardens, Kings Dominion, and Puerto Rico at discounted rates. Langley Air Force Base had an Airshow and one

416

of the game stations was you could win a prize if you picked up a wrapped coin in a tank full of eels. My son who enjoyed picking up frogs and lizards, reached in a selected a coin. The judge unwrapped the coin and it was for four free tickets to Kings Dominion. The judge was more excited than we were because we thought the cost of the tickets all together was $60, but our expression changed when we realized the tickets were worth $200.

Lessons Learned

1. ***Prepare yourself for retirement*** – No matter what job you have, you are going to leave it someday either voluntarily or involuntarily. I selected Ft. Monroe as my last assignment because I wanted to a be a JROTC Instructor after the Army. It worked because I worked in ROTC and JROTC programs for 10 years after I retired.

2. ***Be specific on your requests*** – Ft. Monroe asked for a Signal Officer, but was not specific on what type of Signal Officer they needed for the position. Actuality they did not need any Signal Officer because it wasn't a Signal job.

3. ***Train your people*** – The Iraq War exposed how Non-Combat Units were not as tactically prepared as Infantry or Armor Units. Before the Iraq War, Non-Combat Arm units thought they would get an Infantry or Armor Company to protect them while they did their missions. I warned several of my fellow Officers no Combat Arms Commander will give them one of their companies during a time of war. TRADOC later changed their training for soldiers not in combat units to include more training on tactics.

4. ***Talk to everyone*** – I try to know everyone on any base which I was stationed at. If you ask, people will help. I had lunch with a Japanese Officer in Kuwait and because I spoke a few words in Japanese and asked him to sit with me, he gave me his unit pin.

5. ***Take care of your body*** – A Retirement Officer made a statement which I live by this day. He said "I don't know why retired soldiers let themselves go when they know how to exercise and if you stop exercising then those checks stop".

6. ***Units know what they want, not commands know what units want*** – There were a couple of times I witnessed were a unit requested certain equipment and the command told them they

418

don't need the equipment and gave them equipment which they did not use. The job of the command is to support units.

7. ***Do your own research*** – I should have looked on a map first instead of taking someone's advice for my Yuma, Arizona trip.

OTHER EXPERIENCES

One of the Military's sayings is the show must go on rain, sleet, or snow. It was so cold at Ft. Bragg; I dug a five-foot deep foxhole by myself to stay warm. The command was worried about me collapsing and I told them I used to work in tobacco fields and it was a lot harder than digging a foxhole.

Ft. Leonardwood was so cold, the mucus in my nose froze. I experienced a warm winter in Korea in which the temperature was -14°F. The temperature changes in Iraq drastically from day to night. The temperature was 110 degrees plus in the daytime and other servicemembers told me I would need a jacket at night because the temperature drops down to the 70s. I told them Korea made me immune to cold weather and I never wear a jacket in 70-degree weather. That night when it dropped down to 70, I started shriving and put on a jacket. I couldn't believe I was freezing in 70-degree weather.

Servicemembers see the good and bad in people. My goal when I was sent to a foreign country was to go where Americans didn't go, so I could learn about the history of the country and the culture. People were willing to give me the history of their country because I was respectful and it excited them to know someone wanted to learn about their country and culture without judging it. You must respect other cultures. I have stayed in houses made out of mud, houses without indoor plumbing, ate in restaurants which had no running water, and drunk some of the nastiest liquor in the world to show respect for other people cultures.

Poverty drives people to make drastic decisions which they would have never do if they had a better life. I have been in countries where people bathed in rivers and parents offering their daughters for marriage so their child could have a better life. Seeing things like this makes one become more of a compassionate and understanding person. The main difference between America and other countries is there are more opportunities in America for a person to succeed than other countries.

ATHLETES

The Military is a very physical and demanding job. The perception of the Military to most Americans, is people join the Military because they can't find a job. The truth is Military people have a wide range of skills and the majority of Servicemembers are very smart and athletic. Servicemembers are very competitive. I served with the number one golfer and racquetball player in the Army, wrestling champions, body builders, boxers, athletes, Olympic champions, and a chess Champion.

A few soldiers who I served with choose becoming a soldier over a professional athlete. COL Johnson's golf game was so good that he would have been the one of the few professional Black golfers in today's era. Ricky Parker turned down a contract with the Atlanta Falcons football team. Amateen turned down a chance to becoming a boxing champion. These are just a few military people who choose serving their country over potential fame and fortune.

CONCLUSION

The U.S. Military is the arguably one of the best leadership schools in the world and provides an excellent professional training blueprint. Enlisting in the Army is a decision which launched a trajectory of success, and I have enjoyed a rewarding career as a result. Had it not been for the Army, I would not have traveled the world, learned multiple languages, and immersed myself in different cultures. The American Military is the only career path I experienced that provides extensive travel, global immersion, skills mastery, and hands-on-technical training.

Whereas people pay for the thrill of extreme adventures. I was fortunate to get paid to do it. It was not unusual during a typical work day to jump from airplanes, ride in helicopters, repel down building, pole vault into windows, scuba dive, use boats for water operations, and swim in the Pacific and Atlantics oceans in the same day. I had the opportunity to work with various weapon systems such as anti-tank weapons, machine guns, hand grenades, and a host of other foreign and domestic weapons. I drove multi-million-dollar tanks and operated highly expensive robotics. A day in the life of a soldier is nothing short of amazing.

Achieving success in the military is not an easy endeavor and takes commitment. I was motivated to put in extra work because I remembered what the humongous drill sergeant said when I joined the Army, which is, "America is involved in a conflict every 10 years, and we better take this training seriously". I was always looking for ways to learn and improve myself. I became a voracious reader. I read bibles, dictionaries, USA Today newspapers every day, Army regulations, and studied Foreign Languages. It may sound nerdy to some, but I can attest to reading being the key to discovery, enlightenment, and self-improvement.

I am a firm believer that you can't complain about an outcome if you don't put in the work. I exercised twice a day, five times a week, and walked over 12 miles carrying over 50 pounds of equipment countless times. There were many times I worked seven days a week, 16-hour days, holidays, birthdays, and anniversaries. I was not required to learn Taekwondo, run the Houston Marathon, or participate in the Houston to Austin Bike Ride, but I did this for physical and mental growth. This mindset gave me confidence over fear.

I served in the Army for 20 years, 4 months, and 16 days. Injuries prevented me from serving longer. I am thankful for my military experience and the good times outweighed the bad. I am proud that I have influenced someone to the join the military every year since I retired in 2007. I believe that leading by example and representing the Army in a positive way led to the recruitment of future leaders. The training I received in the military afforded me the best job of my life, which was as a JROTC Instructor at James Kenan High School in Warsaw, NC. This book is about my life in the military. Units, leaders, and regulations have changed since I retired from the Army.

The most valuable lessons which I learned were to respect others, your word is your bond, help the less fortunate, and you can't succeed without help from others. Listed on the following pages are other important lessons which I learned throughout my time in the military.

LESSONS LEARNED

1. The Good Lord only helps those who help themselves.
2. God gives everyone a talent; use yours to better mankind.
3. Leave your job better than when you arrived in it.
4. You may not be the best in your group, but giving your best is the best thing.
5. The titles we earn on Earth don't guarantee a place in Heaven.
6. Bad News travel faster than Good News.
7. Your actions overseas reflect on what people think of Americans.
8. No one wakes up saying they are going to fail, therefore; help them to succeed.
9. If you think you, have it bad, look in the obituaries.
10. A Smile goes a long way.
11. If you are the smartest person in your group, then you are in the wrong group.
12. If someone says watch this then you know something dumb is going to happen.
13. If you don't learn something new every day then you have wasted your day.
14. Have at least three yearly goals: financial, physical, and learning something new.
15. If you don't speak up then who will.
16. Learn another language and you will make a new friend.
17. The person who you think looks like a nobody, may know the answer.
18. You are only passing through on Earth so enjoy it.
19. Don't complain about it; offer a suggestion on how to fix it.
20. Instead of blaming someone for your problems trying looking into the mirror first.

425

21. A father should never live better than his child.
22. Complacency breeds laziness.
23. Respect and kindness open doors.
24. You can't lead from the front if you being towed by the rear.
25. Always have a plan with a backup.

ACKNOWLEDGEMENTS

I would like to acknowledge the service members whom I served with, the community where I was raised, friends, and family members who helped me to have a successful Military Career. I would like to especially acknowledge Marilyn Saavedra, Elliott White, Raymie Soto, and Pam Jordan CEO of Boss Enterprises. This book could not have been completed without their assistance and encouragement. I am forever grateful for these connections which inspired me to write this book.